LIFE DONE DIFFERENTLY

ONE WOMAN'S JOURNEY ON THE ROAD LESS TRAVELLED

LISA JANSEN

For all the kindred souls on the road less travelled.
It's so good to know that I'm not alone.

AUTHOR'S NOTE

This book tells my story, and I've done my best to retell events exactly as they happened. However, my memory isn't perfect, and despite detailed journals from this time, I cannot guarantee that every little detail in this book is correct and exactly what and when it happened. In addition, the book is only my version of events, and other people mentioned might remember events and conversations differently.

The names of all people, and in some rare instances, locations and dates, have been changed to protect people's privacy.

Since I live in New Zealand, and the country is a big part of my story, I wrote this book in New Zealand English. If you are used to reading American English, I hope you can overlook a few "s" where you're used to seeing "z" and other minor differences.

CONTENTS

FOLLOW MY JOURNEY IN PICTURES

If you're keen to not only read about my journey but also see some of it, I invite you to check out the photo gallery on my website. For each chapter in this book, I've selected photos that show the places and events I'm describing to help bring the story to life.

lifedonedifferently.com/gallery

NEW ZEALAND

North
Island

South
Island

PROLOGUE

APRIL 2022

I'm sitting on a bench at the top of the hill miles away from any town, enjoying my packed lunch. There are no signs of civilisation, other than the bench I'm sitting on and the path that took me here. Before me, as far as the eye can see, is the most stunning scenery. Green hills with thick, impenetrable bush, opening up to beaches so golden you have to see it to believe it, and then the endless ocean, a gorgeous turquoise at first, turning into a dark blue further out. I can see the hills of French Pass to the east. With some imagination, I can even see the shape of New Zealand's North Island in the distance in the north.

I'm in Abel Tasman, one of New Zealand's 13 national parks. Abel Tasman is at the north-western end of the South Island on the coast between Motueka and Tākaka. It's small compared to the other National Parks in the country, but it's still almost 24,000 hectares in size. The Abel Tasman track, one of New Zealand's Great Walks, covers the park's entire length, closely following the coastline. It's 60 kilometres in total, and most walk it over four or five days, staying at campgrounds and huts along the way.

I'm not quite that ambitious. As much as I love hiking in beautiful scenery, I also like sleeping in the comfort of my own bed. I'm just on a day trip – but a special one. I'm celebrating my 38th birthday. And I couldn't have asked for a more perfect day. Even though it is the middle of April, which means autumn down here in the Southern Hemisphere, it still feels like summer. It's warm and sunny without a cloud in the sky, and the water is still warm enough to make for refreshing (but not freezing) dips.

I had been in the area for a few weeks and already covered the northern and southern sections of the Abel Tasman Track. Today, I'm walking the middle section, which is said to be the most beautiful – but also the hardest to access. I took a water taxi from Marahau to Torrent Bay in the morning. From there, I'm walking north to Onetahuti, where the water taxi will pick me up again in the afternoon.

It's busy in the park. I love hiking in silence and solitude, so I have to admit I could have done without the crowds. Although, to be fair, what I call a crowd, most would probably call a few people. It's not like we are walking single file along the track. But I'm passing many more people today than I did the previous two weekends walking other sections of the trail. It was to be expected, though. Not only is the weather amazing, but it's also Easter and school holidays. I usually would have avoided popular destinations like Abel Tasman during public holidays, but I wanted to do something special for my birthday.

As I sit there, eating my lunch, my mind drifts back to the last time my birthday fell on Easter weekend. It was five years ago, but it feels like a different lifetime.

Back then, I was a 33-year-old highly successful marketing professional with a bright career ahead of her. I lived in

Auckland, New Zealand's biggest city, in a house with stunning water and harbour bridge views. Every day, I commuted to the city for work, spent the day in the office in front of a computer and then headed home. On the weekends, I went kitesurfing, paddle boarding or on other adventures with my friends – which is exactly what we did for that Easter and birthday weekend in 2017. Back then, I was on track to live a fairly traditional life.

Here I am five years later, 38 years old, on my own, hiking in Abel Tasman for the day before I will return to the campervan that I call home. For the last four and a half years, I have been a nomad, living in my campervan and travelling all over New Zealand. There wasn't much left of the country that I hadn't seen yet. It's amazing, I realise, how even after all this time, I still sit in awe at how beautiful New Zealand is. If anything, I'm more humbled and amazed by it than ever. I guess some things really never get old.

The last four and half years have been nothing short of amazing. There were highs and lows, of course. There have been challenges and setbacks. It felt lonely at times to follow this path that was so different from most people's. I questioned my choices sometimes. There were days when I wished I could just be like everyone else. But given the choice, I wouldn't change any of it. OK, maybe I would change a few little things. There were some moments I could have done without. But then I remind myself that all of it together, made the experience what it was and made me who I am today. If I look at it that way, even the tough times seem worth it. I had been on this incredible journey that had gotten me to this point where I feel more confident and more content than ever. I can feel change coming again. Just like I had back in 2017. But this time, I'm not worried. I know that, whatever happens,

I will make the most of it. I'm confident that whatever life throws at me, I will find a way to be happy.

It feels amazing to have reached this point in my life. But what a ride it has been.

And it had all started five years earlier – the last time my birthday fell on Easter Weekend.

1

DOUBTS

AUTUMN 2017

Auckland

I was in the car on my way home, driving the last few kilometres alone after dropping off my friends. It was the evening of Easter Monday and the end of another epic adventure weekend with the people I called my saltwater family. We had spent the long weekend at Sandy Bay to celebrate Easter as well as my 33rd birthday in the only way we knew how – with time in the ocean, nature walks, great food and even better company.

We had stretched the weekend out as long as we could, and it was dark when I turned into the driveway at home. I was renting a room in a waterfront property in Hauraki Corner on Auckland's North Shore. I loved the stunning views over the water to the iconic Harbour Bridge, but I hated the steep driveway down to the house, especially in the dark. However, the idea of carrying my standup paddle board, kitesurfing gear, clothes and everything else down the driveway wasn't appealing, so I carefully backed down the drive.

As I unloaded the car, I could feel the gloominess that had become a frequent visitor lately building inside me. I was overcome by a sense of sadness that I struggled to understand. I just had the most amazing weekend with incredible people. And it wasn't just a rare one-off. It wasn't just the end of the most amazing weekend, it was the most amazing summer that was coming to an end. We spent Christmas and New Year in Opoutere, a beautiful beach settlement in the Coromandel, celebrating the wedding of two friends with a week-long summer camp packed with daily adventures, great people and lots of sunshine. That was followed by long weekend trips to the Far North and Taranaki. Then, in February, my sister visited from Germany, and we spent two weeks travelling the South Island in a rented caravan. In between, there were kitesurfing days at Muriwai Beach and Orewa, standup paddle boarding missions and potluck dinners – and, of course, Easter at Sandy Bay.

When I wasn't having fun exploring the great outdoors of New Zealand, I worked as the Head of Marketing for a software startup. We were a great team, I was given plenty of opportunities to work on exciting projects, learn and grow, and I was paid well. It was the job I always wanted, and I was enjoying it a lot.

Life was great. Better than great! I had amazing friends, a job I enjoyed and fun hobbies. I was living in a house with sea views, and I was fit and healthy. But, most importantly, I was happy. If someone had told me ten years earlier that this would be my life someday, I probably wouldn't have believed them. I don't think I could have ever imagined that life could be this good. But here I was, living the dream. And yet, there was this darkness building inside of me that hadn't been there just a few months earlier.

––––––

I think it's fair to say that, for the most part, my life had been incredibly normal until that point. I grew up in a small town called Lingen in northern Germany with an older brother and a younger sister. Lingen is what many would call the perfect place to raise a family. It's a pretty little town that's very family oriented. It's big enough to have all the conveniences and attractions you'd need, but small enough to feel familiar and safe. We biked to school with our friends from a young age and played unsupervised on the streets and in the nearby forest with the neighbourhood kids. It's the kind of place where, as a parent, you feel comfortable to let your kids run around outside on their own.

My mum was a teacher, and my dad ran a car dealership and workshop with his brother. We lived in the same house from when I was three, and went on family holidays to the Netherlands – or Northern Africa for something a little more exciting. We embarked on a few shorter camping trips and even tried a longer one once, but thanks to non-stop rain, it was a disaster and we never tried camping for more than a few nights again. Overall, it was a very traditional upbringing. There definitely were no free-spirits, nomads, or vanlifers in my childhood.

I finished school in 2003 and started university in Germany. Like many young people, I was keen to travel and see the world, so I decided to spend two semesters in New Zealand. I can't really remember why I chose New Zealand, but something about it called to me. Maybe it was just the fact that it was so far away. Whatever my reasons, in February 2007, I packed my bags and flew to the other side of the world.

I loved New Zealand from the moment I arrived. It was scary and challenging to be in a new country all by myself, but New Zealand felt right, and I had a great time during that first year. So much so that I ended up extending for another semester – and then for another year and another year after that, and now, as I'm writing this, it's 16 years later, and New Zealand has become home. While that might be what some people would call "Life Done Differently", it didn't feel very different to me. I might have moved to the other side of the world, but there are lots of immigrants with similar stories here in New Zealand, and I still lived a very traditional life. I finished my degree in Management and International Business at the University of Auckland, got a job in market-ing, and settled into a fairly career-focused life. I did well and worked my way up quickly.

All of this led to me being a 33-year-old Head of Marketing of a software startup who lived in New Zealand and enjoyed kitesurfing and other watersports in her free time. Like I said, nothing unusual about that. And nothing wrong with it either. I was happy.

And yet, there was this feeling bubbling away inside of me. At the time, I considered it a sense of sadness – which made no sense given how great life was, but I couldn't find a better word to describe it. The sadness was always strongest when particularly great moments were coming to an end, like on that Easter Monday as I was unloading the car after a fantastic long weekend with my friends. It was almost like I didn't trust that life would continue to be this great, and I felt sad that the future couldn't possibly be as amazing as the present. It felt like things were changing – and I didn't want them to change.

My friends were getting married. Some had already started to have kids. They were buying houses and planning their futures, focused on family life. Somehow, over the last year or two, this bunch of independent, carefree people had turned into ones with grownup jobs, spouses, houses, kids and family commitments. However, when I thought about it, I realised that WE hadn't changed. THEY had. I was still the same carefree, independent person with few grownup responsibilities. "What happened?" I wondered. "When did they all agree on taking these steps together? And why did no one tell me that's what we were doing?" Even as these thoughts went through my mind, I knew, of course, that they hadn't all gotten together one day to plan their lives and agree on a direction – and forgot to tell me. They had just done what most people do at our age. And I hadn't.

So was the sense of sadness because I was feeling left out? Was I sad because I didn't yet have what all my friends had?

Did I want a husband, kids and all those other grownup responsibilities? It would have made perfect sense, yet it didn't feel right.

To be honest, until that point, I had never really thought about whether I wanted a family of my own. It had always seemed so far in the future. I was never one of those women who dreamed of the day she would walk down the aisle in a white dress or the day she would be a mum. I often felt a bit reluctant about the idea of being a mother, but it wasn't like I knew I definitely didn't want kids. I kind of just never really thought about it. Even at 33, it still felt like something far in the future. Whenever I would hear about people my age being pregnant, I would have this initial gut reaction thinking something like, "oh, how scandalous to be pregnant that young". But, of course, that was ridiculous. My friends and I had stopped being too young to be parents long ago.

Regardless of how I felt about kids, there was no more denying that they were becoming a part of my life. We were in that phase where it felt like there was another new baby every time we went away for a long weekend or holiday. Not long, and they would outnumber us. My friends had clearly decided that they wanted families – which probably meant it was time for me to at least have a serious think about it.

That Easter Monday, as I was lying in bed, exhausted yet unable to sleep, was the first time I ever seriously asked myself, "Do I want kids? Do I want a family?" I didn't have an answer. But the question was out there now, and I knew I would have to answer it soon. Whether I could hear it or not, the biological clock was ticking.

I fell asleep that night feeling a weird mix of gratitude for the fun we had and a sense of dread that it won't last. I could feel change coming. And I didn't want things to change.

A couple of weeks later, I was at my desk at work, staring out the window. It wasn't that I didn't have anything better to do, but somehow I struggled with motivation lately.

I'm one of those lucky people who found a profession they enjoy, that they are good at, and that pays well. Maybe because of that, work had become a big part of my life and identity. I was a natural at it, and as someone who had never really been a natural at anything before (except maybe my ability to eat three times the recommended serving size without flinching), it gave me a lot of confidence. I think it's normal to enjoy things we are good at. Who doesn't like being complimented on their achievements and getting positive feedback? I certainly do. I enjoyed the work I was doing, but I think I also really just enjoyed being appreciated, respected and valued. I wanted more of that feeling, so I worked hard and gave it my all. Over time, work increasingly became a big part of my identity. I was Lisa; intelligent, successful, and good at her job. I liked being that person, but there was a darker side to it. At times, it was such a big part of who I was that I was scared of what would happen if I would ever not be good at my job. What if people would stop appreciating me? What if I made a mistake? So I worked harder to make sure that wouldn't happen – and work became even more of my identity.

However, at that point in autumn 2017, I had started to question what it was all for. It was nice to be good at my job, but what was the long-term goal or outcome? What was my motivation to continue to get out of bed every morning to make my way to the office? I was earning good money, but what for?

I watched the people and traffic outside the window next

to my desk. Our office was above a busy intersection in Newmarket, one of the liveliest suburbs of Auckland, New Zealand's biggest city. Cars, buses, cyclists, motorbikes and the occasional truck were driving past outside. On the sidewalks, shoppers, office workers and students from nearby schools were making their way from A to B. It was lunchtime, so the sidewalks were busier than during other times of the day. I wondered if all those people knew what they were doing it for? Did the students know what they were studying for? Did the shoppers know what they really needed and wanted? Did the workers know how they would turn their income into meaning and happiness? Did they all know their 'WHY?'?

In that moment, I wanted nothing more than to go and ask those people what was giving their lives meaning and purpose. Have you ever had an idea that seemed really crazy but at the same time too exciting to ignore? I had one of those that day. I would go and ask random people on the street about their WHY! So I grabbed my jacket and jumped into action before the sensible introvert inside me would have a chance to stop me.

If you have ever tried starting a conversation with a random person on the street, you know it's not easy. Most people probably thought I was trying to sell them something and ignored me like I had ignored countless 'weird' people trying to approach me on the street (I guess that's karma). Those few that stopped and listened to my opening line, which went something like, "could I ask you about what motivates you in life?" generally fled quickly after hearing that. They probably thought I was some religious fanatic trying to convince them of some higher cause and being. In hindsight, I'm surprised I didn't give up at that point. As an introvert, talking to strangers isn't exactly my favourite thing, even when those people actually want to talk to me. Maybe it was because I hadn't really spoken to anyone yet that I had the energy to keep going. However, I clearly needed a new approach.

I decided to get a coffee and come up with a better plan. While waiting for my Flat White, I noticed Ben, a guy I knew vaguely through a shared friend, sitting at one of the tables. I went over to say hi, and as he invited me to sit, I realised this might be my opportunity. I had learned from the quick rejections on the street and approached the topic slightly differently. Basically, I set an expectation up front that things would get a bit crazy. "Can I ask you a weird and, given I barely know you, possibly overly personal question? I promise I'm not trying to sell you anything, and I won't try to convert you to any religion or cult either." I'm not sure if it was the better framing of the conversation or the fact that he literally couldn't leave without me getting up, but I got an answer to my "what is your WHY?" question. I learned that Ben had recently started his own business together with a partner. They had secured seed funding and a significant customer. Everything was going great, but it was also a lot of work. Ben didn't mind. It was evident from how he spoke about the business that his heart and soul were in it. He wanted the company to succeed. Ben wanted to make a difference to customers and employees and, through that, hopefully, become successful as an entrepreneur and ideally wealthy as well – partly so he would be in a good position to start a family with his long-term partner in a few years. That was his WHY. It was all the purpose and meaning he needed in life right now.

Encouraged by that conversation, I decided to keep going. Over the next two weeks, I talked to seven others about meaning, purpose and their WHY. I figured out that sticking to people who at least knew my face was easier than approaching total strangers. So I talked to people who worked in the same building when I saw them on the elevator or people I saw on the ferry almost every day (clearly, approaching people when they couldn't escape was a good strategy).

However, the conversation I remember most from those two weeks was with a total stranger. I noticed her standing at the bus stop outside our office building when I was walking back from getting coffee a few days after my encounter with Ben (yes, I drink a lot of coffee). She was radiant! You didn't have to look twice to know that she was different – and confident. She wore a big colourful dress and had purple highlights in her otherwise grey hair. I thought she might be on the way to a theatre rehearsal or costume party. But at the same time, the way she carried herself and smiled at everyone suggested this was just how she liked to dress. She also seemed like the kind of person who would happily have a somewhat weird conversation with a stranger. Turns out I was right about that.

I found out that her name was Sylvia the Great, which, according to her, "may or may not be her real name". She was 68 and had recently retired. She had five children and, so far, 4 grandchildren and was hoping for more. I told her how much I loved her dress and asked if she had always been into fashion. "You mean if I've always dressed like a crazy person?" was her response. I laughed and nodded. To my surprise, she went on to tell me that she had been a very conservative dresser – and person – until a few years ago. She shared that she had spent her whole life "doing the right thing and looking after other people." She didn't regret any of it, but when she turned 65, she decided to give herself the best gift she had ever received: permission to be crazy and have fun. So now she made it a point to wear bright and crazy outfits every day without worrying about what everyone else thinks, simply because it made her happy.

We could see on the display that her bus was only a few minutes away, so time to get the conversation back on topic. Sylvia the Great pondered my WHY? question for a moment and then replied, "who needs purpose and meaning. What does it mean anyway? My advice is to have fun and be kind. The rest will follow." And with that, she stepped onto her bus, and I never saw her again. But her advice stayed with me.

While not every person I talked to that week was as memorable as Sylvia the Great, they all were interesting in their own ways. However, I can't say I learned anything new. People's answers to what was bringing purpose and meaning to their lives were pretty much what I expected; family, kids, friends, career progression, financial security and status. One young woman talked about wanting to travel the world, but that was about as different as it got.

Not that long ago, I could have related to this. Maybe not the family and kids, but certainly the career progression and financial security. For many years, the drive to learn, progress and get ahead in my career was enough of a WHY to keep me motivated. But I could feel it changing. As much as I still liked being good at my job, it wasn't enough anymore. It certainly wouldn't be enough, on its own, for the next 30+ years.

I started to understand why getting married and having kids is such a natural step for most people. Whether they are consciously aware of it or not, most people probably get to the point in their lives where they wonder what's next, and, let's be honest, starting a family is an easy answer. It's what society expects us to do. It's what we see wherever we look. Many argue it's what we're biologically programmed to want. It also probably goes far beyond just starting a family. In general, most of us live in a society that values conformity. It is so easy to fall into the trap of doing something just because everyone else is doing it. After all, that's what we're expected to do. From a young age, we are taught to fit in, and those who don't often struggle with acceptance. Doing things differently generally isn't encouraged in most situations – certainly not when it comes to having children.

I had long ago figured out that not everyone questions and challenges life the way I do. Not everyone has this urge to explain and make sense of things. Many people seem perfectly happy to simply go with the flow. I envy them sometimes. If you just go with the flow, you probably find yourself happily married with two kids, a mortgage (if you're lucky enough to be able to afford one) and a regular job in your early forties without ever having really asked yourself WHY?, or having considered the alternatives. That path is so ingrained in us that it can be hard sometimes to remember that it is, in fact, a choice – at least for most people from my generation living in the western world. But having kids, in particular, is not only a choice, it is quite possibly one of the most important decisions to make in life.

Having kids is one of the last genuinely permanent decisions my generation makes. With just about everything else, we seem to have more opportunities to change our minds than any other generation before us. While our grandparents and parents usually chose one job for life, it's now incredibly common for people to change jobs and even their entire careers multiple times throughout their life. Moving cities or even countries used to be a huge decision, but nowadays, people move back and forth around the world almost as easily as previous generations used to go on holidays. You can work full-time or part-time – and switch between the two throughout your working life. We get married, divorced and then married again. Everything seems to be possible and flexible. We can make decisions and change our minds in the next year or decade.

You can't do that with kids. Once you decide to have a child, you are a parent for the rest of your life. You can't be a parent for a few years and then change your mind and 'return' the child. You can't be a part-time parent. You might be able to get someone else to look after your children for a few hours, you might even have shared custody with a former partner, but you're still a parent all the time. You still have to provide a good life for them. You still have to consider them in every decision you make. Maybe that's why children give people so much purpose and meaning.

Was I ready for that kind of commitment? Was I willing to give up my freedom – permanently? I did wonder briefly if I was overthinking this. I definitely tend to do that sometimes. But then again, given the magnitude of the decision, I'm more inclined to say that many people are not thinking it through enough.

As I was on the ferry home on the day that concluded my two weeks of asking random people about their motivation, those questions still lingered on my mind. It was a beautiful autumn evening. At half-past five, it was starting to get dark, but there was still enough daylight for the bike ride and ferry trip home to be enjoyable. I loved taking the ferry to work. It took only 10-15 minutes to get from Auckland's North Shore to the City Centre, but I loved being on the water, even for that short time. And during autumn, if I timed it right, I often got to admire stunning sunsets over the Auckland Harbour Bridge on the way home. In addition, the 20-minute bike ride on either side was good exercise – something I probably wouldn't otherwise get on workdays.

As I was waiting for the ferry to depart, my thoughts had shifted from "do I want to commit to children?" to "what else is there?". What do people do with their lives if they don't have kids and start a family? I had to dig around in my memory for a while before I could even think of anyone I knew past 40 who wasn't a parent. I remembered a teacher I had in school almost 20 years earlier. She didn't have kids, which was even more unusual back then. I don't know if it was a choice or a result of circumstances. She was lovely and very popular among students. But I had no idea what gave her life purpose and meaning. I knew she loved theatre. Maybe that was her thing? I thought about a woman who I had worked with a year earlier. She was in her 50s, never married, and didn't have kids. I remember her saying once that she chose not to be a mother, but she didn't go into any more detail. She loved living the good life. She travelled a lot, liked fashion and enjoyed going to fancy restaurants. Thinking about the non-work-related conversations I had with her, I would say travelling gave her a lot of meaning.

Who else? Over the years, I had met a couple of people without kids who seem to have dedicated their lives to their careers and building businesses, but I didn't know any of them well enough to know just how much meaning that was giving their lives. I could imagine that a career-focused life, especially if it involved growing a business from the ground up, could be very fulfilling. Was that what I wanted? A life dedicated to my work? It was certainly the path I was on. If I would change nothing and continue in the same direction, that is probably where I would end up.

I tried to picture it in my mind. What would it be like in 10, 15, or 20 years if I decided not to have kids and instead invest my energy into progressing my career? I would probably get to work on inspiring projects, meet interesting people and work with equally motivated and passionate colleagues and partners. Business, especially the technology-focused area I was working in, was constantly changing, so it would probably never get boring. And I would do well financially. I would earn good money, and without a family to support, I would be able to live a very comfortable life. It all sounded good in theory. And yet, it didn't feel right.

As the ferry arrived in Bayswater and we were getting ready to disembark, it hit me; "I don't want to spend the next 30 years working in an office every day. Yes, I like my work and get a lot of fulfilment from it, but I want more from life."

All the doubts I had over the past weeks, that sense of sadness that kept bubbling up, it all made sense suddenly. The path I was on in life was no longer right for me. But the direction everyone around me had taken didn't feel right either. And it wasn't just about the fact that they were getting married and had kids. It was about the commitments they were making to a certain lifestyle. I wasn't sure if I would ever want kids and marriage, but what I did know was that, right now, I wasn't ready to commit. I wasn't ready to commit to family life, but just as much, I wasn't ready to commit to a career-focused life in the city. The problem was, I didn't know what I wanted.

What do you do with your life if you don't want to follow the traditional path around marriage and family (at least not yet), but a career-focused life isn't what you want either? I decided that it was time to find out.

2

CHANGE
WINTER 2017

Auckland

Lake Taupo

Wellington

Picton

Murchison

Christchurch

S o here I was, 33 years old and with absolutely no idea what I wanted to do with my life. That was a new feeling for me. Until that point, I'd always had goals. I didn't always know how to achieve them, and on more than one occasion, it turned out that I was wrong about what I thought I wanted. Of course, I usually only figured that out after putting a lot of effort into achieving my goals. There were also times when I knew what I wanted and what I needed to do to get it but somehow lacked the motivation to make it happen (like every time I decided to become a yogi but never managed to stick to a regular practice for very long). But not knowing what I wanted was new.

I wouldn't say I was one of those people who always knew what they wanted from life, but I always had goals. Finish school, get accepted into university, study abroad for a while, graduate from university, get a job, do well at my job, get that promotion, learn how to kitesurf and paddle board... You get the idea. That winter, for the first time that I could remember, I didn't have a goal. I didn't know what I wanted. All I did know was that I wanted change. I knew the path I was on wasn't right for me anymore.

How do you change your life? I certainly wasn't new to the concept. In fact, I had gone through a massive transformation in the decade leading up to that moment. I went from being an overweight, unhappy, unhealthy, and at times depressed, student in Germany who was failing classes to being a fit, healthy and happy kiteboarder, outdoor enthusiast and successful marketing manager with a Master's Degree with First Class Honours. I knew how to change. The problem was that this time, I didn't have a goal.

When I turned my life around in my 20s, I had goals. I knew who I wanted to be, and I worked my ass off to become that person. I knew I had to exercise to be fit. I knew I had to study hard to get good grades. I knew I had to invest time into personal growth and self-awareness to gain the mindset I wanted. That's not to say that any of it was easy. All of it required hard work, both mentally and physically, but the fact that the goals were so clear helped. Of course, I didn't appreciate that at the time. It was only now that I wanted change without having such clear goals that I appreciated the value of having them. Hindsight is a beautiful thing.

I played around with different ideas during that winter. I considered anything from simple things like changing my haircut and colour (but I liked having long, blond hair) to much more significant changes like a new career (but I enjoyed my work) or moving to a new city (but what about my friends) or even a new country (but I LOVE New Zealand). Nothing felt right. Nothing felt like it would bring about the kind of change I was after.

I can't remember exactly where I first heard the saying that ultimately pushed me in the right direction, and that has since become a guiding principle in my life.

"If you want change, you have to create space for it."

I wish I could remember how I first heard about it. Maybe I came up with it in some streak of genius. Google seems to think so, given it's my blog post with that same title that shows up at the top of the search results. So, for now, I will claim it as mine. But then again, it doesn't even matter where it came from. What matters is what it means, and what it inspired me to do.

"If you want change, you have to create space for it" is about the idea that for real change to happen, you have to create the space for it in your life. It was about realising that if I would keep working 40-50 hours a week and spend the little free time I had doing the same things I had been doing for the past few years, nothing would change. I would continue on the path that I was on. In addition, it would be tough to figure out what I truly wanted from life if I kept spending all my time trying to succeed in this life I had decided I didn't want.

Here is another saying that has guided me: "It's not about knowing what you want. It's about knowing what you don't want, and then trying new things until you find something worth keeping." I also can't remember where I got this one from (I'm starting to wonder if something is wrong with my memory). The problem with this is that trying new things is incredibly difficult when every minute of every day of your life is already used up. More so, it's challenging to try new things and make space for change when you have bills to pay, people depending on you, expectations to meet, and goals to achieve.

It often feels like so much of our lives is about living up to society's expectations, keeping up and achieving goals, that there is no time for play and experimentation. How will we ever have the time to figure out what we truly want from life if we spend all our time chasing after all the things society tells us we should want?

That winter, I realised that what I really wanted was time. I wanted time to play, experiment and figure out who I am when I'm not chasing after all these goals and ideals I'm supposed to want.

I remember doing the numbers one night. I was working, on average, about 45 hours a week (sometimes more). With a 30-minute lunch break and a two-hour commute every day, I was spending roughly 57 ½ hours earning a living. I've always needed lots of sleep to function well, so that's 56 hours a week spent snoozing. I estimated that I spent about two hours each day doing life admin like cooking, eating, showering and getting dressed, plus another three hours on the weekend for chores like laundry, cleaning and food shopping. That's 17 hours a week. I also liked to start each day with a morning routine that involved reading, journaling and mentally preparing for that day, which took up about 45 minutes each day. So in total, about 136 hours a week are taken up, leaving 32 hours of free time each week. At first, that seemed like a decent chunk. I felt like I could do a lot of new things in 32 hours. However, I quickly realised it's really not that much. Once I caught up with friends, went kitesurfing or did some other outdoor activity, and spent a bit of time reading and relaxing, there wasn't much time left. More importantly, there wasn't much energy left. I learned I might have 32 hours a week to try new things, but I certainly didn't have 32 hours' worth of energy left by the time I got to the free-time portion of the day or week.

At this point, it started to dawn on me that what I really wanted wasn't just time for new things but also energy. It was time to admit that, to make space for the kind of change I wanted, something had to go. Sleeping, eating, showering, and cleaning seemed like things I should definitely keep making time for. I loved my morning routine, so I didn't want give that up. Not seeing my friends and spending less time outdoors was the opposite of what I wanted. That left only one thing: work.

I went from school to university to work without stopping for more than a few weeks for holidays. Ever since I had moved to New Zealand, I had been working hard. I worked part-time alongside my studies, and once I entered the full-time working world, I rarely stopped after 40 hours each week. Maybe it was time to take a break. Perhaps it was time to figure out who I was when my life wasn't dominated by my job.

I honestly can't remember where the idea to buy a campervan to live and travel in came from. It was suddenly just there one day. In the years since, I've often been asked what inspired me to take this step. I feel like people expect me to say something like, "we always went camping when I was a kid", or "a friend was doing it, and it sounded really cool", or even just, "I saw people doing it on Instagram and loved the idea". None of that is true. We may have gone on a couple of camping trips when I was a kid, but they were short ones and overall, my family was definitely more into the resort-style holidays than camping. I didn't have any friends who owned vans, and I didn't even know that #vanlife was a thing on Instagram before that winter. I don't think I ever set foot in a campervan until that year. I had certainly never thought of it as something I would want to do one day. Looking back now, it seems incredibly random. At the time, I don't think anyone in my life would have voted me most likely to end up living in a van down by the river.

Despite it being a somewhat random idea, it felt right from the very first time it crossed my mind. It felt like after months of doubts, uncertainty and searching for answers, the pieces had suddenly fallen into place. It's hard to describe what it's like when something just feels right. It might not make a lot of sense when looking at it with rational and level-headedness, but you know in your heart it's the right thing to do at that specific moment in your life.

The dream was simple. I would buy a campervan, quit my job, give up the room I was renting and live a life of freedom, travelling around beautiful New Zealand. I would spend my days kitesurfing, paddle boarding, reading, writing, exploring and doing whatever else would find me. I would have time and energy to do new things. I would figure out what I want to do with my life and who I wanted to be. I would create the space for change.

The idea turned into a plan pretty much immediately, and I felt like a new person. All the doubts and that sense of sadness from the past few months were replaced with excitement and energy. I felt like I had a new lease on life.

At this point, the sensible thing would have been to do a lot of research and carefully plan the changes I wanted to make. I'm usually a fairly considerate and somewhat cautious person. I'm certainly not Miss Spontaneity, and I don't think anyone would call me impulsive. And yet, in this case, I just jumped right in. Looking back now, I honestly can't believe how unprepared and impulsive I was about it all. It seems crazy and out of character, but I guess I was on a mission, and nothing was going to stop me. Luckily, it all worked out in the end – though not without some challenges. I learned a few lessons the hard way and probably could have saved myself from some setbacks had I done my homework.

All those realisations would come much later. That winter in 2017, I was too excited about my new plan to be sensible. And so I went van shopping.

Thanks to a good job and a relatively frugal lifestyle, I had some savings, and I planned to use those to buy a van and support myself while I took time out from work for a few months. Figuring out how much to spend on a van was a balancing act. On the one hand, I wanted to be comfortable living in it, but on the other hand, I knew that spending less on the van meant my savings would last longer before I had to go back to work. Ultimately, I decided that I would be comfortable spending up to NZ$ 25,000 for my home on wheels.

Build or buy was another critical decision I had to make. After I first had the idea, I pictured myself living in one of those beautiful, custom-built vans you see on Instagram. I also really loved the idea of converting a van myself. Something about living in a home I had built (or at least helped build) appealed, and it would mean that I could design the van precisely as I wanted it. However, while the decision to live and travel in a van was somewhat impulsive, this was when the cautious realist in me won the upper hand again (thank god!). As much as I loved the idea of converting my own van, I had to admit that it probably wasn't the best idea. I didn't have the skills, tools, time or place to do it. If I had tried a DIY build, I probably would have ended up writing a book about van conversion fails instead of one about living in a van. I also realised that, here in New Zealand, buying a ready to go camper is generally cheaper than converting one to the same standard due to the cost of materials. So after a little reality check, I decided I would buy a campervan that is ready to go instead of spending summer trying to figure out how to convert one.

I started by making a list of the things my van must have. I quickly realised that I definitely wanted one that was certified self-contained. A self-contained van is one that you can live in off-grid without having any impact on the environment around you and without leaving any waste behind. This means you must have a toilet on board, a proper rubbish bin, and waste- and fresh water tanks. We have a Certified Self-Contained Standard in New Zealand where vehicles get inspected and get a certificate that confirms they are, in fact, suitable for off-grid living. While there is a bit of ongoing debate about exactly how valid this standard is, I learned that there are places where you are only allowed to stay overnight if your vehicle is certified self-contained. With that in mind, I decided it was a must-have for me. At the time, the regulations around the standard had just changed so that only vehicles where the toilet was accessible, even with the bed fully made up, would be able to get certified as self-contained. I'm also quite possibly the person with the world's smallest bladder so an onboard toilet that was easily accessible at any time was a must-have for me regardless of what any standard demands. As a result, I ruled out the very small vans.

The next thing I thought about was height. I'm almost six feet tall, so if I wanted to be able to stand up in my van, it would have to be a high-top. I thought about this one for a bit, mainly because there was a significant price difference between average height campervans and those with a high top. If I would buy one I couldn't stand in, I would have been able to afford a newer model, reducing the risk of costly maintenance and repairs. However, in the end, I decided that standing height was important to me. I was buying a van to live in, and I wanted to be comfortable. I also figured that, as an introvert who values privacy, I would probably spend a lot of time in the van when others might be happy to sit outdoors, and I was sure I would appreciate the extra space a high-top van provides.

Safety was another factor I considered. New Zealand is generally a very safe place. However, given I would travel alone, I thought it couldn't hurt to be extra careful. With that in mind, I decided I wanted a van where you can walk through from the back into the driver's cabin. That way, I would always have the option to take off without having to leave the van should I ever feel unsafe.

Other than that, the list of what I was looking for was fairly short. I preferred an automatic, but it wasn't a must-have. I liked the idea of a permanent bed. But, in the end, I realised that was something I was willing to compromise on in exchange for having a smaller, more manoeuvrable van. I figured turning the seating area into my bed every night, and back into seats in the morning, wouldn't be such a big deal when you've got lots of time on your hands.

Deciding that I wanted a high-top van, combined with my limited budget, significantly narrowed down the options. Add to that the fact that I wanted to keep it as small as possible so it would be easy to drive even around towns, and I was left with four options: A Mercedes Sprinter, a Ford Transit, a Fiat Ducato or a Toyota Hiace. Out of those options, the Ford Transit seemed to be the most common and most affordable here in New Zealand.

At this stage, I should have looked at as many vans as possible, talked to experts, researched the different models online to learn about their pros and cons, and just generally should have learned about campervans and what to look out for when buying one. I didn't do any of that. Apparently, my sensible cautious side had exhausted itself when it talked me out of converting my own van, and now the impulsive 'I want a van, and I want it now' Lisa was back in charge. After spending a few hours scrolling through TradeMe (New Zealand's eBay), I found a van I liked. It was a 1999 Ford Transit High Top that was factory-built as a campervan. It ticked all the boxes and was within my budget. The only problem; it was located on the South Island, over 1000 kilometres away from where I was living at the time. However, I had noticed that vans seemed to be a bit cheaper on the South Island than up in the north, so I figured I might be able to get a bit of a bargain by buying down south. I thought about flying down to check it out, but the owners had sent me lots of photos, so I knew what it looked like, and I figured I wouldn't be able to tell how good a condition it's in mechanically anyway. So instead, I found a local garage to do a pre-purchase inspection, the owners dropped it off, and once it got the all-clear, I agreed to buy it. For anyone who thinks that's a bit impulsive, you're absolutely right. I swear I'm usually a much smarter and more careful person. I hope it helps if I tell you that I didn't hand over any money until I had met the owners and seen the van. And at least I did get a pre-purchase inspection done. That must count for something.

On the 31st of August, I officially took ownership of my new home on wheels. I flew from Auckland to Christchurch, took a bus out to Rangiora where the sellers picked me up at the bus stop and took me to their home where the van was parked in the driveway. My memories of the next couple of hours are a bit of a blur. I can't even remember what my first impression of my new home was. I think I was too excited and nervous to really take in the moment. Before I knew it, I had handed over the money, jumped in my van and headed north.

I stopped for groceries and then pointed the steering wheel towards Murchison. It was only once I had left the city behind and was cruising along on the open road that it started to sink in. At the time, the coastal road through Kaikoura was still closed due to earthquake damage, so I had to take the longer, less scenic inland route. I didn't mind. I was on an 'I'm a van-owner' high. Everything was exciting and beautiful, and there was this sense of it being the beginning of something amazing.

When I think back to that day, I can't help but chuckle at my naivety. It was this moment in time when vanlife was all about freedom and adventure. I didn't know yet that there would also be challenges and setbacks. I didn't know yet that living in a van came with its own problems and that you can't just park up anywhere you want and spend the night. I didn't know about overflowing freedom camping spots or the total disregard for privacy and personal space that are also part of this life. Don't get me wrong, even now, almost five years later, I still think that the good far outweighs the challenges. But sometimes I miss the carefreeness and naivety of that moment when everything seemed so simple and exciting.

I spent my first night as a vanlifer in Murchison, a small town about four hours northwest of Christchurch. Before I bought my van, I had joined the New Zealand Motor Caravan Association (NZMCA), mainly to take advantage of the heavily discounted ferry tickets. Since I had to take the ferry from the South to the North Island to get back to Auckland, joining the NZMCA was worth it. The association had a property in Murchison where members could park overnight, which is where I spent my first night. My most vivid memory from that first night is how cold it was. While Auckland and Northland – my usual stomping grounds at this time of the year – hardly ever see temperatures below zero, the South Island is a very different story. Of course, given the van I'd just bought was advertised as having a heater, I had assumed the cold wouldn't be an issue when I had planned the trip north. Turns out, that is yet another example of how little I knew about campervans at the time.

As the temperatures dropped in the evening, I tried to get the heather running, following the steps the previous owners had shown me during the handover. Try as I might, I couldn't get it going. After turning every switch on and off at least ten times, I decided to call the sellers and ask for advice. With them on the line, I tried all the switches again without any luck. They told me to turn the main power switch off and on again, which also didn't do anything. Eventually, they suggested it could be a problem with the campground power and advised connecting to another power plug. My response, that I wasn't plugged into power, was met with silence followed by: "Dear, it's an electric heater. It won't work unless you are connected to power." (I could hear them roll their eyes). So that was one of the first things I learned about my van; the electric heater, as well as the microwave and power outlets, only work when I'm connected to power at a campground. Who knew? I swear I'm usually a pretty smart cookie!

Despite the cold, I survived the night thanks to my sleeping bag and an extra fleece blanket I had bought before I left Rangiora. The next morning, I warmed myself up with hot coffee and then continued my journey to Picton to catch the ferry to the North Island that afternoon. Somewhere along the way, I decided to name my van Josie. The name just came to me and felt right. Josie sounded fun and likeable but also strong and maybe a bit quirky. I had a feeling that Josie and I would have some great times together. However, later that afternoon, we had a not-so-great time crossing the Cook Strait in howling winds and massive waves. As a sailor's daughter, I don't easily get seasick, but I got pretty close that day. I was half expecting Josie to be destroyed by the time we got to Wellington, but apparently, she didn't mind the rough sea as much as I did – even the coffee mugs in the cupboard were still in one piece.

After a night in Wellington to recover from the wild ferry ride, I continued my trip north. After two hectic days of rushing north to catch the ferry, I was able to slow down a bit. I had taken a couple extra days off work, so I had two full days to get from Wellington back to Auckland. On the first day, I drove for about four hours to the southern end of Lake Taupō, where I spent the night at the lakeside freedom camping spot.

I remember this being the moment where it started to sink in. I officially owned a campervan! I sat in my new (to me) van, drinking coffee, and it felt like home already.

Josie was a 1999 Ford Transit with a diesel engine and had done just over 200,000km. She had an automatic transmission, which is rare for these vans, but something I really appreciated, especially when having to stop on steep hills, of which there are many in New Zealand. A separate house battery kept the fridge running and the lights on, and was charged via the solar panel on the roof, the alternator while driving and when plugged into power at a campsite. Gas was used for cooking and to heat hot water. Inside, Josie had everything I needed. Behind the passenger seat was the kitchen with a fridge, a sink, a gas stove and storage. Opposite the kitchen, behind the driver's seat, was the little bathroom. Though bathroom is a big word for what it was. There was a toilet and a shower, essentially occupying the same space, and just enough room for me to fit in. I didn't mind. After all, I wasn't planning to spend much time in the bathroom. Next to the bathroom was more storage as well as the aforementioned electric heater and the microwave. At the back of the van were benches on either side that would be my lounge during the day and then turn into my bed at night. Above, shelves provided storage space for clothes, books and other knick-knacks. At the rear, Josie had the two sideways opening doors typical for this style of van. That day at Lake Taupō, I sat on one of the benches, facing to the rear with both doors wide open so I could enjoy the views of the lake. I knew right away that those doors, and the undisturbed views they provided, would be one of my favourite features of my new home. I could already see myself parked up in beautiful locations with open doors, bringing the scenery into my living room.

I remember feeling incredibly happy and content in that

moment. I had just made the single biggest purchase of my life – buying something I knew next to nothing about. Yet, I didn't have an ounce of doubt that I was doing the right thing. I don't think I had ever before been so sure that I was on the right path.

However, the next morning, I got the first taste of the downside of vanlife and freedom camping when one of the fellow campers apparently thought we would all like to listen to his trance music at full volume. If it hadn't been for him, I might have hung around this beautiful spot a bit longer, but as it was, I decided to make an early start and hit the road. After a few stops, I made it back to Auckland by early evening. I parked the van at the side of the road above the house where I was living at the time and just sat there for a while. I didn't want my first van adventure to be over. I didn't want to return to the real world and long days in the office the next day. Luckily, it would only be for a few more months. Soon, it would be summer, and I would start my full-time vanlife adventure. But first, I had a bit of preparation to do – starting with telling people about my plans.

My new home on wheels.

To view more photos from my journey, visit my website.
lifedonedifferently.com/gallery

3

PREPARATION

SPRING 2017

Auckland

It was September, less than three months before my planned departure date, and I hadn't told anyone about my plans yet. I also hadn't really discussed the doubts and uncertainties that had led to the decision to live in my campervan with anyone. That wasn't unusual for me. I'm a very internally-focused person. I usually think things through on my own before I talk about them. Besides, I was worried I would be misunderstood by my friends who were all so confidently following the marriage and kids path in life. I didn't want them to think I was criticising their choices or not supporting them, or that I didn't love their kids. So I kept quiet and dealt with things internally – which is my default anyway.

So far, all I had shared is that I was buying a campervan without going into much detail, knowing most people would assume I planned to use it for weekend trips and holidays. I'd talked about the idea of living in it for a while with two close friends, but even with them, I'd been cautious about what I said. Truth is, I wasn't ready to share my new plan with the world. I was in the honeymoon phase. The idea to live and travel in my van, enjoying adventure and freedom, seemed so exciting and so right. I didn't want anyone poking holes into it. I wasn't sure if people would understand why I was doing this and worried that they would challenge my sanity for giving up a well-paying job and a great life in Auckland to live in a 20-year-old van. I wasn't scared of swimming against the stream. On the contrary, I was excited to be doing so. What I was worried about was potentially having to accept that my friends and people I care about wouldn't be supportive. I was afraid that my choices could mean the end of friendships that meant a lot to me, because I couldn't see how I would be friends with someone who wasn't supporting this plan that had become so important to me. On top of that, I was worried about my boss and colleagues feeling like I was letting them down, and I hated that idea.

Funnily enough, my family was the easiest part in all of this. They all still live in Europe, and with them being so far away, their influence on my life and decisions was very limited. But even without the distance, I wouldn't have worried about my parents disapproving or challenging my plans. It's just not who they are. They've always let me and my siblings make our own decisions, only very rarely voicing strong opinions or interfering. I was sure it would be no different this time. I was a lot less sure about how my friends and colleagues would react to my plans.

But, I knew I had to say something eventually. People would notice once I'm gone. I also wanted to share my journey openly in the hope that it would connect me with others who could relate to what I was going through. About a month earlier, as I was still in the middle of figuring out what I wanted to do next with my life, I'd started a blog called Life Done Differently. I always loved writing, and it had long been a way for me to process things, reflect, and gain clarity. I have written about every significant phase in my life – though in most cases, in personal journals that no one will ever see (at least I hope so!). In this case, I had decided to write publicly – for two main reasons. Firstly, I felt like the world needed more examples of people challenging the status quo and not following the beaten path just because everyone else is doing so. And secondly, I was hoping that it would connect me with like-minded people. Until that point, I had written about my doubts and the search for a different path in life, as well as buying the van, but I hadn't yet shared that I intended to live in the van full-time. However, if I wanted to be authentic, I had to put it all out there – which, of course, I couldn't do until I told the important people in my life in person.

I started with those friends who I thought would most likely support my plan. They all loved the idea and were almost as excited about it as I was – though I think there was a bit of wonder and surprise as well. I should probably point out that I decided to ease people, and myself, into it. I honestly didn't know how long I would want to live and travel in my van, but I had a gut feeling that it would be a while. However, whenever I told people about my plan, I said I would do it for the summer. I figured that way, it would seem less crazy, and it meant that if I didn't enjoy it, I could simply go back to my old life without having to explain anything. Nevertheless, I was planning to quit my job, move out of my rented room and sell most of my belongings that didn't fit in the van, so it was defi-nitely more than an extended holiday.

After the positive response from my friends, I told the guy I was dating at the time. You probably think it's weird, maybe even dishonest, that I had gotten this far without telling him, but we had only been dating a few weeks, and things were still very casual. He did know, of course, that I bought a camper-van. His reaction to that told me he probably wouldn't be the number one fan of my plan, which is one of the reasons I delayed telling him the whole story. Turned out my instincts were right. He was not a fan. In fact, he was the only person who responded openly negatively. In his defence, we met through work and bonded over our shared interest in business and technology startups. He was very career-focused and probably assumed that I was, too. He wasn't outdoorsy and hadn't really met kiteboarder, ocean-lover and outdoor enthu-siast Lisa yet. I can understand how it all came as a bit of a shock to him. Not surprisingly, the relationship ended the day I told him about my vanlife plans.

I'm not going to pretend I was heartbroken over it. I had already started to figure out that he probably wasn't the one for me – regardless of my future plans. I also think the fact that I made this whole plan without even considering whether he would maybe want to come along was pretty telling. I knew in my heart that this was something I wanted to do on my own. In hindsight, I should have just ended it with him instead of telling him about my plans and then making him the bad guy for not supporting me. But, you know what they say about hindsight.

While I wasn't heartbroken about the end of that relationship, his response did make me pause. For the first time since I had the vanlife idea, I had serious doubts. The intensity of his rejection of my plan, the way he called it career suicide, a waste of money, unsafe and utterly stupid, I couldn't help but let it get to me. Was this whole plan riskier than I made it out to be in my head?

I realised I hadn't really thought about the risks until that point. I had worried about people not supporting it, I had considered the possibility that I might not enjoy the lifestyle, and I had worried about the practicalities of the lifestyle (where would I park, do my laundry, get fresh water, etc.). But I hadn't thought much about the risks – the risks that would come with the lifestyle as well as the risks of walking away from my job and settled life in the city.

Would travelling on my own in a van be safe? Truth be told, I didn't spend too much time pondering that question. I have always been good at doing stuff on my own. I moved to New Zealand on my own, I backpacked around the world on my own, and did lots of other things safely on my own that others might consider risky. I've been told on occasion that I have a bit of a "don't mess with me" aura when needed, so I'm pretty confident I wouldn't be an easy victim. Besides, New

Zealand is a very safe country in that regard, and I'm an intelligent, sensible person who doesn't take unnecessary risks (most of the time). Also, I was planning to have good insurance and sign up for roadside assistance, so I would have that to fall back on if needed. Overall, I was confident I would be safe – or at least not any less safe than I was living in Auckland.

Would doing this put my career and financial security at risk? That was a more difficult question to answer, and I pondered it for a few weeks. However, in the end, the answer was simple. First of all, I felt like the risk was minimal. In many ways, I was just taking a time-out for a while (for now). I knew my skills were in demand, and I had a good reputation and network, so if I decided in a few months that I wanted to go back to working a full-time job, I was confident I would find something. It might not be my dream job, but it would pay the bills, and I could keep looking for the perfect job from there. I also had a bit of money saved up, so I could afford to be without income for a while, which made it all feel much less risky. However, what really allowed me to put that question, and any worries that came with it, aside was realising that it didn't matter. At the end of the day, I didn't want to be a super successful career woman. I wanted to be happy. And I knew that taking this break would make me happy much more so than career progression would. So maybe it was risky, but it was a risk worth taking.

Thinking through all of this also made me realise that this whole undertaking didn't have to be that big a deal. I think some people hear about a plan like this, and to them, it feels like this massive, life-changing, permanent decision, full of risks and uncertainty. But to me, it felt more like something I would try for a while. If I like it, I keep going, and if not, I can go back to my old life. Approaching it that way made it seem much less risky and allowed me to enjoy the excitement without getting bogged down with worries.

———

Having put my mind at ease that the risks I was taking were worth it, it was time to tell my boss. Over the past few months, he and I had worked together very closely to redefine the goals and market for the business, and we'd arrived at a point where the strategy was becoming clear, and the opportunity before us was exciting. It was hard to leave just as we'd arrived at this point. I hate letting people down, and I couldn't help but feel like that was exactly what I was doing. I was worried that people might think I didn't believe in the business or that I wasn't proud of what we had achieved. So as you can imagine, I was feeling very nervous about telling my boss and the team. But I just knew that this was something I had to do.

As it turned out, I worried for nothing. My boss and the whole team could not have been any more supportive. They totally got what I wanted to do and were all super excited. And best of all, I didn't even have to resign. After talking through my plans and what the business needed over the coming months, we decided that I would continue doing some work remotely while I was travelling. This was before COVID made working remotely normal, and I felt incredibly grateful that I was given this opportunity. We agreed that I would work 10-15 hours a week while on the road, and then we would re-evaluate at the end of summer. I was thrilled. Not only did it mean that I could continue doing the work I loved and supporting the business, it also meant that I didn't have to rely on savings to cover my costs while I was travelling.

Everything was falling into place, and I was more excited than ever about the summer ahead. However, before I could set off for full-time vanlife, I first had to get my van ready. While I had bought a factory-built camper that had all the essentials for a comfortable life on the road, there were a few tweaks I wanted to make. The biggest challenge was finding a way to transport my standup paddle board and my longboard. Having them on roof racks like you would on a car wasn't an option. First of all, they would block the solar panel and the roof vent, and I needed both. Secondly, it would be impossible to get the heavy boards on and off the roof by myself. I'm tall, but not that tall. So, I needed a different solution.

To be honest, this is another example of something I should have probably thought through before buying a van. Instead, I just bought one thinking I'd figure it out somehow. I found photos online of vans with surfboard racks on the side, which looked like a great option. However, finding someone here in New Zealand to build those for my van proved difficult. I called and emailed countless people. From welders to panel beaters, motorhome manufacturers and repairers, and boat builders, no one was keen to take on the job. Part of the problem was that the top part of my van was made of fibreglass, which, apparently, is hard to work with.

I was looking forward to spending the summer exploring lakes and coastlines on my paddle board and learning to surf on my longboard, so finding a way to take both with me was really important. I could, of course, transport them in the van, but it would be super annoying. They would take up all the room, and I'd have to move them out of the van every time I wanted to use the space – and then there'd be the risk of them getting stolen at night. Just as I was trying to come to terms with the idea that I might have to travel without my boards, I found Vehicle Construction and Maintenance in Auckland. Their "we can do anything" attitude was exactly what I needed. Together, we came up with the perfect design, and they built the racks and attached them to the side of my van. The boards would be secured with lockable straps, which would make them as theft-proof as possible. It didn't come cheap, but it was worth it. And as a bonus, the guys also attached a tow ball at the back where I could attach a rack for my bike so that it would come along on the journey as well.

With that part sorted, I could focus on making myself at home in the van. While I had to walk away from the idea of converting my own campervan, I wanted to personalise the factory-built camper so that it would feel like my home. I got new covers for the couch squabs, put up photos, fairy lights and other nick-nacks and moved in some of my stuff. During October and November, I also went on a few weekend trips to get comfortable with the van and figure out what essentials I needed.

I had set the first of December as my departure day, and with that date fast approaching, it was time to tackle another big part of preparing for the lifestyle change: downsizing. For the past year before I set off, I rented a room in a house. Luckily, that meant I didn't have much furniture and other big items to get rid of. However, I still had a lot more stuff than fitted in the van. I know many people who embarked on a similar lifestyle change find downsizing hard, but I loved it – almost too much so. There was something incredibly liberating about getting rid of stuff. I was tempted to sell or give away everything I wasn't taking with me. But, just as I was about to donate all my winter clothes to charity, luckily, my more sensible side intervened and asked the valid question: "what am I going to wear in winter?" I also had a few books, a small desk and other bits and pieces that had sentimental value and were worth holding on to. I considered asking friends if I could store stuff with them, but in the end, I decided not to burden them with my boxes. Instead, I rented the smallest and cheapest storage option I could find and filled it with everything I wanted to keep but didn't want to take with me. Over the years, that has proven to be a good decision. It means I can leave winter clothes behind in summer and vice versa, have somewhere to store things I want to hold on to but don't have space for in the van, and I'm not burdening friends.

When it was time to move into the van, I made three piles of all the stuff that I still had at the time: Must Come, Maybe and Not Needed. I remember the Must Come pile looking huge. Since I had already made some weekend trips in the van, the essentials like kitchen utensils and some of my clothes were already in the van. I had also already moved in some books, non-perishable food and other bits and pieces. And yet, the pile of everything that still had to go into the van looked massive. There were clothes, shoes, jackets, bedding, towels, toiletries, books, my laptop and other work gear, my arts and crafts box, the tennis racks and balls (which I would never use), and of course, all my sports gear: three kites, a kiteboard, two bars and lines, a harness, three wetsuits, leashes, the paddle for the paddle board, snorkelling gear, bike helmet and a yoga matt. To my surprise, it all fit. The van offered a lot of storage, with massive space under the benches and over the driver's cabin, plus shelves above the benches on both sides. I even ended up taking a few things from the Maybe pile – most of which I never used or needed.

Eventually, as spring turned into summer, the van was loaded, my boards attached on the side and the bike at the back, and it was time to hit the road.

4

FREEDOM

SUMMER 2017 / 18

Spirits Bay

Karikari Peninsula

Muriwai Beach

Bay of Plenty

East Cape

Lake Taupo

The second of December 2017 marks the official start of my full-time vanlife adventures, and I couldn't have asked for a better way to kick off this new phase in my life. I spent the first weekend at one of my all-time favourite places; Muriwai Beach on Auckland's west coast. For the most part, New Zealand's west coast is wild and rugged, while the east coast tends to be much calmer. In other words, if you want a relaxing beach day and a safe swimming spot, east is best. If you want big waves, rough coastlines and less crowded beaches, go west. Muriwai Beach is a beautiful black sand beach that stretches for miles, from the small settlement at its southern end to the entrance to the Kaipara Harbour, 60 kilometres north of Muriwai village. It's worth a visit for its beauty alone, but Muriwai is one of my favourite places because it's an epic kitesurfing spot. It's not for the faint-hearted. On a good day, the wind blows strongly from the southwest, the waves are big, and the currents and rips can be unpredictable. But that's what makes it fun. When you kite out there, you have to be present. Not paying attention for even a second can result in being caught in the waves and tumbling around for a bit before you can somehow find your way up and get air into your lungs. I had some scary moments out there, but many more thrilling and fun ones.

However, on that first weekend in December, my first one as a vanlifer, Muriwai was the complete opposite of what it's famous for – and what I love it for. The sun was shining, there was barely a breeze in the air, and the waves were small and glassy. So, instead of kiteboarding, it was a surfing and hanging out at the beach kind of weekend. I wasn't complaining. It was nice to see this side of Muriwai Beach, and it made for excellent conditions to ease into vanlife. I arrived on

Friday and stayed at the local campground right behind the dunes, providing easy access to the beach. I would come to love this campground, partly because of its location but also for the friendly team, modern facilities, and amazing showers. My friend Lina joined me at the campground for a night, and other friends came out for the day on Sunday. We had an epic time at the beach, catching waves (or trying to, in my case) and hanging out in the sun. Then, Sunday afternoon, it was time to say goodbye. As my friends headed back to their lives in the city, I got ready to begin my big adventure.

My first destination was Lake Taupō, New Zealand's biggest lake, right in the centre of the North Island. The startup I worked for was developing event management and safety software, and the Ironman New Zealand team was putting the platform to the test at the Ironman 70.3 event in Taupō that following weekend. Several of us were heading down to support the Ironman team and see how our app would work in the real world. A lot of hard work had gone into getting to this point, and we were all very excited to see the software used at such a high-profile event. Of course, I didn't want to miss it. Given I was the most flexible and had my own accommodation on wheels, I was sent as the advance team. I arrived in Taupō on Tuesday and spent the next few days getting to know the team and training them on using the app. On Thursday and Friday, the rest of our team made their way down and together, we helped the Ironman team get ready and supported them as much as we could during the event. The weekend was a complete success. Feedback from the Ironman team was great, and we learned a lot from being on the ground with them. However, it was also full-on, and by the end of it, I was looking forward to a few quiet days to recharge. I decided to head east to Ohope at the southern end of the Bay of Plenty region and then make my way north along the coast.

I thoroughly enjoyed my first few weeks in the van. After the busy week in Taupō, life slowed down. I did a few hours of work here and there, but I spent most of my time enjoying life. I tried to improve my surfing (without much success), read a lot, went for walks on the beach or rode my bike, explored new places and drank coffee while admiring the scenery and contemplating life. I found the transition into vanlife surprisingly easy. There were no significant unexpected challenges or things that went wrong, and I felt perfectly safe. Any questions I had were easily answered by a Google search or the CamperMate and the NZMCA mobile apps which listed camping spots as well as dump stations, fresh water refill points, supermarkets and everything else I needed. I remember it all feeling easy and natural. I took to vanlife as if it was always meant to be.

Before starting my vanlife journey, I had occasionally worried about whether I would feel safe while freedom camping. It's one thing to sleep alone in a van when parked up at a managed campground or fenced private property surrounded by others. But would I feel safe parked up in a public spot where anyone could come and go at all hours? Luckily, I quickly realised I had nothing to worry about. Turns out that you're rarely actually alone while freedom camping in New Zealand – at least not in summer. My first freedom camping experience was in Ohope. I found several designated free camp spots in the area on the mobile apps and chose the one closest to the beach. I arrived around mid-day, and only one other camper was already parked up. However, over the afternoon, five others showed up one by one. I chatted briefly with some of my temporary neighbours, who were all lovely. By the time it got dark, I felt perfectly safe and fell asleep without a worry on my mind. And that's pretty much what it was like at most freedom camping spots during my travels. I was rarely alone. If anything, it was often too crowded, especially during the summer months.

Having put my mind at ease about freedom camping, I spent a lot of nights in free spots during the first summer. Though at least once or twice a week, I usually stayed at a paid campground, mainly because I wanted to take a proper shower. While Josie had a shower, it was tiny, and I had to squat to get my hair wet. In addition, showering in the van meant I used up a lot of my freshwater and had to refill constantly. Staying at a paid camp also meant I could do laundry and charge up the van's batteries, so once or twice a week, it seemed worth the $15 - $25 most camps charged.

After a week and a half in the Bay of Plenty, I started to make my way north to spend Christmas with friends on the Karikari Peninsula, which had long been one of my favourite parts of New Zealand. The peninsula, which pokes out on the east coast of the northern end of New Zealand, looks a bit like an upside down version of Italy when viewed on a map, but much smaller. With Doubtless Bay in the east, Rangiputa Harbour in the west and Rangaunu Bay in the north, Karikari Peninsula is paradise for anyone who loves the ocean. You're never more than a few minutes from a white sandy beach. The area is also known for consistent sea breezes, which many find annoying at times, but us kiteboarders love them. As so many times before, we once again had an amazing time. We kiteboarded on Rangiputa Harbour and at Tokerau Beach, had coffees at Carrington Estate and explored the peninsula's many beautiful beaches.

When it was time for my friends to return to Auckland at

the end of the holidays, I continued north. It was a weird feeling. Up until this moment, I'd felt like I was on holiday. For several years now, I'd spent time over the summer holidays with this group of friends, so the last few weeks had felt normal. But when everyone else returned to Auckland and their busy lives, while I headed off in the other direction to continue my life of freedom, it started to sink in that this summer was special. With that realisation came a determination to make the most of it – starting with a couple of weeks off the beaten track in the Far North.

I had been to Cape Reinga at the very northern end of New Zealand a couple of times before, but always for fairly rushed day trips. This time, I was looking forward to taking my time and visiting some of the more remote parts. One place I was particularly looking forward to exploring was Kapowairua / Spirits Bay. In photos, it looked like paradise, and I couldn't wait to see it for myself. So one day in the second half of January, I turned off State Highway 1 in Waitiki Landing and followed a gravel road for 15 kilometres. It was slow going. At the end of summer, the road was in poor condition due to the high volume of traffic over the holidays. I took my time and prayed that the van and everything in it would survive the bumpy ride. However, once I made it over the last hill, and Kapowairua / Spirits Bay came into view, I immediately knew it was worth the time it took to get here. Before me, the bright blue bay and white sandy beach stretched out into the distance. After a quick photo stop, I drove down to the campsite, checked in, and found a spot to set up camp.

Kapowairua / Spirits Bay is an area of great significance for Māori, New Zealand's indigenous people. According to Māori legend, the large old pōhutukawa tree above the bay is where the spirits of the dead depart from this world to return to their ancestral home. Hence the name Spirits Bay, or Kapowairua in the Māori language, which means "catch the spirit". Due to the significance of the area, access to land outside of the campground is restricted. However, I chatted with the Māori camp managers and asked if I could walk up one of the nearby hills. I was given permission to do so, as long as I respected the land by leaving nothing but footprints behind. So on my second day at Spirits Bay, I made my way up the green hills. The higher I climbed, the more spectacular the views got. It was a beautiful clear day, and I could see for miles. Spirits Bay stretched out below me to the west. In the east was equally beautiful Takapaukura / Tom Bowling Bay, behind me were rolling green hills, and in front of me, the endless oceans melted into the horizon.

I was walking along when I suddenly heard animal noises. Expecting sheep or cattle, I turned the corner quietly so I wouldn't frighten them. To my surprise and delight, what waited for me on the other side was a herd of wild horses. There were at least 20 of them, including some foals. Seeing these horses grazing on the green hills with the blue ocean behind them was breathtaking. I snuck around quietly to take some photos without scaring them away, and then sat down on a rock to watch them for a while. By now, they had noticed me, but I kept my distance and they didn't seem to mind me. Every now and then, one would come a few steps in my direction with a look of curiosity, but they always changed their mind before coming too close. It was a magical moment and one that I was sure I would remember for a long time. "Who needs a TV or big city entertainment?" I thought to myself. "I'd rather watch wild horses in paradise."

At the end of January, after an amazing time in the Far North, I started to make my way south again. I spent a few days around Auckland to catch up with friends and then headed south towards the East Cape. When you look at a map of the North Island of New Zealand, you see a bit poking out on the east, roughly halfway up the coast. That's the East Cape. It was the only larger area on the North Island I hadn't been to yet, and ever since I decided to live and travel in my van, I knew it was one of the first places I wanted to visit. The East Cape didn't disappoint. Right after my trip, I wrote a blog post about the region and titled it "New Zealand's unpolished Gem", which I felt perfectly summarises the peninsula north of Gisborne. It's much less touristy than other parts of the country but no less beautiful. Following State Highway 35 from Gisborne around the cape to Opotiki takes you past white sandy beaches, along rugged coastlines, over green hills and through small settlements, all of which make the East Cape a stunning place. I also liked that the locals were welcoming without that, at times, forced friendliness we've become used to in more tourism-focused areas. In addition, in the second half of February, most of the summer visitors had left, meaning campgrounds were quiet, making it easy to find a spot.

I spent a few days in Tologa Bay, famous for the 660-metre-long wharf that stretches out into the bay. From there, I made my way to Tokomaru Bay, where I surfed and paddle boarded in the bay and enjoyed being parked up with uninterrupted views of the coast. One day at Tokomaru Bay, I was sitting in my camping chair outside my van reading, when a couple pulled up in their campervan next to me and introduced themselves as Marie and Thomas. We started chatting, and I learned that Marie was Norwegian and Thomas

American. They'd met backpacking in South America two years ago and had been together ever since. They'd arrived in New Zealand the previous December, bought their little camper and hit the road. They had started in the south and were making their way north. I told them about my favourite places to visit in the Far North, and they gave me tips for when I would make it further south.

Over the following two days that we spent parked next to each other at Tokomaru Bay, Marie, Thomas and I discovered we had a lot in common. Like me, they were in their 30s and didn't want to do the things most of their friends were focused on – settling down, starting families and working to get ahead in their careers. When Marie and Thomas met in South America two years earlier, both had full-time jobs in their respective home countries. They took as much leave as they could each year to go on big adventures, always dreaming of not having to return to their normal lives. "When we met, it was like we were each other's sign to make that dream a reality," Marie explained. "With Thomas, I finally had someone in my life who was pushing me to follow that dream instead of asking me when I would settle down, get married and have kids." Thomas said he felt the same way and explained that when they had to say goodbye in South America, they made a pact with each other that they would use the next 12 months to figure out how they could have a life of adventure and freedom. They had only met a few weeks earlier, so they didn't know if it would be a life together, but that wasn't the point. The goal was to find a way to be able to travel more and see the world – whether it would be together or separately.

Interestingly, both realised that it was easier than they had imagined. Marie was working as an executive assistant and was able to find a job as a virtual assistant pretty quickly.

Thomas is a chef, and those are in demand just about anywhere in the world. Listening to them tell the story of how everything fell into place once they had the right motivation to make their dream a reality sounded very familiar. For me too, things had somehow all worked out as soon as I committed to buying a van and spending time living and travelling in it.

Over the coming years, I would cross path with more people like Marie and Thomas, but I will always remember them as the first 'kindred souls' I met. As I watched them drive away, I felt a huge a sense of relief. "There are other people like me out there!". I wasn't the only one feeling like the typical path in life wasn't right for her. It was a massive relief to know that I wasn't alone in my quest to discover what life has to offer when you don't want to dedicate it to work or kids. Marie and Thomas told me about other like-minded people they had met on their travels. They confirmed that, yes, most nomads are in their 20s or 60s, but there are others in their 30s and 40s who don't want to settle down but instead chase freedom. I was looking forward to meeting those people.

The day after Marie and Thomas left, I said goodbye to Tokomaru Bay and continued north to tick off one of the must-dos when visiting the East Cape; watching the sunrise from the East Cape Lighthouse. The East Cape is one of the first places in the world to see the sun each day, and with the lighthouse being the easternmost point of the cape, it's often named as the first spot in the world to welcome a new day. I spent the night at a campground in Te Araroa and set an early alarm. In the morning, I slowly drove the 20 kilometres out to the lighthouse. The road was narrow and full of potholes, making it tricky to navigate in the dark. I was glad I had left extra early. I made it to the lighthouse car park well before sunrise and set off to walk up the hill. It's a short walk, but with over 800 steps and without daylight, I wouldn't call it easy. Once at the lighthouse, I got out my blanket and my thermos with coffee and made myself comfortable. It would be almost another hour before the sun would be up over the horizon, but the first glimpses of light were already visible. For the next hour, I enjoyed a stunning light show until, eventually, the sun rose and another day began. I stayed for a while after almost everyone else left, thinking to myself "moments like these is what it's all about." Eventually, I managed to tear myself away and walked back to my van at the bottom of the hill.

Once I made it back to Te Araroa, I took a little nap and then set out to explore the village and visit Te Waha-o-Rerekohu, New Zealand's oldest and largest pōhutukawa tree. The massive tree is about 600 years old, and stands proudly in the grounds of Te Araroa's local school. Unfortunately, it was too late in the season to see the tree in bloom. The pōhutukawa tree is also known as New Zealand's Christmas tree because its typical blooming season coincides with Christmas. Every year in December, pōhutukawa trees all over the country turn a bright crimson colour, announcing the beginning of summer. I could only imagine how incredible Waha-o-Rerekohu would look when in bloom. However, even without the red flowers, the tree was an impressive sight.

I spent another day in Te Araroa before I continued west and eventually made it to Ōpōtiki, at which point I had spent two weeks travelling around the East Cape, and I loved every bit of it. I could have lingered much longer, but at the time, I still had itchy feet and wanted to keep moving.

I was loving life that summer. I've loved New Zealand since the day I arrived back in 2007 and always considered it one of the most beautiful places in the world. But this summer was giving me a whole new appreciation for just how beautiful New Zealand is and how lucky I was to have the opportunity to explore it. Everywhere I went, the scenery was stunning, the people were friendly, and there was lots to see and explore. What I loved most was being parked up right by the beach, watching the sunrise from the comfort of my bed in the morning, knowing I had a whole day ahead of me to do whatever I wanted.

If I had any doubts about vanlife before I started, they disappeared that summer. Life was simple and fun and I felt a sense of freedom like never before. I knew without a shadow of a doubt that I was on the right track. There have been many amazing moments since, but I've never felt quite as free again as in those early days. It was a magical time of living in the moment, enjoying the adventure and excitement without a care in the world. It was a brief moment in time when I loved everything about vanlife before I encountered some of the challenges and downsides of the lifestyle. I planned to use my savings over the summer, but thanks to being able to work a few hours each week, I didn't have to. As a result, there were no financial worries either. Everything was just easy that first summer. It was total freedom.

I don't think I appreciated at the time that it wouldn't last. I thought I could live in my van forever if I wanted to and go on living just like this. Of course, I could have done that – but that's not who I am. Looking back now, I realise that it was only ever a matter of time until responsibilities, ambition and expectations would catch up to me, no matter where and how I lived. Sometimes I wish I could go back and relive those first few months, knowing that the feeling of total freedom wouldn't last so that I could soak it up more. But then I realise, if I had known that it wouldn't last, I wouldn't have felt as free as I did. Besides, I wouldn't change anything about that summer anyway. I was already living life to the fullest.

Kiteboarding on Rangiputa Harbour

Wild horses at Spirits Bay

The digital nomad life

The digital nomad life

To view more photos from my journey, visit my website.
lifedonedifferently.com/gallery

5

TIME
AUTUMN 2018

Āwhitu Peninsula

As summer turned into autumn, life slowed down even more. That first summer, I was driven by a desire to travel and see places. I rarely spent more than two nights in one place, always on the move to that next magical spot. While life was much more relaxed than it had been a few months earlier, I was still busy. Between driving, meeting up with friends, working a few hours each week, exploring new places and enjoying all my activities, there wasn't a lot of downtime. I certainly wasn't stressed, but life still felt fast and high energy.

As the days started to get shorter and colder, that began to change. After the initial rush of seeing new places, I was ready to slow down. I started to spend more time in my head, daydreaming and contemplating life. My travels also slowed down. I stayed in one place longer, and the distances between destinations decreased. While that first summer was exciting and fun, this is when the real magic started to happen. I will always remember that autumn for how amazing it feels when you stop rushing and instead give yourself time. For the first time in my adult life, I felt like I had exactly the right amount of time for everything. I wasn't stressed, but I wasn't bored either. I had things to do each day, but I almost always managed to get through my to-do list for the day, usually with time to spare, and my to-do list included things like going for walks and drinking coffee (what can I say, I like making lists). I had time to do my work, and do it well, without rushing because I had ten other things to do. I had time to go for walks on the beach, enjoying the scenery, sounds and smells. I had time to spend an hour drinking coffee while looking out the window or daydreaming without feeling guilty because I should be more productive. I remember how everything started to seem so simple and clear around that time. It felt like fog, that I didn't even know was there, had lifted from my brain.

One of the first things I noticed was how much more focused and efficient I was when working. At the time, work was kind of improvised. I didn't have a good setup in the van, I didn't have regular hours and I was hotspotting off my phone to connect to the internet or relied on public networks in libraries or cafes. Most of the time, I was working sitting on one of the benches in the van, with my laptop on my knees. Any physio would have cringed at my poor posture. Despite this not exactly ideal setup, I was more productive than ever. Things that used to take me two hours only took one, and I'm pretty sure I did some of the best quality work I had ever done during that autumn – despite spending less time on it.

I'd always taken great pride in my work and always felt like I was delivering very high-quality outputs. Focus and efficiency come easy to me, and I have often been able to do things faster than others – at work, that is. In just about every other aspect of life, I'm usually slower than average. I certainly didn't think I had a problem with focus or that my workload was negatively impacting quality. But I guess, sometimes, you don't see the truth until you step out of a situation and look back at it from a different perspective. Now that I had time, I realised what real focus truly feels like. With all the busyness and endless to-do lists gone, I realised how much it had, in fact, impacted the quality of my work and how much more value I could provide when I wasn't rushing.

While I first noticed this change in relation to work, it also impacted other parts of my life. I felt calmer, more content and sharper in a way. The crazy thing is that none of this was something I was looking for when I started vanlife. I always thought I was pretty calm and focused. I thought I was seeing life clearly. It was like I had been vision-impaired without ever knowing it, and now someone had given me glasses, and everything was so much sharper. It's hard to describe what it feels like when the fog you didn't even know was there lifts. I really wish everyone would get an opportunity to experience it at some stage in their life.

With the fog lifted and time on my hands, an idea started to form in my head. I've always loved writing and often thought I would love to write a book one day. I love reading as much as writing and have a lot of admiration and respect for authors. Becoming one would be a major achievement for me. However, it was one of those 'one-day' ideas. Something I might do once I'm retired. I dreamed about it, but I never once seriously thought about actually doing it. I wanted to, but it didn't feel like something that would fit into my life. And so it remained a 'one-day' idea – until that autumn.

The idea for my first book, One Size Does Not Fit All, emerged slowly over several weeks. At first, it was just stuff in my head. I spent a lot of time thinking about my life and my journey up until then. Being free and loving life made me reflect on how far I'd come, and it gave me a new sense of gratitude for how amazing my life had turned out. It took me a while to find my place in the world and to find happiness. I struggled as a teenager and young adult, and it was only over the past decade, since I had moved to New Zealand, that I slowly found myself and created a life that makes me happy. Until that autumn, I never had the time to reflect on my journey and the many lessons I'd learned along the way. But that autumn, I did.

I still vividly remember when these more or less random thoughts and reflections turned into a concept for a book. I was exploring the Āwhitu Peninsula southwest of Auckland city. The area is technically part of Auckland. You can see the famous Sky Tower from the peninsula's east coast, and planes heading for Auckland airport regularly pass through the sky above. However, while part of Auckland, it feels like a world away. The area is remote, and the landscape is dominated by forest, farmland and beaches instead of buildings. You can see the city, but it takes well over an hour to get to the peninsula from central Auckland (and that's without traffic). I had never been there before, which, in hindsight, seems odd. It's a magical place so close to Auckland, and you would've thought I'd been out there for weekend adventures. But the Āwhitu Peninsula is a bit of a hidden gem. I've since learned that many people who have lived in Auckland for years have never even heard of it.

I stocked up on fuel, water and food in Waiuku and then made my way north along Āwhitu Road. I spent a couple of nights at Āwhitu Regional Park, exploring the walking tracks and enjoying the scenery. After that, I drove up to the lighthouse at the northern tip of the peninsular and then made my way back south, stopping in at Hamilton's Gap on the west coast, where I stayed at the popular freedom camping spot for a few nights.

When it comes to scenery and nature, Āwhitu Peninsular is like a mini version of New Zealand's North Island. In the east are white beaches with calm waters, in the west are wild black sand beaches with big swells and dangerous rips, and in the middle are rolling green hills. In April, it was quiet, but in summer, the peninsular can get busy with Aucklanders wanting to escape the city for a while. I loved the beauty and the remote, peaceful feeling of it. There were just enough other people around to feel safe but not so many that it felt busy. I got lucky with the weather most days I was there and enjoyed exploring this beautiful part of Auckland with lots of sunshine which made all the colours look even brighter and more impressive.

It was at Hamilton's Gap on the west coast of Āwhitu Peninsula that my first book was born. The remoteness, the fact that there was no phone or internet coverage, and the stunning, wild, black sand beach made it the perfect spot for ideas and inspiration to flow. I went for long walks on the beach and spent hours drinking coffee while enjoying the views and reflecting on my life. And suddenly, those reflections and thoughts that had been on my mind for the past few weeks turned into an outline for a book. I didn't go to Hamilton's Gap to come up with a structure for a book. At that point, I hadn't even thought about turning it into a book. But there I was, writing down the overall storyline, the different sections and key topics I wanted to cover. It took months to write the book, of course, but that was when it was born. I will never forget that moment as the perfect example of what can happen when you give yourself time and space. I was right in my belief that change would find me if I just created space for it. I didn't start vanlife to write a book, but turns out that was one of the things I really wanted to do – and I don't think I would have ever figured that out if I hadn't given myself the space and time to do so.

My first summer in the van was all about excitement and the 'need to pinch myself to believe it' kind of happiness. However, during the autumn months, a different type of happiness started to settle in. It was calmer and much more about what was going on inside of me than about the beautiful places I was visiting or adventures I was going on, though there was still plenty of that, too. It was a content kind of happiness.

Over the years, vanlife has taught me many valuable

lessons. At times, it felt like the longer I lived this way, the more it was teaching me. However, the most valuable lesson of them all is still one that I learned that very first autumn, and that is; how little I need to be happy. I had gone from living in a waterfront house with stunning views and a spa pool in Auckland to living in an eight square metre tin can. I had walked away from a career that promised a very comfortable life and the ability to afford many luxuries. I went from having a whole wardrobe full of clothes, and shoes piling up in boxes next to it to having 4-5 outfits and three pairs of shoes. I had sold, donated or stored 80% of my belongings. Despite all that, I was happier than ever, and I didn't miss anything. That, in itself, was an incredibly valuable realisation. However, the reason I consider it the most valuable thing vanlife has taught me is because of the implications. When I realised that I didn't need a big house, fancy car, designer clothes or 20 pairs of shoes to be happy, I also realised that I wouldn't have to work 40+ hours a week for the next 30+ years of my life – and that was freedom.

I still vividly remember something that happened when my siblings and I were teenagers. My brother is two years older than I, and my sister is three years younger. I think it would have been around the time my brother started university and was thinking about long-term career prospects. I would have still been at school but doing the odd part-time and holiday jobs, and my sister would have maybe just started one of her first student jobs. We were in the lounge, and I can't remember exactly what we were talking about, but it had to do with jobs, careers and work. At some point, my sister said something along the lines of "Yeah, but who really works 40 hours every week," and said it in a way that implied that she thought it sounded like a ridiculous idea to work that much. At the time, the rest of us thought it was hilarious. I remember my brother and I having laughing fits, and we teased her about that statement for years afterwards. In the right context, someone in the family would probably still bring it up today. It turned into one of those iconic stories that every family has. Why was it so funny? Because we thought EVERYONE works 40 hours a week. That was just a fact of life. My sister questioning that was like someone asking, "yeah, but who really needs oxygen to live." It seemed like such a naïve and maybe even stupid thing to say. To be clear, my sister is anything but stupid! She was referring to part-time and summer jobs while still at school, and in that context, that statement certainly made sense. The rest of us took it out of context and turned it into the joke we all remember today.

In the last few years, I've often thought about that memory – but my view of it has changed completely. It's no longer an example of a funny story but instead an example of how brainwashed we are to see only one sensible path in life. Looking back now, I wish I had taken my sister seriously. Back then, the idea that someone wouldn't work 40 hours a week seemed stupid. Today, the fact that everyone is so stuck on the idea that we have to work 40 hours every week (and often more) seems stupid to me.

It often seems to me that many people work 40 hours a week because they think they don't have a choice. While that might be true for some, it doesn't mean we shouldn't at least question and challenge that concept. Yes, some of us do not have a choice. Unfortunately, some jobs pay such low wages that people have to work full-time (sometimes more) to support their families. I'm highly aware of that and have always felt very grateful that I have a well-paying job. However, I'm far from the only one who is that lucky. During these first few months in the van (and ever since), people have often said things like, "You're so lucky. I wish I could do what you're doing." While I agree that I'm lucky, I also think that most people who said this to me could do what I did if they wanted to. Many employers are increasingly open to flexible work arrangements, including part-time hours, job sharing or hiring contractors. In addition, for many jobs, the hourly rate is enough to be able to get by without working full-time hours – if we are willing to make some sacrifices in our lifestyle (and that's a big if).

Some people aren't willing to make those sacrifices. For them, having a big house, modern car, and exciting holidays are worth putting in the hours at work. There is nothing wrong with that. However, I sometimes wonder if many people work long hours because they have never really considered another option. I used to. Before I started vanlife, it had never once occurred to me that I could work only part-time. The only people I knew that did so were those with other commitments, like caring for family members or starting a business on the side – in which case they were working long hours, just not all for the same company. I never once considered that I could work fewer hours and simply use the rest of the time to enjoy life.

But here I was, living my best life, needing little money to do so. I did some numbers and found that I could live very comfortably and put money aside if I worked 20 hours a week. Even 15 hours would be enough to get by relatively comfortably. I wouldn't be able to afford amazing holidays every year or designer clothes, and it would require me to continue to live rent-free most of the time, but in exchange, I would get something I had realised meant more to me than anything money could buy: time.

It was around this time that I seriously started to think about vanlife as a long-term way of life. I loved living and travelling in my van, but more than that, I loved the opportunities and time it was giving me. It wasn't that I didn't want to go back to living in a house. The important part was that I didn't want to go back to being busy and stressed all the time. I had tasted freedom – and I wanted more.

This was the moment I had known would come. This was where I would truly walk in a different direction than all the people I cared about. It was no longer a matter of taking a time-out for one summer. At this point, my job was still there for me to return to, and most people thought I was just on a long holiday. That was all about to change. After dipping my toes into Life Done Differently for a summer, I was ready to be all in.

Looking back now, I feel like it should have been a big decision. I feel like there should have been a moment where I sat down, thought through my options and made a plan for the future. But that moment never happened. Continuing to live in my van past that first summer wasn't so much a decision as it was an evolution. It just felt like the natural thing to do. It also didn't feel like a big deal at the time. I would just keep living in my van until I didn't like it anymore, at which point I would stop. Yes, I had to tell the business I had been working for that I wouldn't be returning to a full-time role. But I think they already knew that. Since I was still working for them, we had been in touch frequently over the summer and autumn, and they knew how much I loved my new lifestyle. The same applied to all my friends. No one was surprised when I just kept living in my van past that first summer and autumn.

It felt exciting and liberating. I knew in my heart I was doing the right thing, but I would be lying if I wouldn't also admit that there was a bit of fear and doubt. For starters, I was wondering how I would cope with winter in the van.

6

WINTER
WINTER 2018

Tokerau Beach

Kerikeri

Auckland

W hen I decided to continue to live and travel in my van beyond that first summer and autumn, a part of me was concerned about whether I would still enjoy it in winter. It's one thing to love life on the road while the days are long, warm and mostly sunny. But, how would I cope once the days were short and cold and rainy would be the words to describe the weather?

This might be a good time for a little geography and culture overview for those who don't know much about New Zealand. It's a small country in the Southern Hemisphere, southeast of Australia, that about five million people call home. We like to call ourselves Kiwis, so when you hear me mention that word, I'm usually not talking about the green fruit (kiwi fruit) or the flightless bird (kiwi bird) but the people of New Zealand. We have slightly more land mass than the UK, but over 13 times as many people live in the UK – which tells you a lot about our population density and the kind of country we are. We're also fairly isolated down here in the Pacific. Our closest neighbours are Australia and the Pacific Islands, but even those are at least 3-4 hours flight away.

New Zealand is famous for having more sheep than people, it's unpredictable and fast-changing weather and indigenous Māori culture, as well as for providing the back-drop for much of the Lord of the Rings and Hobbit movies, and being good at rugby. However, probably more than anything, New Zealand is famous for its breathtaking scenery. In my opinion, it's the most beautiful country in the world. We've got everything. Both white and black beaches, clear blue oceans, steep mountains, some of which are snow-covered year round, lakes of the brightest blues, seemingly endless fjords, unique wildlife including species you can't find anywhere else in the world, vast rainforests, small towns and big cities. OK, technically, we only have one truly big city, but who comes to New Zealand for the cities. For anyone who loves nature, New Zealand is paradise.

New Zealand is a narrow but long country. We often talk about the North Island and the South Island, but there are actually over 600 islands in total. To be fair, most of them are not populated, unless you count birds and other wildlife. The vast majority of people live on either the North or the South Island, and the smaller islands are generally considered to be part of either of those two big islands. Though those living on some of the smaller islands would probably disagree with me here.

Auckland, in the upper North Island, is New Zealand's biggest city, with about 1.5 million people. It's the only city in the country with a population of more than a million. Our second-largest city, Christchurch, and third, Wellington (the capital), trail far behind with only 400,000 and 220,000 people, respectively.

Because New Zealand is such a long country, it covers several climate zones. Overall, the climate is relatively mild and extreme temperatures are rare. However, the further south you go, the colder the winters tend to be, and sub-zero temperatures (Celsius) overnight are not uncommon anywhere on the South Island. On the North Island, on the other hand, frost and snow are much rarer, with elevated areas and parts of the central North Island being the exception. In other words, if you're living in a 20-year-old van that isn't particularly well insulated, north is the way to go in winter. Since I've lived in Auckland, which is fairly far in the north, for 11 years and have always loved the Far North of our country, spending winter up there was fine by me. Frost and snow are almost unheard of in those parts of the country. I remember back in 2011, we had a cold day in Auckland with a bit of white flurry flying around, and it started an extensive discussion about whether it was snowing (as someone who grew up with proper snow, I argued NO!). 1930 was the last time Auckland saw snow that settled on the ground for a bit. In fact, temperatures below 10 degrees Celsius during the day are rare. In other words, one could definitely survive winters in a van in northern New Zealand.

However, temperatures are only one thing that could make winters in the van challenging. Rain is another big one. While the country's north is milder in winter, it gets a fair share of rain. Parts of the island are covered in rainforest and, well, it's called RAIN-forest for a reason. June, July and August can be very wet, and sometimes you don't see the sun for days. How would I cope with being stuck in the van when it rains for days on end?

One thing was clear; I would not be able to get through winter off-grid. In summer, my solar panel was generally generating enough power to allow me to be off-grid most of the time. However, in winter, when the days are shorter, and we might not get much sunshine for long periods, it was unlikely that would work. At the time, my van only had one 80-watt solar panel and a standard house battery. The solar panel charged the battery, and it was also charged when I was driving via an alternator. That battery then ran my 12-volt fridge, the water pump and lights, and it allowed me to charge my phone, laptop and other devices. I had to be careful with power, even in summer. If it was cloudy or rainy, I sometimes couldn't charge devices, and sometimes I'd have to go for a drive or go to a campground and plug into power to top up the battery. However, most of the time, I had all the power I needed. In winter, that would be a different story. The sun wouldn't shine enough for my solar panels to produce the power I needed, and I didn't want to drive hours every day just to charge the battery. However, there was a relatively simple solution; I would spend more time on campgrounds in winter so that I could plug into power. That way, I could also run my electric heater to stay warm.

Nevertheless, I was unsure how I would cope with winter in such a small space. With the weather less suitable for outdoor living and activities, and the days shorter, I figured I would likely spend much more time inside my van during winter compared to summer days. Would it get a bit claustrophobic after a while? I felt like it might be a good idea to have a backup plan. Luckily, I found the perfect one: Housesitting.

Housesitting means that you look after people's homes and pets while they are away in exchange for a place to stay. It might sound strange if you're not familiar with the concept, but it is a win-win-win. The homeowners get someone looking after their pets, gardens and home without having to pay for it, the pets get to stay in their familiar environment instead of having to go to a kennel, and the housesitter gets a place to stay and pets to cuddle with.

Housesitting is a growing trend globally. More and more home and pet owners have discovered it as a cheaper way to have pets looked after while they are away. At the same time, more and more people realise it's a more affordable way to travel as well as a way to experience the company and love of pets without having to commit to one permanently. As a result, there are now thriving housesitting communities in many countries worldwide. Here in New Zealand, we have several websites and Facebook groups that connect home-owners with sitters. I registered with one of the websites that winter after a fellow nomad recommended it. Lucky for me, housesitters seemed in demand at the time, making me feel confident that I could find opportunities if I wanted to. So there was my backup plan for my first winter as a nomad.

Throughout June, I was still travelling in my van, spending most of my time in the Far North. As expected, the temperatures were relatively mild, and with a fleece blanket, a pair of comfy slippers, and lots of hot drinks, I found it easy enough to stay warm. However, what did bother me was the rain and humidity. There was a week in the middle of June when it rained for several days. I had travelled from Kerikeri to Tokerau Beach further north, hoping to escape the rain, but the weather gods weren't so kind. When it rained for just a day, I usually stayed inside the van. But after 24 hours in my eight square meter home, I needed to get outside, rain or not. I didn't mind walking in the rain. It was fun and refreshing in a way. However, rainy walks meant I had a pile of wet clothes and shoes afterwards – and nowhere to put them.

That week in June, wet gear was piling up, and everything in the van felt damp. There had been some wind between the rain, and I had enjoyed a super fun kitesurfing session at Tokerau Beach, right in front of my van. However, as fun as it was, it meant I now also had a bunch of wet kiting gear in my already damp van – and let me tell you, wet wetsuits do not smell very pleasant after a while. I considered leaving the wet gear outside the van, but I worried it would get stolen. Over summer and autumn, this had never been an issue. Occasionally it rained for a day or two, but before long, it was sunny again, and I could hang everything up outside to dry. But that week in June, all the wet gear was lying in the van, smelling and adding to the damp feeling. The condensation that usually appeared on the windows overnight didn't help the situation either. So, in the end, it wasn't the cold but the dampness that drove me to activate my backup plan.

I ended up housesitting for almost all of July, August and September. I was lucky and got three longer sits of 3-4 weeks each, which meant I didn't have to move around too much and could get to know the pets well. In between housesitting, I did shorter stints in the van. All three of the longer housesits were in Auckland, which was partly a choice. I decided that if I stayed put for winter, I might as well do so near my friends so that I could spend time with them. I was pretty sure I would hit the road again in spring and might not see them for months, so I wanted to make the most of it while I could. In addition, there were lots of housesitting opportunities in Auckland – which isn't surprising when you consider that almost a quarter of the population of New Zealand lives in Auckland. As a result, it was easy to find places.

Escaping the cold and rain was only one of the reasons why I decided to housesit that much during that first winter. Ever since I had the idea for my first book in autumn, I was really motivated to make it happen. It was all in my head, and I was dying to get it on paper. As much as I was loving vanlife and travelling, all I wanted to do at that point was write. It seemed like housesitting was the perfect way to give myself that opportunity. I didn't have to spend time driving and finding places to park. And being in a house meant I had a bit more space to set up a proper work area and to move around. I also love having pets around, so that was another bonus.

That winter, I was still working for the company I had been with full-time before I started vanlife, as well as a couple of other clients from the pre-vanlife days. However, during autumn, I had also won a new client. This was exciting because it was the first new client I got as a digital nomad. I was referred to them by someone I had worked with previously, which is always a good start. But I was still nervous to tell them about my lifestyle. They wanted to engage me as a senior marketing consultant to support and mentor the junior marketing assistant on their team, so it wasn't exactly an entry-level role. How would they feel about a senior marketing consultant living in and working from a campervan? Turned out they had no problem with it at all. They loved it and were more than happy for me to do most of the work remotely, with the occasional in-person meeting in Auckland when I was around. I won another new client that winter who was equally nonchalant about my lifestyle. And this was well before Covid made working from home normal. Remote working was still relatively unusual at the time, and with almost all companies I worked for, I was the only one who wasn't in the office. I was surprised by how easy it was to get new work and how excited everyone was when they heard about my lifestyle. I realised I could potentially have a long-term career as a virtual marketing manager and consultant, which was exciting.

I did learn one valuable lesson that year about being a digital nomad – especially one who does relatively senior work. I figured out that it's better to tell people that I live and travel in a motorhome instead of calling it a campervan. Apparently, many Kiwis who don't know much about the lifestyle think of a people-mover type vehicle with a mattress in the back when they hear campervan – which made some wonder what I did with the money they paid me if I can't afford a 'proper' home. It usually only took a meeting or two for everyone to realise that this lifestyle was a choice for me and not something I did because I couldn't afford to live in a house. But I still started to say that I live in a motorhome whenever I was talking to work-related people. It sounded a bit more mature and was a more accurate reflection of my home on wheels, given it had a kitchen and bathroom.

So that's how I spent my first winter as a nomad; housesitting, writing, working and catching up with friends in and around Auckland. Before I knew it, the days started to get longer again, and I was getting ready for another season on the road.

7

REGRETS

SPRING 2018

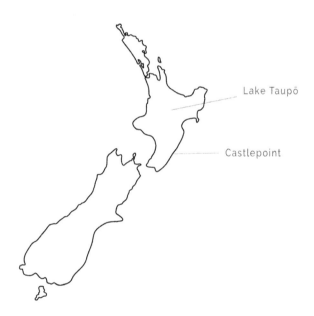

Lake Taupō

Castlepoint

After making it through the first winter without any major issues, I was more confident than ever that vanlife wasn't just a short phase in my life. As I started to travel again in October, I was experiencing a sense of content like never before. I knew I was exactly where I needed to be, doing exactly what I needed to do at this point in my life. It was an incredible feeling. I was perfectly content with the here and now, but at the same time, there were all these possibilities of what the future could look like. It's hard to put into words how I felt in the early weeks of that spring. I felt invincible, like nothing could ever get in the way of me being happy again. I had finished my first book and was going through the motions of reaching out to publishers and agents. I knew the chances of it getting published, let alone selling in significant numbers, were very slim, but it didn't matter. There was this possibility that I could be a writer. I didn't need to be the next Mark Mason or Brené Brown, but, even though I enjoyed my marketing work, I never before loved any work quite as much as I'd loved writing that book. So the idea of being able to make money as an author – even if all the odds were against me – was exciting. But at the same time, it didn't really matter.

The last few months had shown me that I could find work as a virtual marketing freelancer. More importantly, I realised how much I enjoyed working that way. I was more productive than ever, and the opportunities that found me were exciting projects I wanted to be involved with. So even if making a living as a writer would remain a dream, I was confident that I would not only be financially secure but would also continue to be one of those lucky people who enjoy their work. I had my own home, small as it might be, and I didn't have rent or a mortgage to pay or any other significant financial commitments to worry about.

However, it was about more than work and feeling financially secure. After a winter of housesitting, being back on the road came with a sense of freedom and a feeling like nothing could get in the way of living life to the fullest. I felt more assured than ever that I was on the right track in life. It certainly wasn't the path most people around me were on, but it was right for me. However, a meeting with an old friend poked some holes into my feeling of pure content.

Maya, is a former colleague who had turned into a friend. When we'd worked together a few years earlier, we were both very ambitious and working hard to progress our careers. She had stayed on that path while I had taken a different direction. Despite that, we stayed in touch and met up occasionally for coffee or lunch whenever I was in Auckland. When we saw each other that spring, I told her how much I loved vanlife and that I had no intentions of settling down and returning to the traditional path in life. "Do you ever worry that you might regret your choices?" Maya asked at some stage. "I don't think I will", I replied. "I might not progress my career as fast anymore, and I'm earning less, but there seems to be plenty of work for a virtual marketing manager out there. And besides, I don't think I'll ever regret anything that makes me this happy!".

"But what about the future?" she wanted to know. "What if you really end up without kids, and in 10 or 20 years, you regret that choice? By then, it will be too late." I started to understand where she was coming from. Since we had met through work and usually spent a lot of time talking about our jobs whenever we met up, I thought she was talking about giving up my career when she first asked whether I worried I would have regrets. But it was the fact that I was seriously considering not to have children that she was concerned about. She wasn't the only one. The risk of regretting it seems to be the number one objection people hear when they talk about wanting to be childfree. "Don't you worry about being alone when you get old?" is a related and equally common concern. I often thought it was a weird way to approach parenthood. Should we really encourage people to have kids just because they worry about being alone? Besides, having kids is no guarantee that you won't have regrets or end up on your own. We have all heard the stories about older people who feel lonely because their family never visits, even though they are close by. We also live in an increasingly global world. I live very far away from my parents, and so do many others. We won't visit them much when they are old simply because we're too far away. In addition, even though it is still a taboo topic for many, regretting parenthood seems not all that uncommon if you believe the often anonymous posts and discussions in various online forums. Given all this, it seemed odd that people were so concerned those who choose to be childfree might regret it, while you never hear people voice that concern to those who are planning for parenthood.

A part of me wanted to start an argument with Maya that day. I generally have a pretty thick skin and usually don't mind people questioning my choices, as long as it's done out of curiosity and not judgement. But this particular question about regrets always bothered me. It often felt like people thought having kids would be the path to guaranteed happiness, while any other choice is risky and something we might regret. The truth is, there is just as much of a chance of regretting having children. I don't think many people who talk about wanting kids are ever asked if they worry they will regret it. It would probably be considered an inappropriate question. Yet somehow, it was OK to tell those who don't want kids (or are unsure about it) that they need to worry about regretting that choice.

Sometimes I wonder if it was specifically about the decision not to have children or if it was bigger than that. Maybe it's just another example of society struggling to understand and support anyone doing things differently. Over the past year, I'd also encountered people concerned I would regret leaving my promising career. I'd met families who were travelling full-time, and they talked about other people asking whether they worried they might regret not giving their kids a more stable and traditional upbringing. Just a few weeks earlier, I'd met a couple who had recently sold their house to buy a motorhome and travel the country, and pretty much everyone around them was worried they might regret that decision. Talk to anyone who has done anything unusual in life, and they will probably tell you that they were faced with the "don't you worry you will regret your choices?" question more than once. It bothered me that the general belief held by society seemed to be that being different was risky and less likely to lead to happiness.

Nevertheless, as much as I generally hated questions like the one Maya was asking, I knew her well enough to know that it came from a place of curiosity, not judgement. So I tried my best to explain it to her without sounding upset. "It's pretty simple," I said. "I'm not 100% certain yet that I really don't want kids. But one thing I know for sure is that I won't have kids just because I worry I might regret it if I don't. After all, there is no guarantee that having them won't lead to regrets, and I would much rather regret being childfree than regret being a mom. At least that way it's just me who has to live with the regrets and not a child as well. So if anything, the worry of having regrets will stop me from having children." We left it at that. I think Maya could sense that this was a sensitive topic for me, and so we moved on to talk about other things.

I felt confident in my choices and that I was on the right track. However, it was like Maya's question had planted a tiny seed of doubt. What if I would regret the choices I made? The question stayed on my mind that spring. But it didn't stop me from enjoying being back on the road.

I travelled around the upper North Island for most of October and November, revisiting favourite places around the Bay of Plenty, Auckland region and Northland and discovering new ones. Then, in the second half of November, I set off on a trip to the Wairarapa, a part of New Zealand I hadn't spent much time in before. The Wairarapa is the area along the southeast coast of the North Island, between Wellington and Hawkes Bay. It's a sparsely populated region dominated by farmland. However, I didn't come for the farms. Instead, it was the remote coastline that attracted me. Other travellers had told me about the beautiful, isolated beaches along the east coast of the Wairarapa, and I was intrigued. I wasn't disappointed. I spent two weeks visiting stunning beaches along the coast, returning inland in between to stock up on food and other supplies in the towns and villages.

Castlepoint in the northern part of the Wairarapa, in particular, blew me away – figuratively and (almost) literally. It's an almost surreal landscape. There are two bays next to each other, with a lighthouse on top of a cliff in the middle. Rocks and mini-islands shelter the southern bay, creating what almost looks like a lagoon. The area is famous for strong winds, and everything looks a bit windswept, resulting in a rugged, almost mysterious atmosphere. On the day I arrived, I walked out to the lighthouse in the afternoon. It was so windy I was worried about being blown off the walkway.

Unfortunately, the wind was off-shore. I would have loved to kitesurf in this magical place, but that required onshore wind.

My second day at Castlepoint was what had become a very typical day for me. I woke up early, made coffee and then got back to bed to read and journal for an hour or so while I watched the sun rise over the ocean through the windows of my van. After that, I got up, turned my bed into my lounge/office, made breakfast and then spent the next few hours working. I had a meeting with one of my clients to be briefed on a new project and some other work to progress for other clients. By one o'clock, I was done with work for the day. I made lunch and thought about how I wanted to spend the afternoon while I ate. The wind had calmed down, and I decided to head up the hill at the southern end of the bays.

It seemed like a simple afternoon activity. However, it turned into an adventure. At first, there was a relatively well-maintained track, but the higher I climbed, the dodgier the trail got. For the last bit, there basically was no path, and I had to find my own way through the grass and up the rocks. I slipped a couple of times and more than once wondered if I should turn around. But I had gotten this far and didn't want to give up now. I certainly was glad, though, that it was less windy. The previous day, this climb along narrow cliffs with steep drop-offs would have been way outside my comfort zone. As it was, I did make it to the top, though with slightly shaky knees. But I got rewarded with the most amazing views over Castlepoint and the Wairarapa coast. I had brought a thermos with tea, so I sat down and had a cup while I enjoyed the scenery. From above, the lighthouse and the bays looked even more impressive. Beyond it, the coastline stretched into the distance. Rolling green hills that dropped off steeply into the ocean, with the occasional beach interrupting the cliffs, dominated the views in both directions. Once again, I felt incredibly grateful that this was my life.

It was my rumbling stomach that, eventually, made me pack up and start the descent. I made it back down by sliding on my bum for the most part until I reached the visible path again. A group was standing there, debating whether they should go on. "Does the track continue?" one of them asked me. "That depends on what you consider a track," I said. "If you keep going, be prepared to get muddy," I added while pointing at my dirty hands and bum.

When I returned to my van, the growling in my stomach had become more forceful, so I decided to make dinner. My van had a three-burner gas stove but no oven. I sometimes missed having an oven, but I learned to make do with what I had. Besides, I've never been particularly passionate about cooking. I like homemade food, but I don't enjoy spending lots of time preparing it, so I usually stuck to simple recipes. My favourites were those you can prepare in one pot or pan. I also usually made at least two portions, so I didn't have to cook daily. That day, I made a simple stir-fry with chicken and veggies. I was hungry and tired, so it needed to be quick and easy.

After dinner, I checked my emails in case anything urgent had come up with a client while I was out. I replied to a few, but there was nothing I needed to action immediately, so I spent the evening watching Netflix. Some days, I would do some work after dinner, and sometimes I would explore in the morning and work in the afternoon. There also occasionally were days when I had a lot of urgent work and didn't have time to be out and about, just like there were days when I didn't work and spent all day having fun in nature or spending hours reading or writing. Every day was different, but overall, it felt balanced.

From day one of my vanlife adventures, one of the things I loved most was the community. I am an introvert and love spending lots of time on my own. I need it to think, process and recharge. But I also like being part of a community – especially one as diverse as the nomad community in New Zealand. On my travels, I've met people from all walks of life. From young tourists travelling the country for a few months to families living and travelling in big house buses, retirees in expensive motorhomes and caravans, and everything in between. Many of them were people I would most likely have never met in my old life, and I loved this new diversity in my community.

However, there was one thing that bothered me. It was hard to go beyond campground small-talk. I've always been someone who craves deep connection with people instead of just light-hearted fun. I want to really get to know people, and learn about their true selves, not just what you see at first glance. But it takes time to connect with people in that way and learn about their dreams and values and the lessons they've learned along the way. It usually takes hours of conversations, which is hard to make happen when you're constantly on the move, not to mention someone who needs ten hours of alone time to recharge for every hour of conversation. I met amazing people, but I often felt frustrated with the lack of depth of the conversations I was having with them. Luckily, I found a way around that. I started to write stories about other people who were doing life differently. This would later turn into articles for a magazine as well as my own podcast, but back then, in the spring of 2018, I just wrote about different people for my blog. It was the perfect way to get to know people faster. When you go into a conversation with the intention of interviewing them for a story, you get to ask questions that you couldn't really ask someone you had only just met otherwise. After all, you can't really ask someone about their biggest dreams and regrets after chatting for five minutes during happy hour at the campground. Well, to be fair, I guess you could. But it never felt right to me. However, if they know you are coming to ask them exactly those questions, you can get away with it.

I loved hearing people's stories. Among the first people I interviewed and wrote about were activist, politician and off-grid lifestyler Mike, single mum and fellow nomad Julia, engineer, loner and Buddhist Pete, and Liz and Allan, who were using their retirement to walk the length of New Zealand. There were others, including some with whom I had great conversations naturally, without having to use my writer excuse to ask big questions. I learned a lot from these people and would continue to do so over the years that followed.

Interestingly, I learned a lot from people twice my age and older – people I likely wouldn't have encountered much in 'normal' life. When I bought my van, I joined the New Zealand Motor Caravan Association (NZMCA). The association has properties all over the country that offer a safe and usually peaceful place to park for a few days. I liked staying at the NZMCA parks. However, I did often stand out among the community. I don't have any official data on this, so don't hold me to it, but I would guess that the average age of an NZMCA member is probably close to twice my age. There are other younger members, but we are far and few in-between. In addition, solo travellers are far outnumbered by couples. While the NZMCA membership is as diverse as the nomad community on the whole, the typical member is a retired couple in a modern motorhome or caravan – not a mid-30s, single woman in a 20-year-old campervan.

I might be an introvert, but I'm not shy. I almost always made it a point to say hello to my campground neighbours and liked having a brief chat, usually about where we've been and where we're going. Often, my camp neighbours were curious to hear my story, given I wasn't exactly the average person they met on their travels. It were those encounters with travellers twice my age that brought up the topic of regrets again that spring. Whenever I told older people about my lifestyle and the choices I had made, I usually got one of two responses. They would say something along the lines of "I wish I had done what you're doing when I was younger. I regret wasting my best years just working all the time", or it would be something like, "just make sure you prepare for the future. I regret that I didn't save or invest more when I was younger. I wish I could live more comfortably now."

It was interesting that wherever I went, I was equally likely to get either response when I told people my story. I didn't know it yet, but in the years to come, I would often find myself torn between these two extremes. Back then, as I was approaching one year on the road, I was still so in love with the lifestyle and everything that came with it that I didn't think much about the future yet. If some random circumstance had forced me to decide between giving up vanlife for good or living in a van for the rest of my life, always just earning enough to pay the bills, I would have happily chosen the latter. Life was so easy and so much fun, I could absolutely see myself continuing exactly the same way for the next 40+ years.

Nevertheless, the responses I was getting from people 30-40 years older than me made me pause. It made me think of the conversation earlier that spring when my friend asked me if I ever worried I might end up regretting my choices. I still wasn't really worried about regretting choosing a different path in life, but some doubts had started to creep in. However, more than anything I found it fascinating that some people seem to regret certain decisions and others don't – and it seems to have very little to do with their choices or the outcomes. Some people worked hard their whole life to build wealth, leaving little free time, and end up being perfectly happy with that choice, while others regret it. Some people spend a lot of time enjoying life instead of chasing fortune and fame, and some of them regret it later while others don't. What makes some people regret their life choices while others don't? From what I could tell, it seems to have fairly little to do with the outcome, so what does trigger regrets? And the even more important question; how could I make sure I would be among those people who don't have regrets?

I was contemplating this as I travelled from Wairarapa towards the central North Island that spring. It was a chance encounter with fellow nomad Julie-Ann that gave me the clarity I was looking for. Julie-Ann and I had been in touch via email for a few months. She had come across my blog earlier that year and got in touch. She was in her early 70s, had two kids and three grandchildren, and had separated from her husband many years ago. She had a home near Napier in Hawkes Bay, but spent a lot of her time travelling in her Mitsubishi Rosa bus. Despite us not having much in common on paper, we had interesting conversations via email, and when the chance presented itself to meet up at Lake Taupō, we were both excited to do so.

We agreed to meet at the NZMCA park near Taupō. Despite the park being very busy, we managed to get sites next to each other. After registering and setting up camp, we grabbed our camping chairs and got comfortable between our two vans, enjoying the sunshine while drinking coffee and catching up. At some point, I mentioned my observations about regrets and asked Julie-Ann if she had any. Julie-Ann shared that there was a time in her life when she had struggled with regrets. When her marriage fell apart, around the same time that her kids were leaving home, she found herself alone and with too much time on her hands. "During those days", she said, "I often found myself living in the past. I regretted not putting more effort into my marriage, though I also didn't really know what I could have done differently. More than anything, however, I regretted not making more time for myself." After I asked Julie-Ann what she meant by that, she explained that she felt like she had given so much to other people and had spent so much time living their lives with them, that she didn't know who she was, when those people left or didn't need her as much anymore.

Julie-Ann shared that she went through a dark time for a while but ultimately managed to pull herself out of it. "How?" I wanted to know. "How did you turn that around and find a way to look positively into the future again?"

"I realised that, ultimately, having regrets is a choice," was her simple yet profound answer. She went on, "After about a year spent living in the past and regretting things I could no longer change, I realised that having regrets isn't so much about the choices we make. Instead, it's about our attitude towards the outcomes. Regretting things you can't change anymore is a waste of time and energy. So these days, I choose not to get hung up on regrets. Instead, I focus on making the most of whatever the outcome of my choices happens to be."

That conversation with Julie-Ann stayed with me and changed how I think about regrets. I realised that, like Julie-Ann, I could choose not to have regrets. I could live my life, make decisions to the best of my ability, and then make the most of whatever happens instead of dwelling on what could have been. That didn't mean that I would be set in my ways or wouldn't be allowed to change my mind or admit that I got it wrong. It also didn't mean that I wouldn't worry about the future at times, or that I wouldn't invest time and effort into trying to make the right decisions – for now and the future. It just meant that I wouldn't dwell on things that are in the past and that I can't change anyway. Instead, I will focus on making the most of what I got. After all, I will never know what would have happened if I had made different choices. Even if times get tough, it is, after all, possible that life would be even more challenging if I had taken a different path

So that spring, I decided that having regrets is a choice – and that no matter what happens, no matter what choices I make in my life, I will choose not to regret them. Little did I know that this promise would be tested more than once in the years to come. Some things indeed are much easier said than done.

8

ALONE

SUMMER 2018 / 19

Great Barrier Island

Auckland

"Just you, all by yourself?"

The question came from Deb, my camp neighbour at Ambury Regional Park, where I stayed for a few nights at the beginning of summer. I liked to stay at Ambury whenever I was in Auckland. It was only a 20-minute drive from the city, but the campground was surrounded by farmland which made it feel like you're somewhere rural, not in the middle of New Zealand's biggest city. The park had some really nice walks, including one along the foreshore which offered gorgeous views over Manukau Harbour. I also loved being surrounded by animals. While technically a farm, Ambury is more of an attraction than a working farm these days. Families come here for the kids to experience and learn about the different farm animals. That summer, there were pigs, goats, chickens, turkey, peacocks, ducks, some cattle and lots of sheep. I liked being surrounded by all of them. However, my favourites were the two massive Clydesdales horses that could usually be seen grazing in one of the paddocks. I loved watching those gentle giants.

That day, I returned from a stroll around the park to find new neighbours parked next to me. They were standing outside their camper, so I said hello, and we started chatting. Deb and Frank, her husband of many years, were a friendly couple from Tauranga travelling the country as part of their retirement. For the first few minutes, while we were talking, both of them periodically glanced back at my van. I had noticed these looks before. I obviously didn't know what people were thinking, but it always felt like they were waiting for my partner to appear from the van to join the conversation. After all, that is by far the most common scenario; two people travelling together. When that partner didn't show up, it would eventually lead to the "just you?" question.

I've lost track of how many times I heard that question over the years. Sometimes, it was asked for logistical reasons, like when I was checking in at a campground and they needed to know how much to charge me. Other times, like on this day with the friendly retirees from Tauranga, the question was asked out of curiosity, and maybe a bit of concern. My "Yes, just me" response, delivered with a confident smile, was usually met with varying degrees of disbelief, curiosity, concern and admiration. Sometimes, other questions followed. People wanted to know if I felt safe, got lonely, or found it challenging to be out there on my own. Sometimes, people asked if I was hoping to find a partner on my travels – more often, I think, they simply assumed that I was.

In some cases, like on that day at Ambury Regional Park, the question led to a longer conversation. Deb was clearly intrigued and asked if I would like to come in for tea and homemade cookies. Never one to decline homemade cookies, I happily accepted the invitation. And so, for the next hour, I sat in Deb and Frank's modern motorhome, eating cookies while exchanging life stories. I learned that the two of them had three children who were all married, and grandchildren were plentiful. One daughter was living in Brisbane with her family. The other daughter and a son were still in Tauranga, close to the family home. Frank had owned an engineering business, which he had grown successfully, thanks to a lot of hard work. After 30 years focused on raising a family and building the company, the two decided to sell the business and enjoy the years they had left. Theirs is a very familiar story – and the two of them knew it. After hearing that I write a blog called Life Done Differently, Frank joked, saying if they had a blog, it would be called Life Done Normally.

I could tell both of them were intrigued by my choices and lifestyle. They asked questions with curiosity and genuine interest, rather than the disbelief and judgement I had experienced at other times. I was more than happy to answer their questions. I tried my best to explain how I had lived the career-focused life in Auckland, that I had enjoyed that life and was very happy – until everyone around me started to get married and have kids, and I began to wonder what I wanted from life long-term. I tried to explain to them how I struggled to answer that question, and that I just wasn't sure if I wanted to commit to kids and marriage. "For now?!" was Frank's response. I wasn't sure if it was a question or a statement. I'm not sure Frank knew. "Yes, for now", I replied. It was the truth, and yet it felt wrong somehow.

I'm not one for absolutes. No matter how strongly I believe something, there is usually a part of me that is open to the possibility that I could be wrong or change my mind. So even though I never really wanted kids and never dreamed of my wedding day or having a family, I wasn't saying that I definitely didn't want any of that. I was 34 then, so theoretically, I still had a bit of time to make it happen, if it turned out it's what I wanted after all. But at the same time, agreeing to Frank's "not yet" comment felt wrong. I knew it meant something different to Deb and Frank than it did to me. For me, "not yet" meant that I'm not completely ruling out the possibility that there will come a day when I want a husband and kids. For Deb and Frank, it meant that I probably would want it one day. This was the problem with conversations like these.

I never felt particularly offended by questions about being single and not having or wanting kids. I know some people do. For them, these are very personal choices and shouldn't be questioned by outsiders – which is a very valid view. After all, people who do have kids or get married hardly ever get asked these kinds of question. And you could argue that it would be much more justified to force someone to think through the decision to permanently commit to another person or to bring another human into this world than to challenge someone who's decided not to. Nevertheless, as long as people respected my answers and didn't feel the need to argue or tell me how I should feel, I was usually happy to answer questions like these. However, I did often feel misunderstood.

I don't know if it's true or just in my head, but I often felt like most people who asked these questions simply assumed that I was only on my own because I hadn't found the right person yet. Deb and Frank certainly seemed to think so, though they were cautious about expressing this. "Maybe you will meet someone on your travels, and then you will want to settle down and start a family?!" Deb said, and again, I wasn't sure if it was a question or statement. "Yes, maybe. But maybe not," was my response. I left it at that. I didn't feel like I would be able to find the words, right there and then, to make Deb and Frank understand. It's not like they didn't want to. Like many other people I had similar conversations with, they were open-minded and supportive. They wanted me to do whatever would make me happy. It was just that my idea of a happy life was so different from theirs and from what society tells us a happy life looks like, that it was too hard for them to really understand what I was trying to say.

After over an hour of conversation with strangers, I felt drained. I longed for the comfort and solitude of my little home on wheels. I thanked Deb and Frank for the tea and cookies and the lovely chat and said goodbye. We were leaving in opposite directions the next morning and likely wouldn't see each other again.

Back in my van, I felt deflated. As an introvert, conversations with strangers, especially deeper ones, always take a lot of energy, and I feel the need to recharge by being on my own afterwards. But in this case, it was more than that. At that moment, I felt lonely. Not because I was on my own physically, but because I felt on my own emotionally. I loved my life and who I was as a person. I didn't want to change anything significant about me or my life. I just wished there were more people like me. I wished there were more people in my life who were choosing not to get married and have kids. I felt lonely in that moment because it seemed as if everyone around me was perfectly aligned in terms of how they wanted to live their lives – and I was the odd one out. I was the one that didn't fit in, didn't belong.

To be fair, I should probably say that I FELT like I didn't belong. I think at that point, most people around me still believed that all of this was just a phase, that sooner or later, I would follow the same path as everyone else. Of course, I don't know if it was true, but I often felt like people didn't really believe me when I said that I was happy on my own. I think most of them were pretty confident that, eventually, I would find someone, settle down and return to the normal path in life. You never know, I might do that one day. But at that point in my life it definitely wasn't what I wanted.

It's not that I didn't think about it sometimes. If I'm honest, I must admit that I liked the idea of finding someone. I liked the idea of having that person in my life that's always in my corner. That person I can share the load with. I sometimes fantasised about how nice it would be to have someone who looks out for me and takes care of me instead of always having to take care of myself. Sometimes, I daydreamed about having someone to share my life with, including all the ups and downs. When things got tough, in particular, I often found myself thinking that it would be nice to have someone to lean on, to not have to deal with all problems on my own. But what I daydreamed of was what we see in cheesy movies or read about in romance novels, not the real-world kind of relationship. In the real world, relationships require compromise. They require effort and being willing to work through setbacks. Relationships require making time and space for someone else. They require us to give up me-time for us-time – and I just didn't feel ready to do that.

I once made a friend roll on the floor with laughter for a good five minutes when I explained it like this; I like watching TV shows. Most days, I watch an episode or two in the evening. If I couldn't do that anymore, I would miss it, and I would certainly wish at times that I could still relax by watching the latest crime, drama or comedy. However, if I had to choose between not watching any TV ever again or having it running at volume at least eight hours a day, I would choose the former. As much as I like watching a TV show for an hour or two in the evening, I value peace and quiet and being able to work, read or write without any background chatter more. It might sound like a weird comparison, but I felt similarly about relationships. I would've like to have one for an hour or two here or there, but then I wanted to be able to turn it off and do my own thing again. But, of course, that's not how relationships work. Unlike a TV, you can't turn a relationship off when you want time for something else – at least not yet, maybe one day I can have a robot boyfriend who patiently waits in the cupboard until he's needed.

I think that almost everyone who is in a relationship sometimes wishes they could turn it off like a TV for a bit. I think most people in relationships have moments when they wish they could just do their own thing without any regard for their partner or kids. But for most people, there would be far more moments when they wish they had a partner if they were single. Or, to tie it back to my TV analogy, some people would rather have the TV running at volume 24/7 than never be able to watch any TV at all, even if the TV noise is sometimes annoying.

If you look at it in a very analytical way, being in a relationship makes sense as long as the good moments and perks outnumber the times you wish you could turn off or pause the relationship. I've never been in a situation where the benefits of being in a relationship felt worth making the required sacrifices and compromises. I loved my independence and doing things on my own too much – at least for now.

***

That summer, my best friend was getting married. It was the natural evolution of a relationship that started years earlier, and the engagement the previous winter wasn't at all surprising. Rachel had always wanted to get married and start a family, and I was beyond happy to see that dream coming true for her. Her husband had become a close friend, and I was excited and happy for both of them. There was a lot of wedding talk that summer as well as dress fittings, hen's party planning and everything else involved in your best friend getting married, and while all of that isn't my world at all, I enjoyed it. It was exciting to prepare for the big day with my best friend, and I ended up spending a lot of time in Auckland that summer, specifically because I wanted to be there for all of it. However, there was also a certain sadness. I couldn't place it at first. It almost felt like envy, which didn't make sense because I was confident that, at that point in my life, I didn't want that life she was about to embark on.

One day in December, my good friend Tora, and I were planning Rachel's hen party. We met at her house and talked about ideas and made plans. For Tora, it brought back memories of her own wedding and hen's party where Rachel had been her bridesmaid. It was a fun afternoon, and we were both excited for the hen's party and the wedding a few weeks later. As I was driving away later that day, a random thought hit me; I will never have this. I will never be the one my friends plan a hen's party for. The thought came out of nowhere. It surprised me so much that I pulled the van over and sat there on the side of the road, contemplating it.

For anyone hearing this, the situation may seem obvious. It would be easy to think that such a thought suggests that I wanted all the traditional stuff after all – that I did want a wedding and a hen's party. I tried to open myself up to that idea. I think it can be incredibly hard to be honest with ourselves, especially when it requires admitting that we were wrong. However, I also believe that finding true happiness requires honesty, and it requires us to be able to admit to ourselves when we got it wrong – and change. So if this was one of those situations, I wanted to be open to it. If it turned out that I had been wrong about what I want from life, I wanted to figure that out now and not 10 or 20 years down the road.

But as I sat there by the side of the road with traffic rushing past me, I knew deep in my gut that I hadn't been wrong about what I wanted. I knew I didn't really want a wedding and a hen's party. It was something else that had triggered that sense of sadness. I realised that envy did feel like the right word, but it wasn't envy for their lives. What I envied was that my close friends were on the same path in life. They were making very similar choices – which also happened to be the choices most people make and that society presents as "normal". I envied that because, in my mind, it meant that they understood each other and automatically supported each other. Rachel and Tora had planned each other's hen's parties. They had been each other's bridesmaids. Soon, Rachel would turn to Tora, who already had a daughter and was expecting the second child, for pregnancy and parenting tips. No one would plan my hen's party. No one would be my bridesmaid. I wouldn't be bonding with them over pregnancy and baby talk. Later, they would have playdates and joint family holidays. When their lives would be turned upside down by the demands of young children, and they wouldn't have as much time for friends anymore, they would have their kids, partners and hectic lives to distract them. Meanwhile, I would have more time than ever and would be consciously aware that my friends don't have as much time for me anymore.

At this point, I had been parked on the side of the road for almost an hour, so I decided to head to my parking spot for the night. As I was driving, still thinking about all of this, a thought came to me. "Maybe this is why so many people eventually change their mind about marriage and kids?" Five or ten years earlier, several people in my life, male and female, said they didn't want marriage and kids or were at least unsure about it. Most of them had changed their mind at some stage, and I had often wondered why. One friend, in particular, had been adamant she didn't want kids for as long as I could remember. However, the previous year she excitedly announced she was expecting her first child. We weren't very close, so I don't know what was going on in her life and heart at the time, but when I talked to her a month or two before the baby was born, I got the impression that she was very happy about soon being a mum.

That day, as I was parking up for the night, I felt like I understood, for the first time, why so many people change their minds about marriage and kids. This is another one of those things that I obviously don't know for sure since I can't read people's minds. For all I know, most of them might have changed their mind for very different reasons. But that day, it kind of made sense to me. I could see how being in this situation where everyone around you is on the same path, making similar life choices, could make you change your mind and want the same thing. I could see how the need for belonging, community and "fitting in" could be stronger than the desire for independence, freedom and sleeping in on weekends. So what did that mean for me? Would I change my mind? Would I ultimately choose fitting in over freedom?

The remainder of that second summer in my van flew by. I spent New Year and the first few weeks of 2019 on Great Barrier Island with a group of friends. Great Barrier Island is a magical, remote place about 100km east of Auckland. Some of my friends had been going there for summer holidays since before I became part of the group, and it was a tradition I was more than happy to join. This was my third summer on the island, but the first with the van. We always stayed at the campground at Medlands Beach, which, in previous years, involved tents, air mattresses and mid-night trips to the dark long drop toilet when nature called. Having the van brought a touch of luxury to the experience.

We had a great time exploring land and sea, sharing camp dinners and enjoying the sun. The van gave me extra flexibility and made it easy to do my own thing for a few days here and there. I took advantage of that, spending a few nights exploring other parts of the island on my own.

By the time I got back to Auckland at the end of January, the wedding was only a few weeks away, and final preparations were in full swing. I stayed close to Auckland, so I could be there for the final dress fitting, the hen's party and other bridesmaid duties. However, I got out of the city every chance

I got. Before we knew it, the big day was here, and shortly after, summer was coming to an end.

I never made a final decision on where I stood on the marriage and kids question that summer. On the one hand, I was confident that it wasn't what I wanted from life , but on the other hand, some questions and doubts remained. In the end, I figured the best I could do is live my life in a way that makes me happy, remaining open to possibilities, staying true to myself – and then seeing what happens.

With that attitude, I said goodbye to Auckland and headed south to explore the southern part of the North Island while the weather was still nice most days. After all the emotions I had to work through that summer, I felt a renewed sense of excitement for vanlife and was looking forward to travelling and exploring for the next few months. However, life had different plans for me.

9

ROLLERCOASTER
AUTUMN 2019

The best way to describe the autumn of 2019 is as a rollercoaster ride. It started with the excitement of being on the road again and looking forward to months of exploring. From there, things went downhill quickly, followed by one of the highest highs and more ups and downs after that.

After leaving Auckland at the end of summer, I planned to head south via Hawkes Bay on the east coast, spend a bit of time around Wellington and the Kapiti Coast and then follow the west coast north to Taranaki. I got as far as Wellington.

While I was in Wellington, it was time for my van's six-monthly Warrant of Fitness (WoF) check. All vehicles that drive on public roads in New Zealand need regular fitness checks to ensure they are safe. How often such inspections need to be done depends on the age of the vehicle. Since Josie was 20 years old, she needed to be inspected every six months.

So one morning while I was in Wellington, I made my way to a testing station and waited patiently in line for a while. Despite that fact that I arrived early, there was already quite a queue. In situations like these, being in a campervan is awesome. While everyone else was sitting in their little cars without much too do, I made breakfast and coffee and did some work, hopping into the driver's seat every now and then so I wouldn't lose my spot in the queue. Eventually, it was Josie's turn. I handed over the keys to the inspector and made my way to the waiting area. About half an hour later, I saw the inspector walking my way with a serious look on this face that didn't promise anything good.

With a sombre tone he informed me that Josie had failed the safety check. And she didn't just fail a little. She failed big time due to rust. In a maritime climate like New Zealand, rust is a widespread issue. I know this now, but back then, I was oblivious to how much of a pain it can be. There were some minor signs of rust in the months leading up to this day, so I wasn't entirely surprised to hear about rust issues. However, I was completely unprepared for how bad it was. The inspector decided to show me by giving the step by the passenger door a big kick, only for it to crumble away under his foot. I almost returned the favour by giving him a good kick in his sensitive parts. How dare he treat Josie like that!

I was devastated, of course, but I tried to stay positive. I'm a very solutions-focused person. My default response to problems is to jump into action and do something about them. I'm not someone who gets hung up on negative emotions or feels paralysed when things get tough. If anything, I'm guilty of the opposite. I've probably at times been guilty of not dealing with emotions because I was already focusing on fixing whatever was bothering me. Staying true to my style, I jumped into action after getting the rust news. At that point, I thought all I had to do was find someone who could fix the van. Yes, it would delay my travels and probably set me back financially, but that wasn't the end of the world. I could travel to Taranaki another time and work more over winter to make up for the cost of fixing the van.

So the next morning, I got on the phone. Over the next two hours, I talked to at least ten panel-beaters and rust repair specialists between Wellington and Auckland. All were either completely booked out for 4-6 weeks, couldn't do the work, or were so hostile and rude that I didn't want to trust them with my van. Given Josie had failed her WoF, I had to get her fixed within four weeks. After that, she would no longer be road legal. So waiting 4-6 weeks to get the repairs started wasn't ideal. On top of that, there was no way to tell how long the repairs would take or how much they would cost. As I learned that day, the problem with rust is that you generally can't see most of it until you start looking. So someone might start the repair thinking it would take a week or two, only to find the issue is much bigger than initially assumed.

One of the places in Wellington I talked to didn't have the capacity to do the work for several weeks but said they would be happy to take a look now to give me a better idea of what I'm dealing with, so I took the van there. The guy who inspected Josie was super nice, but he didn't have good news for me. He thought the issue was fairly major and went as far as suggesting it might not be worth getting it fixed. I thanked him for his time and advice and left. I made it a few hundred metres down the road before I pulled over and cried. I don't cry often. Usually, I'm focused on finding a solution instead of dealing with the emotions at hand. But in this case, I had tried finding a solution, and it had only made it worse – at least that's how it felt at the time. When I woke up that morning, I thought all I had to do was find someone to fix the van. Now, there was doubt about whether it could even be fixed.

I spent the rest of the day feeling sorry for myself. I loved that van, and the idea of losing her was hard to take. I also didn't have anywhere else to stay. Without Josie, I would essentially be homeless. I knew I was being a bit dramatic. I had friends I could stay with for a while, I had enough savings to afford renting a place if needed, and I could always work more to make up for the cost of it all. The rational part of me knew that I would be alright. But that afternoon and evening, as I sat in my van that was apparently falling apart around me, I didn't feel very rational. I just felt sad and frustrated.

The next day, I decided I needed to get out of the city and to my happy place – the ocean. So I made my way north to Ōtaki, where you can camp right on the beach. Parked up with stunning views and salt in the air, I could feel my positivity slowly return – just for the next blow to knock me over.

I was checking Facebook and had a couple of notifications. Two of them told me that friends in New Zealand had marked themselves safe (remember that old Facebook feature? Not sure if that's even still a thing). At the same moment, I noticed posts from other friends that didn't promise anything good. There were a couple that had nothing but hearts or sad faces. Some had "Christchurch" followed by hearts or sad emojis. Clearly, something had happened in Christchurch. My first thought was, "not another earthquake". Back in 2010 and 2011, two severe earthquakes had hit Christchurch. The second one in February 2011 killed 180 people and destroyed much of Christchurch's city centre. At this point in March 2019, the city was still rebuilding, and the earthquakes were far from forgotten. However, it wasn't another earthquake that shook Christchurch and the world that day.

I opened the news app on my phone to find out what was going on, and there were the unthinkable words in big, bold letters: Terrorist Attack in Christchurch. For a second, I thought surely this must be a mistake. They must have the wrong Christchurch or somehow got it wrong in another way. The words terrorist attack and New Zealand simply did not go together for me.

Don't get me wrong, New Zealand has its fair share of problems. Our domestic violence statistics, for example, are shocking. But a terrorist attack? It shook me to the core. New Zealand had been my safe haven, my paradise, my happy place. I love this country more than I had ever loved Germany, even though that's where I was born. For me, New Zealand is associated with beauty, kindness, safety, and love. For something as violent as a terrorist attack to happen here was hard to comprehend. Of course, terrorist attacks, or any kind of violence for that matter, are always tragic, senseless and difficult to comprehend, no matter where they happen. But this one hit close to home. My heart broke a little that day.

Fifty-one people lost their lives in the Christchurch mosque shootings on 15 March 2019. May they rest in peace.

I ended up staying at Ōtaki Beach for a few days. I felt like I needed time to come to terms with what happened. However, in a way, the van troubles provided a welcome distraction from the tragic events in Christchurch, and so I started to face the challenges head-on. I decided that Auckland would be the best place to deal with the situation. In Auckland, I had friends I could stay with, it would be the best place to find housesitting gigs if I needed a place to stay for longer, and it offered the most options for repairers and rust experts. However, I also decided to take the long way back north. At that point, I had no idea what would happen next. For all I knew, these could be my last few weeks in the van for a while, or maybe even forever. The rust issues wouldn't go anywhere, and given how bad it was, a couple more weeks wouldn't change anything. So I headed north via Taranaki and took my time. It wasn't quite the same with these issues hanging over me and the devastating events in Christchurch continuing to be on everyone's mind. Nevertheless, I managed to find some joy in the scenery and adventure. I followed the famous Surf Highway along the coast, stayed in a few small villages on the way and eventually made my way to New Plymouth on the northern side of the Taranaki Peninsula. From here, I continued north to Auckland.

As all of this was unfolding, I shared what was happening on my blog and Facebook page, and received many lovely messages of support and encouragement – as well as some advice that turned out to be invaluable!

When Josie failed her WoF, the inspector asked me how I had managed to get a WoF for her six months earlier. I didn't think much of it then, but the question kept popping up in the days that followed. Everyone who saw the van, or even just heard how significant the issue was, asked who had done the previous WoF and why rust wasn't mentioned then. According to the experts, rust of this extent does not just appear overnight. It would have been building up for years, and they all thought it should have been pretty obvious six months ago. When I shared all of this on Facebook, several people suggested that I file a complaint with the garage that did the Warrant of Fitness six months earlier and passed Josie without mentioning anything about rust. They had not only done the WoF but also some significant engine repairs at the same time, so they spent quite a bit of time with and under my van. According to the experts, it would have been hard to have missed the rust, and the fact that they passed the WoF showed great negligence.

With nothing to lose, I followed their advice. While travelling along the coast of Taranaki, I sent a carefully worded email to the garage to inform them of the situation and the advice I had received that suggested they are partly responsible. I had asked one of the rust experts who inspected the van recently to write a letter stating that, in their expert opinion, this level of rust should have been picked up during a WoF inspection six months earlier, and I attached that to the email. I got a reply quickly, asking me to bring the van in so they could take a look themselves, which I did once I got back to Auckland. They inspected Josie, asked a panel beater they trusted to take a look, and then agreed that the issue was significant. At this point, they got their insurance provider involved, who took the lead in assessing the situation. I had to take Josie to more people for inspections – and then I waited. Several weeks had passed since the van failed the WoF, so it was no longer road legal. The chances of it being repaired became slimmer by the day, and I had to accept the fact that I would have to farewell Josie. It was a bitter pill to swallow and for the first time since I started vanlife, I was wondering whether I had made the right decision. I didn't have enough money at the time to buy a new van, and with the insurance provider dragging their feet, there was no way of knowing if and when they would accept and settle the claim – and if so, how much money I would get. In other words, I was homeless and had no idea what the coming months would bring.

It was without a doubt the toughest time in my vanlife journey so far. The uncertainty was getting to me. I felt like I was stuck and relied on other people, namely the insurance company, to decide my fate before I could move on.

Three things made the situation better. Firstly, I was lucky enough to find housesitting gigs from early April, so I had somewhere to stay once the van was no longer road legal. Secondly, the garage I filed the complaint with was very motivated to do their best to make things right and loaned me one of their courtesy cars, so I had a vehicle to get around. They also offered to store Josie until the situation was resolved, which made things easier for me, given I would be moving around a bit between different housesitting gigs. Thirdly, and most significantly, right in the middle of all this drama, I got the most exciting news.

———

At the end of March, as I was making my way north along the Taranaki coast with my rusty van, I got an email from a publisher in the UK who said they were interested in the book I'd written the previous year. After I'd finished writing it in autumn, I'd spent hours researching and contacting agents and publishers. If you think writing a book is hard, try finding a publisher for one. As I'd learned that previous year, there is quite a process to it. You need to find the right publishers or agents, prepare a proposal in the correct format (often publishers and agents have their own guidelines), follow specific processes for contacting people, and then hope someone bothers to read your email and proposal. I knew that it would be a long shot. After all, only a very small number of all the books written each year get picked up by a publisher. Luckily, in this day and age, there is the option to self-publish, which was my plan B. However, I wanted to try the traditional route first. I reached out to dozens of agents and publishers. Most of them never even replied. I was almost ready to give up and go down the self-publishing route when I got the email from Morton's Media Group, a small publisher in the UK.

I was at a campground outside New Plymouth when I got the email that said they thought my book was great and they were interested in publishing it. My first reaction was total joy and excitement. However, that was quickly followed by doubts creeping in. I was part of a few writer communities, and I had heard many stories about people who call themselves publishers ripping off authors. I won't bore you with the details of how the publishing industry works, but essentially there are two types of publishers. Genuine traditional publishers will pay authors an advance for their books (tiny ones for first-time authors like myself) and then royalty for sales (again, often a small percentage for an unknown author, but it's something). In addition, they will cover the cost of editing, design, marketing, printing and distribution. In exchange, the publisher will 'own' the book. Then there are so-called Hybrid Publishers who offer the services of the traditional publishers (editing, design, distribution, etc.), but authors need to pay for these services. In exchange, authors keep ownership and rights. The problem with hybrid publishers is that some disguise themselves as traditional publishers. They approach authors saying they want to publish their book, and just when you get excited, they inform you that you will have to pay for their services. In addition, there have also been some scams where people pretend to be publishers or professionals that provide services to authors, only to be never heard of again once the author has transferred money.

All of this went through my mind after I got the email from Morton's Media Group. With shaking hands and a heart that was definitely beating faster than normal, I did a Google search. It established that they are real, and as far as I could tell, they seemed to be a genuine traditional publisher. However, I still felt nervous about it all. To make matters worse, it was a Saturday morning. Given the publisher was in the UK, I knew it would be Monday night or Tuesday morning before I would get a reply to the questions I sent back. Needless to say, I had an anxious few days and nights.

The following week, it became clear that it was real. Further background research confirmed the publisher and the people I was dealing with had good reputations. In addition, the draft contract they sent through was what you would expect a traditional publishing contract to look like, including an advance payment, royalties and no expectations for me to cover any of the costs associated with publishing the book. Once I realised that, the initial excitement returned. However, that was quickly followed by feeling overwhelmed by the detail and legal language in the contract. I took a few law papers at university and dealt with contracts in my professional life, but I knew nothing about publishing agreements and laws. I realised I had been so focused on trying to find someone interested in publishing my book that I'd never even thought about what I would do if it happened. So I spent hours reading up on publishing laws online and trying to figure out what is and isn't normal and what rights I can expect to have as the author.

There were a couple of things in the contract that I wasn't 100% comfortable with, but I was super nervous to say so. I'd dreamed about writing and publishing a book one day, and in the past year, as I wrote One Size Does Not Fit All, that dream had started to become a real possibility. I don't think I ever enjoyed anything as much as I enjoyed writing that book, and seeing it published would be a huge dream come true for me. However, I was nervous that too many questions and trying too hard to negotiate details in the contract might lead to the publisher deciding that I was too hard to work with and taking it away. It's probably a feeling familiar to anyone who has ever negotiated a contract for their dream job.

Luckily, the publisher was great. They patiently answered all my questions and were willing to change the agreement based on my suggestions. Although, I must admit, if I had to do it all again, I would probably get a legal professional involved to review the contract and give me advice. However, at the time, I didn't know any lawyers familiar with publishing laws, and I was worried the delays that finding one would cause might result in the publisher losing interest.

So, on the 31st of March, with a little bit of a queasy feeling but mostly lots of excitement, I signed the publishing deal for my first book. I had made it back to Auckland by then and was spending the weekend at Muriwai Beach with my best friend and her newlywed husband, who had recently purchased a small camper. It was great to have my best friends there to celebrate what I consider one of the most significant achievements of my life. The book didn't turn into a bestseller, but back then, I could dream that it would. Besides, it didn't even matter. Nothing could take away the fact that I wrote a book which is available as an actual printed book that would forever live on my bookshelf.

After the devastating van news and the trauma caused by the terrorist attacks in Christchurch, this was the high I needed – as well as the distraction. I was given four weeks to finalise the manuscript. After that, it went to the editor, and I spent a few weeks working through their feedback and suggestions. It was the perfect way to keep busy and positive while all the van drama was happening in the background.

Speaking of the van drama. With a roof over my head thanks to housesitting opportunities, a vehicle to get around and a book keeping me busy, the biggest challenge was the uncertainty and the lack of communication from the garage's insurance provider. Weeks went by without any progress. Every time I called to get an update, I was promised there would be progress within a few days – but then nothing happened. More than once I was close to tears when hanging up the phone. This was a nerve-wracking time for me. I had never been through a process like this before and wasn't sure what to expect. The long delays and lack of communication made me feel like I couldn't trust the insurance provider. I was worried that they were delaying things while trying to find a way to dispute the claim.

Eventually, about eight weeks after I filed the complaint, I had enough. I channelled all my anger and frustration and sent a strongly worded email saying I had discussed the issue with my lawyer, and if there wasn't a resolution, or at least a clear plan and timeline to get to one, within the next week, they would hear from my lawyer. I didn't have a lawyer, but I figured I could find one if needed. In the end, I didn't have to. A week later, at the end of May, I received a settlement offer that I was happy to accept. It was bittersweet. On the one hand, I was glad that the situation was finally resolved, but on the other hand, it also meant the definite end of Josie. However, getting the settlement money meant I could afford to buy a new van, which was the most important thing. After all, as stressful as this situation had been, I was more certain than ever that I wanted to continue vanlife. Knowing I could do that, and do so soon, was a big relief.

Part of the settlement deal was that I would take responsibility of 'disposing' of Josie. I didn't like the word 'disposing', but agreed to take her back. So on a Wednesday at the end of May, I picked her up from the garage where she had been parked up for almost two months. I listed her on Trademe (New Zealand's eBay), for a fraction of what I bought her for and with a very clear and honest description of the issues. Within an hour I had an offer from someone who wanted her for parts. I liked the idea that Josie would help other vans stay on the road longer by providing them with those parts of her that were still in good condition. Kind of like the campervan version of organ donation. And so in the first week of June, I said my final goodbye to Josie and watched the new owner drive off with her. I felt lots of different emotions in that moment. I had so many great times with Josie and was incredibly sad to see her go. But at the same time, after all the drama, I was relieved that this chapter of my life was now closed and I was happy that I could move on.

So, in the end, the rollercoaster ride that was autumn 2019 had a happy ending – or at least as happy an ending as a season that involved a terrorist attack and losing my home could have. Nevertheless, I was hoping that winter would be a bit less temperamental.

10

NORMAL
WINTER 2019

Auckland

After the rollercoaster ride that was autumn, my life in winter 2019 could almost be described as normal. I was living in houses, worked lots, and struggled with a super sore back – which apparently is one of the most common health issues of the modern office worker. The only thing that made it less ordinary was that I lived in three different houses and that it was all just temporary while I was looking for a new van.

Back in May, before I knew the outcome of the van situation, I committed to several months of work and housesitting. At the time, I didn't know if I would get any payout from the garage's insurance and, consequently, didn't know when I would be able to afford a new van. Therefore, when friends and friends of friends asked if I could house and pet sit for them over winter, I was more than happy to do so. The fact that I was offered three four-week housesits with only a couple of days in between felt like a sign. At least I would have somewhere to stay. Similarly, when I had the opportunity to take on more work, I jumped at it. That way, I could save up and afford a new van in time for summer, even if I got nothing from the insurance company. In the end, the insurer did pay, and I didn't need to housesit and work for that long, but I had committed, and I'm not one to back down from commitments. Besides, even though I didn't technically need the work and housesits anymore, both still turned out to be a blessing.

Working a lot meant I was building up savings which would give me more freedom in the future. I was working for a few different clients at the time. The work was diverse, and I enjoyed it. As a bonus, I could do most of it remotely, so I didn't have to deal with Auckland traffic. In addition, knowing that I had somewhere to stay until the end of August meant I could take my time finding a new van.

I thought a lot about what kind of van to replace Josie with. Given the insurance payout plus the money I was making from working so much that winter, I would be able to spend a bit more on a van if I wanted to. I thought about getting something larger. I liked the idea of having a permanent bed and just generally more space. But a bigger vehicle would also come with downsides. It wouldn't be as easy to drive, especially around towns, and parking would be harder, too. Josie was almost like a car in that regard. She fit into most standard car parks, and I could drive her just about anywhere a car could go. The other big question was how I would transport my paddle board and longboard. Most bigger motorhomes are too wide to carry the boards on the side like I had done with Josie. They would be pretty high, so getting them on and off the roof on my own would be even less of an option. I had loved having my boards with me during the first 18 months of my travels, so leaving them behind wasn't something I was willing to consider. The side racks on Josie were perfect, and I was keen to get the same setup for the next van. That limited my choices.

The only larger motorhomes that would allow carrying the boards on the side without going over the maximum permitted width were Toyota Coaster or Mitsubishi Rosa type minibuses. They are longer than a Transit van which creates more living space, but are only slightly wider, so the side racks would be an option. While I liked the look of them, I did not like the price tags. Thirty-year-old Coasters and Rosas in decent condition were selling for $50k to $60k sometimes more. Clearly, I wasn't the only one who liked the look of those buses. While I could have theoretically afforded to spend that much, it didn't sit right with me. I had heard too many stories of people who had to invest in significant repairs, even with these buses that generally have a reputation for being sturdy. I didn't want to spend that kind of money on a camper and then risk having to spend thousands more on repairs. Good quality or not, a 30-year-old bus is a 30-year-old bus. There would be a good chance of it needing significant repairs and maintenance work. In addition, most of these small buses didn't have a permanent bed, at least not while also having a permanent seating area, so I wouldn't gain all that much.

That left me with only one real choice; another high-top van similar to Josie. Initially, I was very reluctant to consider another Ford Transit. From conversations with panel beaters and others in the know, I had learned that Josie was far from the only Transit with rust issues – which also explained why they were often a bit cheaper than other, similar vans. Apparently, it was a widespread issue (though Transits certainly aren't the only vehicles that have rust issues). So I looked at Mercedes Sprinters and Fiat Ducatos, which are similar in size. The problem was, they are much harder to come by and more expensive – and come with their own issues. A friend had a Ducato that was causing her headaches and sleepless nights due to engine and gearbox issues. I heard from other people that both Ducatos and Sprinters can be costly to get fixed if something goes wrong. Due to them being a lot less common than Transits here in New Zealand, parts, especially second-hand ones, are harder to find, which can delay repairs and increase costs. In other words, there would be no guarantee that future vanlife would be free of van trouble no matter what I bought. Transits are far from perfect, but at least they are very common in New Zealand, so it's usually easy to get parts and find people who can do repairs when needed.

I had learned a lesson or two from the Josie disaster, though. I took my time, looked at several vans, talked to experts, and researched on the internet. I learned that Ford Transits built after 2002 are less prone to rust. That doesn't mean they don't have rust issues, it just seems less common and less severe. Nevertheless, I was still hesitant. I looked at a Mercedes Sprinter and two Fiat Ducatos that winter. The Sprinter was very run down on the inside and had done well over 300,000km. Despite that, the owner still wanted $40k for it. One of the Fiats looked promising but didn't do well during the pre-purchase inspection. It had several oil leaks, and the inspector said a few things look pretty worn and might need replacing soon, including the brake-pads and tires. Despite this, the owner wasn't willing to lower the price, so I walked away. The second Fiat looked nice enough, but I had a funny feeling about the owner. They didn't seem genuine and had only bought the van a few months ago, making me wonder if they discovered issues and are trying to sell it instead of fixing them. Finding a new van was proving harder than I had thought.

As the days started to get longer again, announcing the end of winter, I was getting impatient. I wanted a new van, but after weeks of looking, I still hadn't found the right one. While living in houses was nice for a while, and I loved having pets to cuddle with, I couldn't wait to be back on the road.

With every day that passed, I felt more like I was getting pulled back into my old life. All those valuable lessons I had learned over the past 18 months seemed to be slowly slipping away. Despite having realised how important free time was to me, I found myself committing to more and more work. Despite knowing that promotions and success in the traditional sense wouldn't make me happy, I found myself comparing my career progression to my peers again. Despite having learned that I don't need much to be happy only a year earlier, I found myself getting caught up in consumerism again.

One day, I was driving home after a client meeting in town, thinking to myself, "I should stop at the mall". Only when I pulled up outside the shops, did I ask myself what I actually needed. I decided to get nice shoes and maybe a new dress for client meetings, so I got out of the car and went inside. It was busy in the mall, even though it was a weekday. As I made my way through the crowd, I suddenly stopped. "What am I doing here?" I asked myself. I don't actually need fancy shoes or a new dress. I had nice clothes I could wear to work meetings and, besides, I planned to live in a van again in a few weeks. I definitely wouldn't need fancy shoes or dresses then. I realised I had been on auto-pilot. I had stopped at the mall not because I needed anything but because that's what people do in Auckland.

It was scary to realise how quickly I had reverted to old behaviours. Despite all the amazing insights I had gained during my 18 months on the road, all it took was a few months back in Auckland, surrounded by billboards, subliminal messaging and people chasing wealth, and here I was, at the mall, getting ready to spend my hard-earned money on things I didn't need. I left the mall that day without buying anything, but I couldn't help but wonder how many other things I had done on auto-pilot that winter without noticing.

A few weeks later, I met up with my ex-colleague-turned-friend, Jason. We had worked together several years earlier when we were both starting out in our careers and eager to get ahead. Since then, he had taken on a senior leadership role in a startup business many considered one of the most promising up-and-coming New Zealand companies. Meanwhile, I was technically homeless and didn't have many work-related successes to show for myself. In many ways, he was living the life I thought I wanted back when we had worked together. Hearing about his achievements and career-focused life, I couldn't help but feel inferior. I wouldn't have admitted it to anyone, but a part of me felt like I was lazy for not working as much as he did – and almost everyone else around me. I knew I didn't want that kind of life, but after nearly four months back in Auckland, a part of me thought I should want the ambition and achievements Jason clearly had.

Thoughts like that had been extremely rare since I left Auckland in my van more than 18 months earlier. For over a year and a half, I had been confident in my choices. Confident that wealth and career success are overrated – especially when they come at the cost of personal time and freedom. For over 18 months, it had been easy to follow my own path and ignore everything else. But being back in Auckland that winter, living a relatively normal life, I found it harder and harder to hold on to that wisdom and confidence. At times, it was hard to remember all the lessons I had learned and that, ultimately, success isn't about wealth, titles or career progression but about being happy. If you had asked me six months earlier, I would have sworn that I will never be pulled back into that kind of life where my self-worth depends on how much I work and earn, but here I was.

That winter, I learned how strong the pull of normal can

be. How even if you break free and get away from it for a while, you're never really free. As soon as you're back in the normal world, with all its traditions, expectations, pressures and ways of doing things, you have to fight to keep a clear head and to stay connected to your true self. Otherwise, consumerism and the rat race will swallow you up again.

Despite that realisation, I felt like I just had to push through. I told myself I'd be back in a van soon, but until then, I had work commitments to fulfil. And so I worked long hours, didn't get out into nature enough, and overall, felt like life was pretty boring. To make matters worse, I developed a really sore back. I'm pretty sure it was a result of poor posture when working. Given I was moving around so much, always staying in other people's houses, I didn't have a proper work setup. Most of the time, I worked at kitchen tables, on couches or on the floor. I didn't have a very ergonomic work setup in the van either. In fact, it was probably worse than any kitchen table. However, it's not that big of an issue when you only work 10-15 hours per week.

During some weeks that winter, I spent 40 hours and more behind the computer, and my back wasn't happy about it. I found a chiropractor who practices something called Network Spinal Analysis (NSA), a form of chiropractic care that focuses on connecting with the nervous system to free tensions around the spine. NSA had helped me tremendously a few years earlier when I had persistent shoulder pains after a kitesurfing accident. I was hoping it would do the same this time, but I wouldn't be so lucky. While the treatments helped, the pain never went away completely. For weeks I experienced constant pain whenever I moved. Kitesurfing and surfing were out of the question. I went for short walks several times a day and did some simple stretches, but that was it as far as movement was concerned.

The only thing that kept me positive that winter was knowing that I would be on the road again soon – and the fact that I was progressing as a writer. The content for my book was finalised in late June. In July, the publisher and I worked on the cover, and I loved what the designer came up with. We also worked on marketing ideas and the pitch for the book. All of it was very exciting for me as a first-time author. In addition, I had also started writing regular articles for the magazine Motorhomes, Caravans & Destinations. Earlier in the year, I reached out to the publisher, offering a story I had written about my trip to Great Barrier Island. They accepted and published it and, soon after, asked if I would be keen to write for them on an ongoing basis. Of course, I was keen. I was only contributing one story per month, sometimes two, so it wasn't enough to pay the bills. But I was making money as a writer, and I loved writing stories about the places I visited and the people I met.

While the book and articles helped, they weren't enough to keep me positive long-term. As I moved for my third and last housesitting gig at the end of July, I was getting truly desperate. I wanted a van. This was when I started to consider Ford Transits again. I had explored all other options without any luck. For every one Sprinter or Fiat Ducato for sale in my price range, there were three or four Transits. In addition, I was worried that I would spend many more months waiting for the right Sprinter or Ducato to come along – and then there would still be no guarantee that I wouldn't have issues with it.

So, when a good-looking Transit came up for sale in Auckland in early August, I made an appointment to check it out. I drove out to Albany where the sellers, a lovely older couple, were living in a retirement village. Bob and Judy had owned the van for about two years. It was their first camper and they enjoyed the lifestyle so much that they decided to upgrade to something a bit larger, so the small van had to go. Bob showed me around the van and patiently answered all my questions. It was obvious that they, and the previous owner who had owned the van for almost 10 years, had looked after it very well. There even was a folder with receipts and a full service history dating back almost ten years.

The van was built in 2003, meaning it was a few years newer than Josie, and research suggested it should be less prone to significant rust. Overall, the van was similar to Josie. It had the same layout with the kitchen behind the passenger seat, the bathroom and storage behind the driver's seat and the two long benches at the back that turned into a bed at night. But this van also had a few advantages compared to Josie. Firstly, it had a slightly longer bed, so I would no longer have to sleep diagonally. It also came with a gas heater which would be super handy in winter. In addition, the driver's cabin was slightly larger, which meant I could get the seat back further and would be a bit more comfortable. Finally, while the van had done over 200,000km, a new engine had been put in just over 50,000km ago, reducing the risk of significant engine problems. I liked the look of it and took it for a test drive with Bob in the passenger seat. I was a little nervous as it had been a while since I last drove a manual. But luckily, my brain still remembered and I got through the test drive without any hiccups. Once we returned, I asked Bob if I could have a few minutes alone in the van. I sat down in the back and asked myself; "does this feel like my new home?"

I ummed and aahed about it for a few days. Josie had taught me how quickly you could lose a lot of money when buying older vehicles. I got lucky that I got an insurance payout, but chances are that won't be the case next time. On the other hand, I really wanted to have a van again, and I realised that nothing in my price range would be perfect and guaranteed trouble-free. So I decided to take the Transit for a pre-purchase inspection. It brought up a few minor things, like the fact that it needed a new tire and windscreen wipers, but nothing major. The seller offered to get those things fixed, and I decided to buy the van.

I was super excited to have a home on wheels again. However, the feeling was different the second time around. There was a lot of joy and excitement as I took ownership of my second van, but I also couldn't shake feelings of doubt and worry. Would this one turn out to be a dud, too? Would I have significant problems with it like I had with Josie? I definitely had lost some of my naivety about the lifestyle. When I bought Josie, I had no idea of all the things that could go wrong. I was blissfully ignorant. It was all excitement and no worry. This time around, there was a bit more worry. The thing is, it's not just about the money. Yes, having to pay for expensive van repairs was super annoying, but the part that bothered me most was the uncertainty and hassle. My van was my home and my car. Imagine you discovered a major issue with your house and couldn't live in it for days, possibly months. No one can tell you for sure how long it will be. Then, on the same day, your car breaks down, leaving you without a home or a vehicle. That's what it's like when you live in your van and have issues with it. It's stressful. And now that I had been through it, I was no longer blissfully ignorant. I knew it was only a matter of time until something would go wrong. I was planning for it financially, ensuring I had enough money put aside to pay for repairs and accommodation if I needed it. But money wouldn't take away the hassle and uncertainty.

Nevertheless, despite some worries, I was super excited to have a van again. It was mid-August by the time I took ownership of it, which meant I only had a couple more weeks of housesitting left before I could hit the road again. I used those weeks to make myself at home in my new van by adding some personal touches and personality to the interior and planned my travels for the coming spring. I also tried to come up with a name for my new van, but nothing felt right. Josie had felt so natural and I decided to wait until the same thing happened for my second van instead of trying to force it. However, it never did happen and so The Van became its name. I admit, not the most original name, but somehow it stuck. And so on August 26th, I moved into The Van and hit the road for vanlife 2.0.

The new van. It looks a lot like the old one.

The inside of the new van.

To view these images in colour, and more photos
from my journey, visit my website.
lifedonedifferently.com/gallery

11

CONFIDENCE

SPRING 2019

Fletcher Bay &
Port Jackson

Coromandel

Waihi Beach &
Bowentown

Remember that sore back that was troubling me throughout winter? For weeks, my back hurt every time I moved. I had seen different physios and chiropractors, and while it helped a little, the pain never went away – and it always got worse as soon as I stopped treatment. It was impacting my life significantly. My favourite activities, like surfing and kitesurfing, were out of the question, and even longer walks were often painful. The constant pain was getting to me, and I found it difficult to stay positive. Worst of all, there was no end in sight. No treatment seemed to really work, and the doctors and health professionals I was seeing were running out of ideas. So as winter turned into spring, I was excited to be back living and travelling in a van, but I was also worried about how the back would cope, and when I'd be able to live life to the fullest again.

Well, I woke up after the first night in my new van, and the pain was gone. After weeks of pain and soreness, it simply disappeared after one night in the camper. Poof. Gone! Just like that. I had another appointment with my NSA chiropractor a couple of days later, and I thought she wouldn't believe me. But, she actually thought it kind of made sense. She explained that many issues in our bodies could be traced back to our nervous system. Clearly, my nervous system was tense throughout winter. Now that I was back in the van and living the way I wanted, my nervous system had relaxed, and the pain had disappeared. Regardless of whether there was a scientific explanation, I still considered it a little miracle – and more importantly, a clear sign that I was back on track to living the way that's right for me.

With the back pain gone, vanlife 2.0 was off to a great start, and it only got better from there. With a renewed sense of adventure and a desire to explore and see new places, I travelled all over the North Island that spring. I left Auckland and headed to the Coromandel Peninsula. I had heard great things about Port Jackson and Fletcher Bay at the northern end of the peninsula and wanted to check them out.

I stocked up on food, fuel and water before leaving Coromandel town, knowing that there wouldn't be any opportunity to get supplies where I was going, and then headed north. The further I drove, the narrower the road got – and the more stunning the views. I have to admit, at some point I seriously questioned how safe this drive was. The road had turned into gravel a while back and was so narrow that passing was only possible in certain spots. Lots of turns made it tricky to see oncoming traffic and the steep drop-off next to me meant that any mistakes would likely end badly. But, I kept going – partly because there weren't many options to turn around, but also because I knew other nomads who had driven this road in much larger RVs, so I figured it must be safe.

Eventually, about an hour and a half after I left Coromandel town, the van and I safely arrived in Port Jackson where a beautiful, almost empty, beachfront campsite awaited us. I stayed in this bit of paradise for a few days before moving on to Fletcher Bay and then making my way south via the east coast of the Coromandel to Waihi Beach and Bowentown.

After that, I spent October in the Far North. It had long been one of my favourite parts of New Zealand, and I was excited to return. I kitesurfed on Rangiputa Harbour, tried my best to surf Shipwreck Bay (with limited success, I still wasn't getting any better at surfing), and spent time with friends who had recently moved to Ahipara and other friends who came up from Auckland for weekend trips. Then, in early November, I started to head south and spent the next six weeks crossing the length of the North Island to Wellington and then back up again via Wairarapa, Hawkes Bay, and the East Cape. I guess you could say I well and truly made the most of being back on the road.

The further I travelled that spring, the more I reconnected with my true self. After a winter in Auckland, where I had felt like I was being pulled back into a normal life with all the pressure and expectations that come with that, I was relieved to find it easy to disconnect from all of that once I was on the road again. I switched the busy city for quiet, scenic campgrounds and busy work days for ones spent exploring in nature. All the fears about not achieving enough or not being successful that had reared their heads during winter faded into the background as I reconnected with the lessons I had learned during my first 18 months of vanlife. I slowed down again, reduced my workload and spent a lot of time reading and daydreaming or going for long walks. Before I knew it, I was back to feeling as confident as ever that the life I had chosen was right for me.

Another absolute highlight that spring was the launch of my first book. The book was published in October, but it took several weeks for the package with my paperback copies to arrive, thanks to it getting lost somewhere along the way. The wait was worth it, though. Finally holding my book in my hands in November was a magical moment. What made the achievement even more special was the support from my friends. My friends Rachael and Peter hosted a book launch party at their house one weekend in November when I passed through Auckland on my way south from the Far North.

A few weeks after Rachel's wedding earlier that year, I had confided in her that I sometimes found it hard not to have all the same big life moments that they had, such as engagements, weddings and the birth of children. I'd told her that I sometimes felt like my biggest moments in life didn't seem to have the same value in society – like my achievements were less significant just because they weren't the same as everyone else's. I didn't want a wedding or a baby, but I sometimes wished to have those big moments everyone values and celebrates so much. Not having them and not getting the support and acknowledgement that comes with them made me feel disconnected at times.

Being the amazing friend that she is, Rachel took my words to heart and hosted a party with all our friends to celebrate the launch of my book. Everyone showed up. We had an awesome afternoon and evening, and it meant the world to me that my friends made the time to celebrate that achievement with me. At that point, many of them were in the throes of raising young kids. With them being busy and me being away so much, we saw each other less frequently. Truth is, we had started drifting apart. I kind of always knew that would likely happen and had accepted it as a side-effect of my choices. However, all of them making the time to show up that day to celebrate something important to me made me feel loved and supported – and confident that even if we saw each other less, we were still connected and would be there for each other when it mattered.

———

That spring, I also met Logan. He was a fellow nomad who had a van similar to mine. Our paths first crossed at a campsite in Coromandel town, but it wasn't until we met again at Fletcher Bay a few days later that we started chatting. It was a beautiful day, and we sat outside in our camping chairs, enjoying the views, drinking coffee and talking about vanlife. We had a lot in common. Logan started vanlife a few months before me. Like me, he was looking for freedom and adventure, and found it travelling the country in a van. His background was different, though. While my life had been fairly conventional before vanlife, Logan's had always been untraditional. He spent many years travelling through Asia before coming home to New Zealand. He never committed to one career. Instead, he had done a wide range of odd jobs, gathering experiences and skills along the way. While I was passionate about my work and enjoyed doing it, for Logan, work was what he needed to do to pay the bills and buy food. He would often work for a few months, save as much as he could, and then travel until he ran out of money. While I can't see myself living like that, I found his stories fascinating and admired him for the bravery it took to live like that without any real safety net.

As an introvert, I often find it hard to fully enjoy meeting new people. There is always a part of me that worries about not being able to get away when I need to. I fear that people want more of my time and energy than I can give – and that it will lead to me disappointing them and letting them down. I often genuinely enjoy chatting with people for a while, but after an hour or so, I start to run out of people energy and crave solitude. In my experience, many extroverts find that hard to understand and feel offended or rejected when I excuse myself or cut catchups short. However, Logan was a kindred soul. But unlike me, he was unapologetic about it. I would often come up with excuses why I needed to leave because I was worried about hurting and disappointing people. Not so Logan. After about an hour of us chatting that day at Fletcher Bay, he got up, said he was going to have a look around, and walked away. I imagine others might have felt rejected and disappointed by not being asked if they wanted to come along, but I felt relieved. I sat in silence for a while, enjoying the solitude and sunshine, and then went on a walk myself in the opposite direction.

That was the first taste of what I later learned was typical Logan. He did his own thing without any apologies. A part of me admired that confidence immensely. I was certainly following my own path in life, and most people would say I was confident and not easily swayed by other people's opinions. However, I often felt the need to justify my decisions and needs. I spent a lot of time thinking about how my actions might impact others and worried about disappointing or inconveniencing the people around me. Logan didn't burden himself with those concerns. His mantra in life was, "I am who I am. Take it or leave it."

I think it was that confidence that I was attracted to. In a way, the fact that he did whatever he wanted, no matter what, gave me the freedom to do the same. For maybe the first time in my adult life, I was completely honest and 100% myself with another person. If I needed alone time, I would just say so. If I didn't want to do something Logan wanted to do, I would tell him, and we would each do our own thing without any hard feelings. If we were hanging out together in my van and I wanted him to leave, I would say so – even if it was late and we were already in bed. It was liberating and weirdly comfortable.

Logan and I travelled together for almost two weeks after our first meeting in Fletcher Bay. Up until that point, I had only very rarely teamed up with other nomads and when I did it was only for a few days. Most of the time, I preferred travelling on my own. But it was different with Logan. In a way, we both still mostly did our own thing, meeting up at campgrounds in the evenings.

One morning in Bowentown, I got up early to watch the sunrise from the beach while Logan was still asleep. As I sat there, reflecting on the last few weeks, I found myself wondering; "Could this be it? Could Logan and I have a future together?"

I didn't have a very good track record with relationships. Somehow, I had always felt better and happier on my own. But I hadn't completely given up on the idea that maybe one day I'd meet someone and want to be in a relationship. I liked the *idea* of sharing life with someone. I just had never enjoyed the *reality* of it so far. Maybe this was it. Maybe this was how romantic relationships could work for me. Two introverts who need lots of space and were completely honest with each other about what they want and need.

After those initial two weeks, we went separate ways, both wanting to do our own thing. We met again a few weeks later in the Far North and a few more times that spring and summer. We had a lot of fun together and great conversations about vanlife, freedom and the meaning of life. But it didn't take long until I started to see the darker side of his unapologetic ways.

It started with little incidents, like the time he parked right in front of another RV at a freedom campsite to get the best views, and then blared his music loudly when they complained. Or how he always refused to pull over to let traffic pass that was building up behind his slow van on steep and winding roads. Or the time he refused to cook a vegetarian meal when we met up with other travellers for dinner who didn't eat meat. They were all just little things, but together they started to tell a story.

The confidence I was attracted to in the beginning more and more began to look like selfishness and stubbornness. I realised that there is a fine line between being confident about who you are, and how you want to live your life, and being unapologetic, inconsiderate and overly set in your ways.

Whenever Logan and I disagreed about something, there was no way forward. He wouldn't listen, wouldn't change his mind about anything. He wasn't even interested in hearing other people's views. He would rarely do anything he didn't actually want to do, even if someone asked him kindly and as a favour.

When we first met, I admired his confidence and unapologetic approach to life. I wished I could be more like that. But by the time we met up for the fifth time, that attraction was fading. I realised that, while I wanted to be confident, I also wanted to be kind, considerate and open-minded. I realised I wanted to be the kind of person who does her part to make life better for everyone, not someone who always just looks out for herself. I wanted to meet people from different walks of life, hear their stories and ideas and learn from them. I wanted to be open to new ideas, ways to improve myself and to changing my mind.

I also realised that, while honesty is important in relationships, it needs to be balanced with kindness and consideration for each other. Two people who are completely honest and one hundred percent accept each other just the way they are, sounded like a good thing in the beginning. However, I quickly learned that it's not a sound basis for a relationship, at least not for me. As much as I liked doing my own thing, I realised that a relationship in which both people are just doing their own thing all the time, hoping that occasionally both want the same thing at the same time, isn't exactly fulfilling. As much as I would have liked to say otherwise, I had to admit that a happy relationship would require compromise, consideration and a general willingness not to do your own thing ALL the time.

I remember the day a lot of this clicked for me. I had parked up in a beautiful spot and was writing in my journal.

Writing has always been a way of thinking and processing for me. I often figure things out by writing about them, so I wasn't surprised that the same happened in this case. I still have the journal from that time. There is a long entry where I'm working through my feelings, coming to all of these conclusions. At the end of it, I wrote in big, bold letters. I'D RATHER BE ON MY OWN FOR NOW!

I told Logan the next day. We sat outside in the sun reading, when I used the cliché "we need to talk" line and told him that I thought we should stop seeing each other. I told him that I respected his independence and strength but that I had realised it wasn't making me feel good anymore. He understood. You can call Logan selfish and stubborn, but he always gave other people the same freedom and respect that he demanded for himself. He rarely adapted his life and priorities to others, but he also didn't expect anyone else to adapt theirs for him. If I wanted to go separate ways, he would support that and let me go. And so the next day, we hugged goodbye and headed off in opposite directions.

After my experience with Logan, there was no denying that a relationship worth being in would require compromises. I had accepted the fact that I wouldn't be able to be completely free and independent while also being in a relationship. And I wanted to be free and independent – at least for now. I didn't give up on love that spring. I didn't give up on the idea that I might one day find someone and be in a long-term relationship. But at that time in my life, I needed to do my own thing. I simply wasn't ready for the compromises that a relationship would require. I wanted to be free and independent. I wanted to figure out who I am and what matters most to me before I make room for someone else in my life.

Logan and I stayed in touch for a while, as friends more than anything else, but it wasn't the same anymore. Each time we saw each other, I found him harder to be around, and eventually, we stopped meeting up. However, I'm grateful that we met that year and for the time we had together. When I met Logan, I still questioned many of my decisions. I often felt the need to explain myself and consider how my choices impact others. Before meeting Logan, I often wished I could just be one hundred percent confident in who I am and how I live my life. Logan showed me how treacherous a path that is, and how quickly too much confidence can turn into selfishness and stubbornness. It made me realise that a certain amount of doubt and consideration for others is good and desirable.

I learned to make peace with doubts. I came to accept that to be the kind of person I want to be – confident, kind and open-minded – I sometimes need to doubt myself. Doubt didn't mean I was on the wrong track or needed to change. It just meant that I was open-minded. In a way, you could say I became more confident about my doubts – which set me up to continue following my own path.

12

PRIORITIES

SUMMER 2019/20

Mangawhai Heads

Great Barrier Island

Waihi Beach

After spending spring zig-zagging all over the North Island, I took the van over to Great Barrier Island for the traditional summer trip with my friends. Great Barrier Island is technically part of Auckland, but it feels like a world away. For starters, it takes 4-5 hours on the car ferry from Auckland to get there. You can also fly, which is much faster, but obviously not an option when you want to take your campervan. Fewer than 1,000 people live permanently on the island, but many more come to visit each summer. However, due to its remote location and limited access – there are only a certain number of ferry spots and seats on planes – it's one of the least crowded summer spots in New Zealand, which is one of the reasons why I love it so much.

We set up camp at Medlands Beach, like we did every year, and enjoyed island life. We will all remember that summer as the windy year. While the region is usually relatively calm over summer, this year, we had one windy day after another. As a kitesurfer and sleeping in the comfort of my van, I loved the wind. However, my friends, who were sleeping in tents and aren't all kitesurfers, were less enthusiastic about it. Nevertheless, we had a great time, and three weeks on the island passed way too quickly.

I had been part of this group of friends for about six years now and considered them one of the best things that ever happened to me. Not everyone who was part of the group made it to Great Barrier Island that summer, but there were still 13 adults and a bunch of kids. Many in the group had been friends for years. I had met everyone about six or seven years earlier when I was working with one of the guys. I had just started kitesurfing, and since many of them were kitesurfers, we started hanging out. In 2013, I joined the summer trip to Great Barrier Island for the first time, and we've had many amazing adventures together since.

However, over the last few years, things had changed. On my first trip to the island in 2013, we were a bunch of singles and mostly unmarried couples. Now, six years later, our group was made up of six families – and me. I love my friends, and I love their kids. I feel fortunate to have friends who didn't let kids stop them from still being very active. They still go surfing, kitesurfing and on other adventures all the time, just with a few kids in tow now. I also enjoy watching the kids grow up, and can't wait to see the amazing people they will become. But I couldn't help feeling a bit like an outsider on this trip. I once again found myself wishing there were more people like me. I wished that not ALL my friends had chosen the traditional path, leaving me behind as the odd one out. It didn't help that it was such a windy year. Wind means kitesurfing. In the past, we would have all been out on the water together, having the time of our lives. This year, only one of the couples had even brought their kitesurfing gear. The others didn't have space to bring everything they might want, and since kitesurfing isn't a very family-friendly activity (it's not a lot of fun to hang out on the beach in 25 knots of wind to look after your kids while your partner is kitesurfing), they prioritised other gear. I kited and explored a lot on my own that year, which was fun, but not quite the same.

One day, I drove over to the west side of the island to go kiting. Once again, I was on my own. I had a great time, but I still wished my friends had been out with me – like they had been in the past. Afterwards, I made coffee in the van and stared out the window for a while. I felt lonely. Despite travelling mostly on my own I don't often feel lonely, but in that moment I felt a strong sense of disconnectedness. My amazing friends were only a 20 minute drive away. I had seen them this morning and would see them again for dinner tonight. And yet they all felt miles away. They were close in distance, but emotionally, I felt further apart from them than ever. It's hard not to feel like an outsider when you're the only single in a group of families.

I started to think about how much everything changes when people are in committed relationships with kids. When I looked at my friends, it sometimes felt like nothing had changed at all, and the next minute, it felt like everything had changed. They were all still active people. They all still did many of the same things they did as singles. We still did weekends away together, and everyone still loved watersports, going on missions and hanging out together. And yet, it all felt different.

I realised that summer that what had changed was less visible than how everyone spent their time. What had changed were priorities. My best friend, Rachel, was the perfect example. She moved to New Zealand around the same time I did. Neither of us has family here. When we met, we were both single, and friends were the most important people in our lives. Friends were our top priority. Then, Rachel met Peter, her future husband. Over time, he became her top priority, and friends moved to second place. After a few years, they got engaged and then married. Around this time, his family, who are based in New Zealand, started to become increasingly important in Rachel's life. Suddenly, she couldn't come kitesurfing with me anymore because of family responsibilities and Christmases and other holidays were spent with family instead of friends. And it wasn't just her. Many of my other friends were also less available for spontaneous kitesurfing sessions or other activities because of kids' birthday parties, family commitments and a whole range of other reasons. They had other top priorities.

That summer, Rachel and Peter were expecting their first child. Of course, the child would immediately became the top priority, and everyone else would move further down the rankings, including friends. On top of that, there was getting ahead at work, buying houses and doing all those other things most people do in their 30s. Over the six years that we had been friends, Rachel's priorities had changed completely. Meanwhile, mine were still mostly the same. I still spent my time kitesurfing, exploring and enjoying the great outdoors, while she chose to spend her time on family and 'grown-up-life'.

Don't get me wrong, I'm not complaining about my friends. They are great. Rachel, in particular, always gets in touch regularly, no matter how busy her life is, and never leaves any doubt that our friendship is important to her. It's not like friends are any less important to her now than they were six years ago. It's just that several other people and goals were even more important. And I guess that's how it should be. When you start a family, your partner and children should be your top priority. However, just because I understand it doesn't mean it was always easy to accept. As much as I love my friends' kids, I sometimes missed the days when we were all each other's top priority, and our main goal in life was to have fun together.

Looking back, I think this was one of the reasons why the idea of living and travelling in a van seemed so attractive. At the time, I thought it was all about figuring out who I am and how I want to live my life. But I probably had also started to realise that everyone's priorities were changing away from friends towards family – and I wanted to find something that could fill the gap that left in my life. With my friends having less time for spontaneous missions and adventures, I wanted something to distract me from the fact that I was scared of being left behind. Maybe unconsciously, I knew that my friends wouldn't continue to provide the same amount of excitement and purpose as they had in the past. They all started to have new top priorities, and I wanted a new top priority as well. And so vanlife and travelling the country became my top priority.

I'm really glad that it did. If I had stayed in Auckland for these years during which my friends' priorities changed so much, I would have probably felt lonely and maybe even resentful at times. I would have been much more aware of how much less time my friends have. As it was, I had my own incredible journey. I was living my best life and loved it. I wasn't sitting around hoping for someone to have time for me. Instead, I had taken matters into my own hands and filled the time with adventure and beauty. I actually often forgot how much everyone's lives had changed – until I was reunited with that group of friends, like for that summer trip to Great Barrier Island.

As the weeks on the island were coming to an end, I reminded myself that there were other people who had chosen a life similar to mine and had similar priorities. There aren't many, but they do exist, and over the last two years, I had met some of them. Once I returned to the mainland, I made an effort to meet up with one of them. Ava and I had connected earlier that year. She is only a couple of years older than me, single and childfree by choice, and lived in a house bus that she'd converted herself. We were also both self-employed and passionate about our work, which is rare in the nomad community where many consider work a must-do, not something they enjoy. Ava and I bonded over our shared values, priorities and lifestyles. We had met up a few times and regularly talked on the phone, and I had come to value her friendship a lot. It was great to have someone in my life who had chosen a similar path.

This time around, we met at Waihi Beach, about two hours southeast of Auckland. We spent a few days parked at the beach, going for dips in the ocean to escape the summer heat and chatting about our lives and plans. Like me, Ava felt no urgency to get married or have kids. For both of us, the future was a blank page with unlimited opportunities. Of course, you could argue that marriage and kids don't necessarily limit your options in life. However, for most people I know, they do. Being married, or in a similarly committed relationship, means you need to consider someone else's values, goals and preferences. And you might be perfectly aligned when you commit to a life together, but people change. A few years after the honeymoon, you might find yourself wanting different things from life – and you'll have to compromise. Similarly, kids don't have to slow you down or stop you from living life as you want. However, for most parents, their kids become their top priority and what's best for them is often more important than what the parents might want or need for themselves.

People like Ava and I have a level of freedom that most people with (young) kids simply don't have. We are unattached. We can spend the next few years living the nomad life without worrying about how the lack of stability might impact our kids. If we decide that we want to live in the jungle in Indonesia for a while, we can do that. And, yes, of course, you theoretically could do that with a partner and kids, but I think we can all agree that it would be much more complicated. First of all, your partner needs to want the same thing. And then you need to figure out how to make it work for the kids. How to ensure they get an education, have friends and are happy. So it might not be impossible, but most parents wouldn't simply decide to change their whole life overnight just because they feel like it. Ava and I can.

Of course, there are many benefits to having a partner. If you do happen to both want to do something crazy, like moving to the jungle in Indonesia, doing it with a partner can make it less intimidating and possibly safer. However, for people like Ava and myself, who are good at doing things on our own, that wasn't valuable enough to make up for the lack of independence and the ability to design our lives without compromise.

At the time, I often felt weird talking to my married with kids friends about the future. I almost felt guilty for rubbing in how easy and free my life was and how many possibilities I had while they were stuck with their partner and kids. I knew they didn't see it that way at all. I got the strong feeling they were all happy in their relationships and wouldn't want it any other way. I was happy for them and was in no way criticising their choices. I knew they wouldn't be happy living my life, just like I wouldn't be happy living theirs. But still, it often felt hard to talk about my dreams, priorities and the future with people whose dreams, priorities and future were so different from mine. Luckily, I had met Ava. We were very different people in many ways, but our lives were similar at the time, and so were our dreams, priorities and plans for the future.

During those days at Waihi Beach in early 2020, we spent hours just chatting about life and our plans. We both dreamed of maybe owning some rural land one day. We both wanted a simple life. But we both also wanted to do well in our careers and be financially secure. Most of all, right now, we wanted to be free and independent. We wanted to travel and see the country – which is exactly what we were doing.

After the beach days with Ava, I headed back to Auckland to pick up my little sister from the airport. She was living in the UK at the time, but was visiting friends in Australia. Of course, I wouldn't let her come all this way without spending a few days with me in New Zealand. This was her fifth visit since I had moved here 13 years earlier, but it was the first one since I had moved into my van. My sister is my favourite person in the world, and I was super excited to have her here and show her vanlife. We headed up to Mangawhai Heads and set up at the campground right on the estuary with amazing views of the dunes and ocean. We had decided to go to one place and stay put instead of travelling around. This time, she only had a few days in New Zealand, and we wanted to spend that time catching up and having fun instead of driving around and trying to find places to stay. Mangawhai Heads was the perfect spot. The estuary and ocean are right there, the town centre with some shops and cafes is within walking distance, and there are a couple of excellent walking tracks. The weather was amazing, and we spent our days swimming, paddle boarding, walking and relaxing while catching up on each other's lives.

Sharing my van with someone else, even just for a few days, was an interesting experience. My van was built for two people. There were two seats, and the bed easily converted into a big double that offered enough room for both of us. Nevertheless, being so accustomed to having the van to myself, it took a bit of time getting used to another person. In the first couple of days, we kept bumping into each other when moving around the van. But it didn't take long to get into a rhythm and figure out that only one of us could move at a time. Making the bed at night and turning it back into the lounge in the morning was especially challenging with a second person in the van. We quickly figured out that it works best if one of us does the conversion while the other waits outside or sits in the driver's cabin. However, that was all a small price to pay for having my sister visit. We were also lucky that the weather was terrific, so we spent a lot of time outside. I was glad I could show my sister the best sides of vanlife. I think she enjoyed getting a taste of it, but I don't think she will follow my example and live in a van herself any time soon.

Her and I are close – or at least as close as you can be when you live far apart. We are very different personalities, but at the same time, we have a lot in common – including the fact that we were both in no rush to get married and have kids. That year, she was 32, and I was 35. In other words, we were both at that age where many of our friends either already had a family or were heading that way. Neither of us had a strong urge to follow that path, but we weren't a definite no to either marriage or kids. We talked a lot about that as well as the sense of feeling like an outsider sometimes in a society where almost everyone else is following a very similar path. Like me, my sister was experiencing the changing priorities among her friends, and it was nice to talk to someone about it all who could relate and who I felt that close to.

Our days together passed way too quickly, and before we knew it, it was time to head our separate ways. My sister was flying back to Australia and then home to the UK, and I headed towards my next big adventure: A three-months South Island road trip. Well, that was the plan anyway. But once again, the universe had different plans. It was February 2020, and the whole world was about to change.

13

STUCK
AUTUMN 2020

Whatamango Bay

Christchurch

Dunedin

Autumn started with me getting stuck in the mud. At the time, I thought it would just be an unlucky incident (as well as a funny story), but it turned out to be the theme for the whole season. But let's start at the beginning.

After I dropped my sister at the airport at the end of February, I headed south. Ever since I started travelling in my van, I had dreamed of an extensive South Island road trip. Now the time had finally come. I was planning to spend three months down south, maybe longer if I could take the cold that winter would bring. New Zealand offers stunning scenery no matter where in the country you are. However, when it comes to beauty, most would agree that the South Island beats the North Island. I had travelled on the South Island twice before, once when I first came to New Zealand 13 years earlier and a second time in 2017 with my sister. Those two trips had given me a taste of all the south has to offer, but they were nowhere near enough to see everything. There were many parts of the South Island I had never been to and many more I only visited briefly and was looking forward to exploring more. But first, the ferry crossing.

After my very uncomfortable and scary ferry sailing two and a half years earlier, when I picked up my first van, I was nervously checking the weather forecast in the days leading up to my scheduled crossing. I worried for nothing. This time around, I couldn't have asked for a better day. The sea was calm, and the sky a brilliant blue. About two hours after leaving Wellington, we entered the Marlborough Sounds – the reason the ferry is the best way to arrive on the South Island. The Marlborough Sounds is an extensive network of drowned valleys created by a combination of rising sea levels and land subsidence. The steep green hills, countless picturesque bays and blue oceans are among New Zealand's most stunning scenery. The ferries from Wellington to Picton – the only way to travel by car between the two islands – enter the sounds south of Arapaoa Island and then follow the Queen Charlotte Sound to Picton. On a nice day, this journey is breathtaking, and I was lucky to get one of those days. I stood outside on the deck, admiring the ever-changing scenery around me. In some of the bays, I could see little houses, many of which are only accessible by boat and need to be entirely self-sufficient. That is probably why most of them are holiday homes. Only a few people live permanently in these remote parts of the sounds.

For almost two hours, our ferry glided through this paradise, and then we docked in Picton, and I was officially on the South Island. It was late afternoon by the time we arrived, and I didn't feel like driving far, so I made my way to the nearby campsite at Whatamango Bay. And that's where I got stuck for the first time that autumn.

While I arrived on the South Island on a beautiful day, it had rained quite a bit the week before, and the grass on the campground was wet and muddy. Of course, I only figured that out once my wheels were spinning in the mud without getting any traction. A quick inspection made it clear that I would not be able to get out on my own. There was only one other camper around, and while the owners were very friendly, there was no way they would be able to pull me out with their RV without getting both of us stuck. So I made my way to a nearby house, hoping someone had a truck.

Two things are worth pointing out at this stage. Firstly, getting stuck is just part of New Zealand life. I don't know anyone who has lived in New Zealand for a few years and has never been stuck, seen someone else get stuck or helped pull someone out – most people can tick 'all of the above' on that list. And no, it's not that I surround myself with particularly reckless people. Go anywhere in New Zealand where cars are allowed to drive on the beach, and if it's a busy summer day, I can almost guarantee that you will see someone get stuck within a few hours. Maybe it's because we love the outdoors so much. Perhaps it's the "she'll be right" attitude Kiwis are famous for. Maybe it is simply that Kiwis learn as kids that getting stuck is just a part of life and nothing overly dramatic (most of the time) that they take risks that others wouldn't. However, to be fair, tourists visiting New Zealand are probably just as likely to find themselves stuck in the sand or mud, so it's not just a Kiwi thing. For whatever reasons, getting stuck is nothing dramatic in New Zealand, and at that point in my life, I was in good credit. I had pulled out others who had gotten stuck twice with the old Nissan Terrano truck I drove before I had a van. With getting stuck being so common, I was confident someone nearby would have the vehicle, rope and know-how to get me out.

And the second thing to point out here is that whoever said it's a man's world has clearly never been a damsel in distress. I approached the first house with a friendly but slightly helpless-looking smile (an essential part of being a damsel in distress), and within two seconds, the older gentleman who opened the door was in full 'saviour' mode. He didn't have a truck strong enough to pull out a camper, but he knew two people nearby who did. He asked me to come in and introduced me to his equally lovely wife, who offered me tea and cake while her husband made some calls. Half an hour later, two friendly locals showed up with big trucks, enough ropes to pull 20 vans out of the mud and excitement in their eyes. I was providing the entertainment they had been looking for. After a round of cake for everyone, we walked over to the campground, the team of experts assessed the situation, made a plan and five minutes later, the wheels of my van had solid ground beneath them again. I thanked everyone profoundly and handed out bottles of wine – and they thanked me for giving them something to do and a story to share. I guess you call that a win-win.

———

After a couple of nights at Whatamango Bay (in the solid, non-muddy part of the campground), I continued my journey. I planned to spend the next 2-3 weeks travelling south along the east coast all the way down to the Catlins. This was an area I had fallen in love with when I visited briefly with my sister three years earlier, and I was looking forward to returning and spending more time. After a few weeks in the Catlins, I planned to make my way inland towards Central Otago and famous Queenstown and Wanaka and then head north via the West Coast. If all went to plan, I would make it to Nelson in the north of the South Island before it got too cold. However, nothing went to plan that autumn.

Three weeks after I left Whatamango Bay, I had made it to Dunedin on the east coast of the South Island, about 700km south of Picton where I had driven off the ferry. We were in the second half of March, and news headlines worldwide were dominated by one topic: Covid. New Zealand had about 30 known cases of Covid at this stage, and there were some restrictions for people coming into the country, including the requirement to self-isolate for 14 days. However, life still seemed mostly normal. But of course, we saw the headlines from Italy, Wuhan, New York and other parts of the world where the virus was spreading rapidly. As a response, on March 20th, the borders were closed for most foreigners. It seemed like a smart move at the time, given what was happening in the world. However, despite those initial restrictions, it all still seemed so far away at that point. I, for one, was utterly oblivious and, in hindsight, naive about how much Covid was about to impact our lives.

On March 21st, I published a blog post about how normal everything still was and how little impact the virus was having on me and my life. Literally within an hour of the blog going live, the New Zealand government released a statement asking us to stop all non-essential domestic travel. For someone whose lifestyle is all about travel and whose home has wheels for just that purpose, that was a major curveball. And it hit me out of nowhere. Up until that point, I had not for a second considered the possibility that I would no longer be able to travel around New Zealand. We were all asked to return home and stay there – but that's easier said than done when you don't have a home in the traditional sense.

The next few days were stressful. On March 23rd, while I was still in Dunedin, the government announced that two days later, on March 25th, New Zealand would move into what was called Covid Alert Level 4 (the highest level). We were told that in Level 4, everyone should stay home as much as possible. Schools, public buildings and facilities, cinemas, museums and all shops and businesses that were not considered essential had to close. Only supermarkets, health care facilities, petrol stations and a few other companies would be allowed to operate under Level 4. In other words, the days of Covid not impacting life in New Zealand were well and truly over.

I'm a member of several Facebook groups for Kiwis travelling in RVs, and there was much discussion about what to do. Most people who had a traditional home decided to return there for the time being. For those of us living full-time on the road, things were a bit more complicated. Posts from people all over the country indicated that some campgrounds had decided to close while others allowed those already there to stay, but wouldn't welcome any new people. At the time, I was parked up at a New Zealand Motor Caravan Association (NZMCA) property in Dunedin with about 25 other campers. Nothing brings people together like unexpected, dramatic events, and so throughout the day, we all checked in on each other and debated what to do. Most of us agreed that the worst-case scenario would be to stay put where we were. There was water and a dump station at the park, so technically, we had everything we needed for a longer-term stay. However, that plan was ruined shortly after, when the NZMCA sent out an email to members informing us that all parks would be closed and all members were asked to return home. There was that word again; "home".

For the first time since I had started vanlife, I missed having a traditional home. I felt very exposed. All of a sudden, it had become undeniable that I was part of a minority – one that clearly wasn't at the top of anyone's mind while making Covid-related decisions. The government was busy planning and announcing support for employers and employees, for homeowners who were worried about covering their mortgage, for parents who were essential workers and relied on childcare to do their jobs, for students who wouldn't be able to attend school or university but still needed to learn, and for a wide range of other groups. No one was talking about support for people who lived and travelled in RVs. We were on our own. If I'd had the money in the bank, I might have actually bought a house right there and then, just to have a safe place to go and wait out the storm. But I didn't have the money.

I thought about returning to Auckland but realised it wouldn't make a difference. I still wouldn't have a 'home'. Sure, friends would have welcomed me, but then what? I figured I'd rather be in my van than be someone's guest for who knows how long. Besides, at that point, I still thought it might all be over in a few weeks, and I could continue my South Island road trip so I didn't want to go too far. However, I still had to find somewhere to stay for the next few weeks.

A week earlier, I had passed through Christchurch on my way south along the east coast. While there, I met Sarah, who was a long-term resident at the campground in New Brighton. We had been in touch over social media for a while, and it was great to meet in person. We clicked right away and had lots to talk about. So when I had to find somewhere to hunker down and wait out the Covid-storm, the campground in New Brighton was the first place that came to mind. I thought it would be nice to stay somewhere I knew at least one other person, even if we had only met for the first time a week earlier. I also knew a couple of other people in Christchurch, and generally, it seemed like a good place to be during a crisis. It is the South Island's largest city, and just about everything you might need is right there. I called the campground, and luckily they confirmed that they would stay open, and I was welcome to come and spend lockdown there. However, I would have to get there within the next 48 hours. After that, they would not be allowed to let new people in. So I got into the driver's seat and headed back the way I had come only a week earlier.

I arrived back at the campground in New Brighton on March 24th and made myself comfortable. While I still had some hope that I would be able to continue my South Island travels before winter settled in, the realist in me knew that I would be here for at least a few weeks. So there I was, stuck for the second time in a few weeks, just not in mud this time, but in Covid Lockdown.

These few weeks in late March and early April were extremely stressful. To an extent, everyone in New Zealand (and around the world) probably felt that way. There was so much uncertainty about what was happening, and seeing the news and pictures from around the world was scary. Living in a van, and realising that no one in power was considering how decisions were impacting full-time nomads, added to the stress. A part of me was scared that, any day now, the government would announce that all campgrounds have to close, without any regard for the fact that some people didn't have anywhere else to go.

I was also scared of what would happen if I got Covid. Those of us who were fully self-contained were asked not to use the campground showers and toilets and instead use the facilities in our campers. However, there were several shared spaces that I couldn't avoid, like the laundry and the dump station. I had to be able to fill up fresh water and get rid of waste water at least once a week. How would I do that if I got sick? Of course, sickness was a concern even before Covid, but I never had to worry about passing a potentially dangerous virus on to others. If I got the standard flu or some other health issues, I would still use facilities like laundries and dump stations, and I would be happy to ask others for help if needed. However, Covid was different. In those early days, when the news of death and overflowing morgues in other parts of the world dominated the headlines, and no one knew much yet about how the virus spreads, I would have felt very uncomfortable about using shared facilities should I get sick. I would be too worried I would pass it on to someone else.

For all these reasons, I felt on edge for the first few weeks of lockdown. However, after a while, I calmed down and settled into it – and life slowed down. It's not like my life had been hectic before then – far from it, actually. Most of the time, my life had been fairly slow ever since I left the career-focused world in Auckland two and a half years earlier. But this was different. It wasn't just my life that slowed down. The whole country slowed down. People suddenly had time for leisurely walks and long phone calls in the middle of a work day. Traffic was reduced significantly, and people generally seemed to be in less of a rush. There was a kind of comfortable sense of community, a sense of "we're all in this together". People gave each other that knowing nod and smile when out on walks. Most stood patiently in line at the supermarkets – something I found hard to picture being the case during normal and busy times. And every day at 1pm, the whole nation tuned in to watch the daily government update like it was the most addictive TV show ever made.

Lockdown was an interesting experience. As an introvert, the lack of social interaction wasn't a problem for me. In fact, I probably had fewer social interactions in my everyday life than many people had during lockdown. However, I was worried about getting bored. Not because of a lack of social interactions, but because of a lack of things to do. Work had pretty much stopped completely within a week or two of New Zealand going into lockdown. There was a lot of uncertainty for most businesses at the time, which resulted in any non-essential expenses being culled – and as a contractor, I was an easy expense to cut quickly. In addition, none of my clients were considered essential businesses, so they were all trying to figure out how to work from home. I wasn't overly worried about it from a financial point of view. There was support from the government, and I also had enough savings to support myself for a while. Besides, with everything closed, there wasn't much to spend money on. However, work would have been a welcome distraction and a way to keep busy during lockdown. Without it, I needed to find other ways to entertain myself.

One of the reasons I had decided to come to the campground in New Brighton for lockdown was its location. New Brighton is one of Christchurch's seaside suburbs, located about eight kilometres east of the city centre. It's famous for the pier that stretches out into the ocean and that claims to be the biggest ocean pier in Australasia. The campground is in the southern part of the suburb, on what could be described as a narrow mini-peninsula. The beach is in the east, a large estuary in the west, and the mouth of the estuary in the south. As a result, the campground was about a two-minute walk from the estuary and five minutes from the beach.

I figured if I have to be stuck for several weeks, I might as well go where I can I surf, kitesurf and paddle board. Unfortunately, that plan fell apart a week or so into lockdown when watersports were officially banned due to being considered too risky. The argument was that if we get ourselves into trouble, we would rely on others to be rescued – which would put them at risk of being harmed during the rescue operation as well as of being exposed to Covid. To be honest, I disagreed with that. I felt that me going kiteboarding would be safer than someone who hadn't done any exercise in who knows how long getting their bike out of storage and racing down a nearby hill just because they didn't have anything better to do. However, even after 13 years in New Zealand, I still had German genes, and we all know how much Germans like to stick to the rules. As much as I wanted to get in or on the water, I simply couldn't bring myself to break the rules.

Luckily, I had my friend Sarah and her dog Bruno. We became what us Kiwis termed bubble-buddies (selected people who you were 'allowed' to socialise with during lockdown) and went for long walks together every day. The two of them were the biggest blessing. I had learned long ago that movement and fresh air are fundamental to my well-being. Despite knowing that, I don't think I would have had the discipline and motivation to go walking on my own in the same neighbourhood every day for over two months. In addition, Sarah and I had amazing conversations on our walks, discussing the current events and many other big and small topics, which made each day so much better and the whole lockdown experience more enjoyable. Sarah and Bruno, my lockdown buddies, will always have a special place in my heart.

However, there is only so much walking you can do in a day, and without work or my watersports to keep me entertained, I had to get creative. So I re-designed all my websites, tidied the van (multiple times), started a podcast, and crocheted little fish to make an aquarium. One day, about four weeks into lockdown, I was having a coffee break after finishing a little red fish for the crochet aquarium, and I thought to myself, "I'm actually really enjoying this whole lockdown experience." The thought surprised me. If someone had told me a few months earlier that I would be stuck in one place for who knows how long, I wouldn't be allowed to do any watersports, most public places would be closed, and I wouldn't have work to keep me busy, I would have said that sounds like my worst nightmare. But here I was, five weeks into it, and enjoying it. It was nice not having to think about where to go next or where to park for the night. I loved all the little creative projects I was working on, and it was nice not to have the option to work, so there was no guilt about not working enough. Most of all, I enjoyed the podcast, though. For each episode, I interviewed other people who were doing life differently. I asked them about their lives, the decisions they had made and why, and the lessons they learned along the way. The interviews were always fascinating conversations that I enjoyed a lot. If it hadn't been for lockdown, I don't think I would have made the time to launch a podcast. Once again, I realised that good things happen when there is space for them in our lives – just that I didn't voluntarily create the space this time, but it was created for me.

———

By the time May rolled around, it looked like New Zealand was getting on top of Covid. Case numbers were down significantly, and with the borders closed, Covid wasn't coming in. On May 4th, no new cases were reported for the first time since New Zealand had gone into lockdown. Restrictions were eased step by step, and by mid-May, it was clear that we would soon be allowed to travel domestically again. Surprisingly, I had mixed feelings about it.

On the one hand, I was, of course, happy that New Zealand had managed to get on top of Covid and that life would slowly go back to normal, and I was also excited to travel again. But another part of me had gotten quite comfortable in New Brighton. I had made good friends, and ever since watersports were officially allowed again in early May, I had made the most of being so close to the water. I also realised I enjoyed not having to make all those little decisions that travellers have to make every day; where to go next, where to park, where to get water, where to buy groceries, where to find a dump station, and so on. Life on the road was simple in many ways, but it was also very complex and intense in others. I enjoyed having a break from all of that.

Maybe that is why I stuck around for almost a week longer than I had to. But on May 20th, a week after New Zealand moved into Alert Level 2 and domestic travel was allowed again, I said goodbye to my friends in New Brighton and hit the road.

It was getting cold on the South Island, so I decided to head north – but I took my time. Over two weeks, I travelled from Christchurch to the Nelson Lakes, spent a few days in Nelson and then made my way to Picton to catch the ferry back to the North Island. I didn't have much of a plan for winter other than getting to warmer parts of the country – in other words, keep going north.

14

AMBITION

WINTER 2020

Auckland

I made it back to Wellington via the ferry in the first week of winter and continued north. After a stop at ever-beautiful Lake Taupō, I veered east towards the Coromandel Peninsula, where I met up with Ava and another friend for a girls weekend in Whitianga. Afterwards, I continued north towards Auckland. In a way, it was weird that I kept returning to Auckland, given I didn't like the city much. There isn't anything wrong with Auckland. It's a lovely city and probably fares pretty well compared to other large centres around the world. Auckland has many beaches and parks, and you never have to go far to see the ocean. It has all the conveniences and entertainment options of a big city, such as malls, restaurants, and lots of different events. There is a lot to be said about Auckland, and I enjoyed living there for 11 years, but at the end of the day, I'm just not a big city girl. I found Auckland too loud and too busy (and don't get me started on the traffic). After being away for two and half years, it felt more overwhelming than ever.

So why did I keep coming back? People! And sometimes for work, but mostly the people. Auckland had been home for such a long time, and it still felt like the closest thing I had to a base. Most of my friends were still living in Auckland, and I liked spending time with them whenever I was back in town. This time, there was an extra special someone who pulled me back to Auckland. My best friend, Rachel, had given birth to her first child in March, just before lockdown, and I was looking forward to meeting her – and of course, spending time with mum, too. I might not have a strong desire to be a mum myself, but I was excited to be aunty Lisa.

I walked into Rachel and Peter's house without knocking. They knew I was coming, so I just let myself in and announced my arrival with a quiet hello in case the baby was sleeping. Luckily, she wasn't, and I was welcomed with a much louder "HELLO" back, followed by hugs and even a little smile from baby. We spent the next few hours catching up. Rachel and I regularly spoke on the phone, but it was always better to talk in person. She told me all about motherhood, and I told her about my travels and my plans for winter. We cooked dinner together and watched a movie. I spent the night in the guest room, as I often did when I was in town. It was nothing special, but it was lovely to be back. As I was lying in bed that night, I thought, "this is why Auckland still feels like home." Rachel and Peter had moved since I last saw them. But although I had never been in this house before, it already felt familiar. I always felt so welcome in their home, no matter where they were living. I considered myself incredibly lucky to have friends like that. We might be on different paths in life, but I knew we would always support each other and always be there for each other.

I ended up floating around Auckland for most of winter. I did some housesitting here and there and spent time in the van in between, but I never went very far. Surprisingly, the drive to travel and explore wasn't very strong that winter. I would have thought that after being forced to stay put for two months due to the Covid lockdown, I would have itchy feet and be excited to travel and explore again. But it was almost the exact opposite. In a way, lockdown had shown me the perks of staying put. I had come to realise that it's kind of nice not to rush around the country all the time. However, there was more to it than just needing a break from travelling.

I generally wasn't in the best headspace that winter. Somehow, I had coped well with lockdown mentally and physically – much better, in fact, than many others – but now that life was returning to normal in New Zealand, I struggled. Everyone else was happy that lockdown was behind us and was busy embracing the return of personal freedom, while I found it hard to feel positive that winter. Turns out, lockdown did have an impact on me. It just took a while for me to feel the consequences. Somewhere throughout lockdown, I had stopped looking after myself, and now I was paying the price. While I had enjoyed my daily lockdown walks with Sarah and Bruno, it wasn't anywhere near the level of activity I was used to. It certainly wasn't the level of diversity in activities I usually had. On top of that, like so many others, I had overindulged in food during lockdown – which is no wonder when going to the supermarket is literally the most exciting thing you do all week. For as long as I can remember, I have had a problematic relationship with food. I was very big as a teenager and young adult. I lost a lot of weight in my mid-twenties, but I had been stuck in a vicious cycle of extreme dieting followed by over-indulgence, followed by extreme dieting and back to over-indulgence ever since. With the over-indulgence came guilt, low self-esteem, and a general feeling of not being my best self. The following year, I got help and managed to break free from this vicious cycle, but that winter, I was still right in it. And I was in an over-indulgence phase. I was eating poorly, wasn't getting enough movement and was neglecting other positive habits like making time to read and write and spending time in nature. As a result, I didn't feel very good about myself.

Looking back now, it was probably a bit of a perfect storm that made me feel less optimistic and happy that winter. Covid had not only forced me to stay put for two months, which resulted in neglecting self-care, but it was also causing devastating headlines around the world and created a level of chaos and uncertainty that I – like many others – found scary and hard to cope with. Add to that the fact that it was winter which meant cold, wet and short days. I have always been a summer person. I find my mood is automatically better when the sun is shining. So all-in-all, it wasn't the most inspiring atmosphere.

On top of that, sometime in the winter of 2020, my old frenemy, ambition, caught up with me. I certainly wouldn't say that I have always been an ambitious person. In fact, when it comes to any kind of physical activity, I'm probably one of the least ambitious people ever (which is a good thing given my complete lack of talent for anything physical). However, I am ambitious when it comes to being good at my job and progressing my career. That ambition had gotten me far. Within a few years of finishing university, I had worked my way up into management roles and was earning good money. It was that money which allowed me to buy a campervan, and that was now giving me the financial security that I didn't have to worry if I ever struggled to find enough work right away. It was also that ambition that made me work hard as a freelancer, which resulted in happy clients who sent more work my way and recommended me to others. But that same ambition also led to me neglecting my well-being at times. More than once in the past, I put my job first and hadn't taken the time to do the things that make me happy.

The decision to live and travel in my campervan was partly about getting away from that ambition. I knew that I needed to get away from my demanding office job if I genuinely wanted to prioritise my well-being and figure out who I wanted to be and how I wanted to live my life. If I had stayed in that busy, career-focused environment in the city, my ambition would have most likely always led to spending all my spare time working instead of discovering what really mattered to me.

Up until that winter, the plan had worked. With the pressure of work and career progression removed from my life, I had found a whole new level of happiness and contentment. Sure, there was a period the previous winter when I felt myself getting pulled back into the career-focused life in Auckland. However, that was mostly a result of external messages and less about internal ambition. When work was slow over summer and then dried up completely during lock-down, I wasn't worried. It felt like ambitious Lisa was a thing of the past, and nomad Lisa was all about time, adventure and freedom with little ambition for career progression. But you know how they say that most things we run away from will catch up with us sooner or later? Well, that winter in 2020, my ambition caught up with me.

When I first started vanlife, work wasn't much of a concern. I was glad I was given the opportunity to keep working for the startup I had been part of since before vanlife, as it meant I didn't have to use up my savings and could travel for longer. I was also excited when I won a couple of new clients during that first year in the van because it showed me that this could be a long-term thing. But for the first two and half years in the van, work had been on the sidelines. I enjoyed it and put a lot of effort into ensuring I did a good job, but I only worked 10-15 hours most weeks. I didn't have much ambition beyond doing an excellent job for the projects that came my way and earning enough to cover my bills. However, in winter 2020, that changed. I had been on the road for a while now, and I started to think more about the future. How much longer would I want to live in a van? Was vanlife forever? And if not, what would I want to do afterwards?

Even though I had been living like a carefree nomad for the last two and half years, my true nature is much more conservative. As much as I value freedom and adventure, I also value financial security and having options. From day one, it was always important to me that vanlife would be a choice, not something I had to do. I met people on my travels who were living in vans because they felt like that was the only thing they could afford. There was something very different about these people. Most travellers I met were content, positive people. Many had that spark in their eyes that told you they were happy. Most of those people I met who didn't live in mobile homes for the fun of it didn't have that spark. Instead, their eyes looked tired and defeated. I had promised myself long ago that I would do everything in my power to ensure vanlife would always be a choice for me. In fact, I didn't just want vanlife to be a choice. I generally wanted to have options in life. Freedom for me wasn't just about travel and adventure, it was also about having the financial freedom to live the way I wanted to – whatever that might mean at different times in my life.

Over the last few years, I learned that I didn't need much to be happy. I didn't know if I wanted to live in my van forever, but I was pretty sure I would never need a big house, fancy car and designer clothes to be happy. I knew I would be very comfortable with a simple life. However, even a simple life costs money. And while I like simple, I'm also not ashamed to admit that I do value certain 'luxuries' like a secure, warm and weatherproof roof over my head, ideally with running water and electricity (whether it comes with wheels underneath or not). And the occasional holiday, nice dinner out or new pair of shoes wouldn't be bad either. Most of all, I didn't want to worry about where the money to pay the bills or put food on the table would come from.

Ever since I started vanlife, I had earned enough money to cover my expenses, and I had even been able to save a bit. But it was nowhere near enough to give me a sense of financial security for the long run. I knew that if I wanted to be in a strong position financially, sooner or later, I would have to earn more. However, for the last few months, the opposite had happened. When Covid hit and New Zealand went into lockdown, all my work was put on hold. Initially, I hadn't been too worried about it, given I had savings to fall back on. However, as my ambition caught up with me and convinced me that I needed to start putting more money aside for the future, I felt more urgency to find new clients and projects. As a result, when things began to pick up again, I jumped at all the opportunities offered to me. Before I knew it, I had more work than I wanted or needed.

I have always felt so incredibly grateful for the fact that I had a job that I enjoy, that I'm good at, and that was in demand – and more recently, that I had clients that were supportive of my lifestyle and happy for me to work remotely. I know I'm very lucky in that regards. In many ways, that winter was no exception. I had great clients, the projects I worked on were interesting, and I enjoyed the challenges they presented. But it was just too much. Being the ambitious perfectionist that I am (when it comes to work anyway), I wasn't satisfied with simply doing all the work. I needed to give 120% to everything I did and then some. I didn't just want to do a good job; I wanted to do an excellent job – for every project and every client. That attitude had gotten me far in my career, but that winter, I started to feel its dark side.

I felt stressed and overworked, but it was hard to see the need for change at first. After all, I was doing what made sense and what society expected me to do. I was in my mid-30s, and after a few years of prioritising fun, I had the opportunity to make up for it by working lots and building up savings. Everyone around me seemed to think that's exactly what I should be doing. I remember mentioning to a few friends how stressed and unbalanced I felt at the time. Somehow, those conversations always ended up being about how lucky I was to have so many opportunities and that working lots now and saving was a good thing as it would give me more freedom in the future. I don't know if I pushed the conversations in that direction, trying to convince myself that I was doing the right thing, or if the people I talked to led us that way. Either way, everyone I discussed it with agreed that I was lucky and that I should work a lot while the opportunities were there. During the conversations, I agreed with it too, but somehow it never felt genuine. Yes, I was lucky that I had these opportunities. And yes, saving money now would give me more options in the future. But what was the price for all that?

I remember hanging up the phone after one of these conversations with a good friend. Like everyone else, he told me that I was doing the right thing by focusing on making money for a while and accepting all available jobs. After we hung up, I thought to myself: "Why are none of my friends telling me that my happiness should be more important than making money?". I quickly realised that the more important question was: "Why wasn't I telling myself just that?" Yes, I want financial security, but shouldn't happiness be more important?

In August, I stayed at a friend's house in Muriwai for a few weeks while they were away on a South Island holiday. The small beachside village in the northwest of Auckland is where I had spent my first weekend as a full-time vanlifer almost three years earlier, and I had been back many times since, usually staying at the campground. Muriwai is one of those stunning, wild, black sand beaches for which New Zealand is famous. I love kitesurfing at Muriwai Beach, but it's also a great spot to go for a walk on the beach or up the hill to enjoy the views. So when my friends asked if I would like to stay at their place while they went away, I excitedly accepted and was looking forward to a few weeks at the beach. But work, and my ambition, got in the way of making the most of it.

I remember a particular Thursday in my second week in Muriwai. It had been what was a typical day that winter. I woke up, started work and basically didn't stop until after the sun had set. During the rare breaks, I ate chocolate and junk food to cheer myself up and to have at least something fun in my day. On this Thursday, I looked out the window in the afternoon only to see a couple of kitesurfers down on the beach. "Why was I not down there?" I thought to myself. I didn't even know it would be windy because I hadn't checked the weather all week – and I usually always keep an eye on the wind forecast. It was starting to get dark, so it was too late to join the kitesurfers. I couldn't believe I was living in Muriwai Beach, Auckland's kitesurfing paradise, and I had missed a chance to go. As I stood on the deck, longingly watching others have fun in the waves, another realisation hit me: "I haven't left the house in three days!". I couldn't believe it. Yes, the weather had been a bit average with lots of rain, but still, there had been plenty of opportunities to get out for a short walk. But for the last three days – and in many ways, the last three months – I had been so caught up in my work that I had forgotten everything else. I decided right there and then that this couldn't be the way to go. Yes, I wanted financial security, and, yes, I wanted to deliver excellent work for my clients, but not at the cost of my well-being.

How did I get here? For the last two and a half years, I had lived this amazing life of freedom and adventure, swearing I would never return to that old, stressful life I used to have. But here I was, more stressed than ever. I realised that after years of prioritising my happiness, I had swung straight back to the other extreme.

I have never been very good with balance or healthy middle ground. I have always been an all-or-nothing kind of person. As a student, I was always either at risk of failing or getting straight As. I either exercised six days a week or not at all. I either ate only junk food or no junk food at all, and while I haven't always been very good at keeping up with weekly cleaning chores, my big spring-clean would give Martha Stewart a run for her money. I shouldn't have been surprised that work followed a similar pattern. I had gone from super ambitious and busy to completely relaxed and carefree, just to swing back the other way. I realised it was time to do something about it. I didn't want to spend the rest of my life swinging between total freedom and totally stressed. While it might be one way to satisfy my ambitious side and achieve the financial security I was after while also having time and adventure in my life, the price was too high. I didn't want to be unhappy six months a year. I wanted to be happy year around.

I realised I needed to find a better balance. And so that became my goal for spring.

15

BALANCE
SPRING 2020

Kai Iwi Lakes

Frensh Pass, Elaine
Bay & Okiwi Bay

Marlborough Sounds

O ver winter, I had come to realise two things. Firstly, my career ambition hadn't disappeared when I discovered vanlife, it had just been dormant for a while, waiting for the right time to make a comeback. Secondly, as much as I loved freedom and time, I also valued financial security. To tell you the truth, I grappled with these realisations for a while. A part of me wanted to be this carefree nomad who just floated through life, happily living pay check to pay check, without worrying too much about the future. I had this idea in my head that life would be easier that way.

In September, I met up with fellow nomads Bianca and Chris at the Kai Iwi Lakes in Northland. The dune lakes on the west coast of the North Island are famous for their crystal clear water and are a paradise for kayakers, paddle boarders, swimmers, water skiers, as well as hikers who will enjoy the walk around the lake or the track over the hills to the west coast beach. I was looking forward to spending a weekend there with Bianca and Chris, who I had crossed paths with at a campground near Nelson a few months earlier. Their van was almost the same as mine, so when we were parked next to each other, we started chatting. They were around my age, and both had, unfortunately, lost their jobs when Covid hit. However, instead of losing sleep over it, they decided to make the most of it by travelling the country in a campervan. They had bought the van at the end of lockdown and were only in their third week on the road when I first met them near Nelson in late May. We had stayed in touch, and when we realised we were both travelling in Northland, we made plans to meet up at the Kai Iwi Lakes. I was curious to hear how they were enjoying vanlife, now that it had been a few months.

Bianca and Chris were the perfect example of two care-free nomads without a worry in the world. In a way, I couldn't believe they had only recently started vanlife. They seemed like the kind of people born to live this way. Everything was always easy going with them, nothing was a big deal, and it was hard to picture either one of them ever being stressed. Chris was a web developer, and after losing his job with an agency during lockdown, he had found some freelance projects. From the way he talked about his work, it was obvious that travel and adventure were his priority right now. He ignored phone calls from clients and risked missing dead-lines in favour of going exploring and having fun. The Kai Iwi Lakes area didn't have very good internet or phone signal, so I made sure to plan the meetup for a weekend and told my clients that I would be offline on Friday and Monday. Chris hadn't even considered whether there would be internet coverage or not. He just lived his nomad life as he pleased, and whenever he had time and internet access, he considered doing some work (if he felt like it).

Bianca worked in hospitality before Covid and had an equally relaxed attitude. The two of them were open about the fact that money was tight, but it didn't seem to bother them. They had invested most of their savings into the van and had little to fall back on. One day, as we were walking the track around the lake, I asked them if they weren't worried about what would happen if the van needed repairs or if they ran out of money for other reasons. "What's the worst that could happen?" was Bianca's response. "Worst case scenario, we have to find work somewhere and stay put until we have enough money to keep going."

A part of me envied them for their relaxed attitude to all of this. I was certain I was much more financially secure than those two, yet I worried way more about it. Bianca and Chris's way of life looked so simple from the outside. I couldn't help but wish I was more like them. But I'm not, and I realised that it's time to accept that. I'm simply not someone who can live day-to-day without a care for the future. I may have been able to do so for two and half years, but that was the exception, not who I really am. As we kept walking around the lake that day, my mind drifted back to the people I had met for whom vanlife wasn't a choice but a necessity – those people who had long ago stopped loving vanlife and would have given it up for a safe and secure house in a second if they had the option. They often seemed exhausted and certainly weren't among the happiest people I had met on my travels. I realised that if I didn't plan for my financial future, I would risk ending up like them. And that was something I was keen to avoid. As much fun as the carefree last couple of years had been, it was time to get real and plan for the future.

Shortly after that long weekend at the Kai Iwi Lakes with Bianca and Chris, I caught up with a friend of mine who was a financial advisor. It seemed like an excellent way to get the ball rolling on making a plan for the future. He told me that the first step would be figuring out my goals. After that, we could work backwards to determine how much I would need to save and invest to achieve those goals. I found the process valuable but also challenging. Once again, most of the standard guidelines and templates didn't really work for me. The average 36-year-old has a partner who, ideally, also contributes financially, a family to support and dreams of retiring in luxury – ideally before turning 60. None of that was me. I didn't have to support a family, and I sure as hell don't need to retire in luxury – especially not if the way to get there involves working 40+ hours each week. I didn't even really want to retire early. I wanted to live while I was young. I don't mind still having to work a bit in my 60s or even 70s if it means I can spend time in my 30s and 40s enjoying life. After all, I can probably still sit at a desk and stare at a computer screen when I'm 60. What are the chances I can still kitesurf or climb mountains? Sure, some people still do those activities at that age, but it's usually those who have been doing them their whole life, not those who spent most of their 30s, 40s and 50s at a desk.

I had met many older people on my travels who often said they envied me for everything my body was still capable of doing. They missed out on some of the best sights and experiences along the way because they weren't fit and capable enough anymore to get there. I didn't want to be like that. Even now, in my prime in my 30s, I had difficulty getting up some of those mountains with epic views. Given my family history of low fitness levels and several health issues, I felt the chances of me doing all of that at 70 were pretty slim. I know for some people, the goal is to work hard for 20-30 years and then retire early and enjoy life. Nothing wrong with that, but I would rather have a good balance for 50 years and have time for both work and play throughout my whole life than dedicating decades to one and then the other.

I tried to explain this to my financial advisor friend. He was your typical career-focused family man, motivated to build wealth and get ahead. So needless to say, he probably didn't find it easy to relate to me. He was nodding his head, but I'm not sure he really understood. Sometimes, I wonder if people don't truly realise the price they pay for all this wealth they accumulate. Sure, retiring wealthy at 55 sounds great. Who wouldn't want that? But I wonder if people realise what it takes to get there. Most of us don't simply inherit the money, win the lottery or make a couple of lucky investments. For most of us, if we're not already rich at 35 but want to retire wealthy at 55, the way to get there is through hard work — lots of it. You have to dedicate the best years of your life to work hard – and it still requires a bit of luck, too.

During my travels, I have spent a lot of time in parts of New Zealand that are popular holiday spots. Kiwis love the bach life. A bach is a kiwi word for a holiday home, and if you want to be considered well-off in New Zealand, you need to own at least one bach. However, whenever I was in one of those bach towns, I couldn't help but feel like many were getting very little use. Even in summer and on weekends, many would often be empty. Most of these baches are in epic locations, right by the beach or mountains. Whenever I would see a deserted bach in a great spot, I would think to myself, "if I owned a bach like this, I would be here all the time." But the thing is, most people who can afford beautiful baches in stunning locations can only do so because they spend their time working in the cities instead of chilling at the beach. It's ironic, isn't it? You work hard to afford a good life and don't have time to enjoy it. And by the time you do, you might be too old to make the most of it. Of course, there is also the other extreme. Some people make lots of time to enjoy life and then realise they aren't financially prepared for rainy days or retirement, and end up struggling. I didn't want to be in either position.

So here I was, caught between craving financial security and wanting to enjoy my life instead of working for the potential of being wealthy in the future. I realised that what I needed was balance. Too bad that balance and healthy middle ground have never come easy to this all-or-nothing girl. Luckily, my financial advisor friend was there to help me figure it out. Once I had convinced him that I don't need to retire in luxury at 55, he helped me come up with a plan that would give me a certain level of financial security in the long run while still allowing me to continue working part-time hours and enjoy life while I'm young (if you can still call yourself young at 36).

Here in New Zealand, you can't talk about investing, retirement planning, passive income and financial security, without the word property coming up sooner or later (usually sooner). Kiwis LOVE property and investing in property. For many New Zealanders, your life isn't complete until you own at least one property. We're quite literally obsessed with the property market. Hardly a day goes by without some property-related story in the news, and I know many young people who are stretched to the limits financially because the desire to own a house is so strong that they end up with a mortgage they can barely afford.

I never quite understood that obsession with property. Maybe it's because I didn't grow up here, or perhaps it's just another thing where I'm different. Either way, I had never felt that urgency and drive to own property. I had also never seriously thought about property as an investment strategy. It sounded expensive, risky and like it could be a lot of hassle if you end up with the wrong tenants. However, talking through my options with my financial advisor friend, as well as some other friends who had a lot of experience in this space, I started to understand the benefits of property investment – and I realised that it wasn't as far out of reach for me as I had assumed, thanks to the fact that I had worked lots the last two winters and hadn't paid rent in almost three years. I'm not a property investment expert, so I won't bore you with the details here. Long story short, I worked out that if I buy an investment property and continue to make modest deposits into KiwiSaver, New Zealand's retirement saving scheme (cute name for a retirement savings program, right?), then I would be financially secure. I wouldn't be super wealthy, and I wouldn't be able to retire at 55, but I would have enough money to retire in my sixties and live a simple but comfortable life – and that was all I wanted.

The good thing with investment property is that your tenants help pay your mortgage. So even though buying property would leave me with a lot of debt, the amount I would have to contribute each week to pay it off felt manageable. I was confident I would be able to cover it even if work was slow for a while. The other thing I liked about buying an investment property was that it would give me more options in the future. Whenever I thought about how I might want to live in 5, 10 or 20 years, I had many different ideas. The one thing they all had in common was that most banks would not consider them sensible investments. I thought I might want to buy a bigger motorhome one day, or maybe switch to a caravan and truck. I also like the idea of owning a rural piece of land somewhere quiet or living in a tiny house and leasing land. I had no idea at the time what I really wanted long-term, but I knew I would have a hard time getting a loan for most of my ideas, unless I had decent securities. An investment property would be that security.

So, after working through all of this over several weeks, I decided to buy a house. I wanted something low maintenance, so I opted for a house and land package. A brand new build would include a builder's warranty, and the chances of something needing to be fixed were lower. My limited budget narrowed down the locations I could afford quite a bit, and in the end, I landed on Rolleston, just outside Christchurch on the South Island. The house would be built the following year and, once ready, would be about as normal a house as you can imagine. It would be a lovely family home in a new, family-friendly subdivision with a park across the road and a school nearby. As far as investment properties go, it ticked all the boxes. Apparently, it's precisely the kind of house 80% of Kiwis dream of living in. I had absolutely no desire to ever live in that house – or one like it. But, I wasn't buying a home, I was making an investment.

Nevertheless, I felt a sense of pride for being able to afford a house by myself and without having slaved away in an office for many years. Yes, I had worked lots the last two winters, but if I looked at it over an entire year, I only worked an average of about 25 hours per week. I was fully aware that I was lucky to have a well-paying job, and I felt grateful for that. However, I knew the main reason I could afford a house was that I hadn't paid rent in almost three years. So in many ways, this was just another example of something that vanlife made possible.

I felt much better after having worked all of that out. I now had a plan that would give me the financial security I was craving without needing to give up my freedom. Yes, I had a bit more pressure to generate income, but it was a level I felt comfortable with. As far as finances went, I had found the right balance. But finances wasn't the only thing I had to balance better.

———

My biggest problem throughout winter was that I worked so much that I didn't have time for anything else. The craving for financial security was one of the reasons why I had accepted so much work, but there was more to it. I genuinely enjoyed most of the work I was doing and occasionally said yes to too many projects simply because I wanted to do them all – and being a perfectionist, I then wanted to do all of them really well. However, I realised there also was another element that played a part: guilt. I often felt guilty that I wasn't working more. I knew that it was society's ideals and norms at play again. We're expected to be busy in life to be 'worthy'. The expectation is that we either work at least 40 hours a week or look after children or elderly family members. Even many moms who work part-time say they often feel guilty that they don't work more – even though they already have a full-time job as a parent. So it's probably no surprise that I was feeling pressure from society to work more. Sometimes, when work was slow, I would lie to people, telling them I spent more hours working than I actually did. I'm not proud of it, but I felt like people would judge me if I was honest. Everywhere I looked, people were busy, either with work or with childcare, or both. Being busy seemed almost like an achievement. As if being busy is a direct reflection of how worthy or important we are.

I knew that if I wanted better balance in my life, I had to somehow overcome that way of thinking. I had to break free from the belief that busy equals worthy. As it turned out, that was a lot easier said than done. To this date, I find myself getting caught up in being busy. Somehow, it feels good to be busy, even though I know it's not good for me. At the end of a busy day, I feel accomplished and important, and that's a good feeling. However, while I didn't manage to fully let go of the 'busy equals important' mindset that spring, I did get better at setting some boundaries around work. I was planning to spend the summer travelling on the South Island (hopefully without any Covid disruptions this time), and I knew if I wanted to enjoy that time, I needed to reduce my workload. Luckily, one big project was naturally coming to an end, and even though there were opportunities for me to do more work with the same client, I decided to decline the offer – which wasn't easy, given I had just committed to buying a house. I also set better expectations with other clients, being more explicit about when I'm available and when not.

I can't claim I solved the work-life balance issue for good that spring. There would be other times when work would take over my life again in the years that followed. But I made some steps in the right direction, and I solved the most urgent issue at hand; reducing my workload to make more time for other things.

With my finances in order and a reduced workload, I was ready to tackle the third area in my life that needed better balance; self-care. Luckily, that one came naturally. As winter had turned into spring, I started travelling again. With that, plus the reduced workload, I was automatically more active and spent more time in nature, two things I've learned are crucial to my well-being. I also started to eat better again and made sure I had time to read and journal most days. I remember thinking how weird it is that self-care is so simple and yet so easy to neglect. I realised, once again, that all it took was five things for me to feel good. I had to spend time in nature, be active, eat well (which doesn't mean perfect all the time), journal most days and make time to learn (which I usually do through reading). It seems like such a simple formula, yet I'd fallen off the wagon more than once. I promised myself that I would be more mindful of this and make sure I make time for these things next time life got busy. At the time, all of these things just fell into place naturally, and before I knew it, I was back to living my best life on the road.

While I was working on balance that spring, I also started to travel again. As it turned out, Covid hadn't killed my travel bug, it just needed a little rest. After winter spent mainly in Auckland, I was excited to hit the road again. I went north first for a few weeks to catch up with friends, including Bianca and Chris at the Kai Iwi Lakes. Then, at the beginning of November, I started to make my way south. After my big South Island road trip earlier that year had been so rudely interrupted by Covid, I was ready to give it another go. Thanks to that hard and fast lockdown in April and May, New Zealand had managed to stamp out Covid. Our borders were closed to visitors, and citizens and residents had to spend two weeks in managed isolation after arriving, so Covid wasn't getting in. While the rest of the world was continuing to struggle with the virus, we were living mostly normal lives. I hoped it would continue like that for summer.

I arrived back on the South Island in early November and decided to spend a few weeks exploring the Marlborough Sounds. Once again, I had a beautiful ferry ride, and enjoyed most of the trip outside on the deck, admiring the scenery around me. I was looking forward to exploring more of this beautiful part of the country. I drove up Kenepuru Road and spent a few days at the beautiful DOC campsite at Kenepuru Heads. From here, I explored on foot and on my bike. I walked sections of the famous Queen Charlotte Track, visited Punga Cove and Furneaux Lodge and several other beaches and coves in the area and biked down some of the gravel roads that looked too steep and narrow for my van. When I was ready to move on, I made my way to Okiwi Bay, Elaine Bay and French Pass on the western end of the Marlborough Sounds. I was lucky to have mostly stunning weather and loved being back in the south.

It was the perfect warm-up for what would be a beautiful summer, followed by an epic (but bittersweet) autumn.

16

BEAUTY

SUMMER 2020/21

Lake Tekapo
Kaikoura
Christchurch
Oamaru
Dunedin

Have you ever stood somewhere in stunning scenery feeling overwhelmed and in total awe of how beautiful parts of the world are? That summer, my third on the road, I had one of those moments at least once a week, sometimes daily. I've always known New Zealand's South Island is beautiful, but that summer, I discovered just how stunning it truly is. I will do my best to paint the picture for you, but I probably won't do it justice.

After spending the last few weeks of spring in the Marlborough Sounds, I made my way down the east coast towards Kaikoura. A friend of a friend who lived there had asked if I could look after her two dogs while she visited family over Christmas. I'd driven through Kaikoura the previous year but only had time for a quick stop back then. However, I liked what I saw. Since Kaikoura was on my list of places where I might want to settle one day (mainly because ocean view properties are still somewhat affordable), I thought housesitting in the area would be an excellent opportunity to see if I liked living there.

The house was just north of the township in a rural area with views of the ocean to one side and the mountains to the other. When I first arrived, I thought they had built the house the wrong way around, given the big deck was facing the mountains instead of the sea. However, a week or so later, I understood why. The prevailing easterly winds would have made an ocean-facing deck uncomfortable a lot of the time. Furthermore, I discovered the beauty of mountain views during my time in Kaikoura. The peaks looked different every day. I spent a lot of time sitting on the deck, drinking coffee while watching the clouds float around the summits.

It was an unusually cold December that year. After a

particularly chilly and rainy day, I woke up the next morning to the most stunning views of snow-covered mountain peaks to the west that turned into green hills in the north and then the bright blue ocean to the east. "Yup, I could live here!" I thought to myself.

When I wasn't drinking coffee and enjoying the views, I explored the area on foot, bike or paddle board. Kaikoura is famous for the many seal colonies in the area. Wherever there are rocks along the oceanfront, there are usually seals. One day, I took my paddle board over to the south side of the peninsular, where the waters are often much calmer than on the north side. As I paddled around the rocks, several seals came by to check me out, including a big one who, for a second, looked like he wanted to knock me off my board, before changing direction at the last minute. There were seals everywhere, lying on the rocks in the sun, staring at me with those big round eyes. Seals look incredibly friendly and are by no means dangerous animals, but I was also very much aware that if they felt threatened, they would attack and could cause some damage. Besides, this was their home, and I was just visiting. So I kept my distance and left it up to them how close they wanted to come.

Another day, I walked parts of the Mt Fyfe track. Mt Fyfe is the dominant peak northwest of Kaikoura, and the views from the top are said to be incredible. However, the way up is hard work, and I didn't have the energy or experience to go all the way that day. Nevertheless, I decided to start walking and see how far I would get. I followed the super steep and slippery dirt road up through the forest for over an hour. To be honest, this first section of the track was pretty dull for the most part. However, whenever there was a gap in the trees, I got to admire beautiful views. I made it to just above the tree line that day, where I stopped for lunch and enjoyed the scenery for a while. I wasn't even halfway up to the summit, but already the views were breathtaking. In the north, I could see the Marlborough Sounds, where I had been a few weeks earlier, and even the outline of the North Island in the distance. In the east, the beautiful coastline stretched before me, seemingly endlessly to the south. It had been hard getting even this far, and I was glad I didn't have any ambition to go any further, so I turned around an made my way back down.

Kaikoura is a famous surf town, and I had hoped to get a chance to work on my surfing while there (I had made embarrassingly little progress in the last three years...). However, I found the surf breaks just a little too intimidating. Kaikoura's beaches are beautiful, with the dark rocks and sand meeting the clear blue waters, but the rocks poking out everywhere mean you need to know where you're going or risk damaging your gear and yourself. I watched the surfers at the famous break north of town for a bit, trying to work up the confidence to go, but I just couldn't get there. As confident as I was when kiteboarding, surfing was a different story – which is partly why I had made such little progress. If some of my surfer friends had been there, I definitely would have gone in, but I didn't have the confidence on my own. So I resorted to watching others instead, which was beautiful, too.

In the end, that was the only thing I didn't like about Kaikoura. The beaches just weren't very user-friendly. For the most part, they were super steep, with big waves smashing onto the rocky shores most days. They aren't safe swimming spots even for experienced ocean people. The beaches aren't great for walking either, due to being mostly rocky, not sandy. So while Kaikoura had the ocean, views, waves and wind that I would be looking for if I ever decide to settle down somewhere, this little town on the east coast of the South Island is probably not going to be the spot. But I had a great time anyway.

———

After my weeks in Kaikoura, I continued south. I spent a couple of weeks around Christchurch, catching up with my lockdown buddies, Sarah and Bruno, as well as other friends. From here, I had planned to continue straight down the coast to Dunedin to pick up where Covid had stopped me in March. However, as I was making my way along the coast south of Christchurch, a heatwave hit. It had been an unusually cold summer for most of the South Island so far, and it was like the weather gods wanted to make up for it in a matter of days. One day, it was 36 degrees even at five o'clock in the evening, and the lowest that temperatures were forecasted to fall that night was 27 degrees. The previous day and night had been only slightly colder. As much as I loved my tiny home on wheels, a van is not a great place to be when temperatures are that high. It gets extremely hot in these vans. And you can't really park in the shade when you rely on solar power to keep your fridge going – and you need a fridge when it's that hot, how else will the ice cream stay cold?

I was lying spread out on a blanket in a bit of shade outside of my van, trying to catch as much as possible of the light breeze in the air, when I decided to check what the temperatures were like in other parts of the South Island. Maybe I could escape this heat wave. It didn't take me long to figure out that Lake Tekapo, which was only 90 minutes away but 700 metres higher, had a much more pleasant 28 degrees, and it was expected to drop to 22 overnight. I had been to

Lake Tekapo once before, almost 14 years earlier, during my first year in New Zealand. I didn't remember much other than the famous chapel and the dog statue by the lake. The area wasn't on my list of must-see places for this trip, but I was desperate to escape the heat. So I got into my hot van, turned down the window (the only 'air conditioning' on offer), and headed west. And that is how I discovered what is now one of my favourite parts of New Zealand.

I was driving along State Highway 8, away from the coast. I was tired after a few nights of poor sleep due to the heat, so I didn't appreciate the scenery around me as much as I might have at other times. However, that changed when I drove over a hill and Lake Tekapo came into view. Tired or not, the view of the lake with the mountains around it simply could not be ignored. I pulled over on the side of the road and had one of those "I can't believe how beautiful the world is" moments. Lake Tekapo has this intense turquoise colour that makes it look more like a tropical beach than a mountain lake. I later learned that it got this colour from a particulate called rock flour, which is rocks ground into a fine dust by glaciers on their way towards the lake. This rock flour is suspended in the water and causes the incredible colour.

The scenery before me was so beautiful that I didn't even care anymore if it was actually colder or not. I knew I wanted to spend some time here, and I couldn't wait to get out on the lake on my paddle board. After I had soaked up the views for a bit, I realised it was, in fact, a much more comfortable temperature, and I was grateful for this cherry on top. It was getting late, so I made my way down to the lake to the New Zealand Motor Caravan Association (NZMCA) park, where I planned to spend the next few days. The park was right by the lake, and even though all sites with the best views were taken by the time I arrived, I got a lovely spot with a little bit of a lake view. And when others left the following morning, I managed to grab a lakefront site. After breakfast, I got the paddle board out and cruised over the lake. The water was so smooth, I almost felt like flying. It was cooler at the lake than it had been at the coast, but it was still a hot, sunny summer's day, so I decided to go for a swim. Excited about the idea of diving into this magnificent turquoise water, I jumped off my paddle board – only to have the air knocked out of my lungs. As I learned that day, glacier lakes are freezing even when the air temperature is 30 degrees. However, once I got air back into my lungs and started moving a bit, it was very refreshing.

That afternoon, I biked into town. Lake Tekapo is a sleepy little village at the best of times, and that year, in the absence of international tourists (our borders were still closed to keep Covid out), it was particularly quiet. I had a look around, stopped at the famous church and the dog statue by the lake and treated myself to a Flat White. "I could live here." I thought to myself. It was a familiar thought. Since I'd started travelling around New Zealand, I'd discovered many places that I could see myself calling home one day. However, this was the first time I felt that way about a place that's not by the ocean.

I spent the next few days exploring the area. I walked up to the observatory at the top of Mt John, enjoyed more paddle boarding sessions on the lake and cruised around on my bike. I absolutely loved Lake Tekapo. However, eventually, I decided to keep moving, vowing to be back again soon. Since I had already come this far inland, I decided to continue to Lake Pukaki and Twizel and then make my way back to the coast via State Highway 83.

If I thought Lake Tekapo's colour was breathtaking, Lake

Pukaki was out of this world. The lake at the foot of New Zealand's highest mountain, Mt Cook, has an even more intense turquoise colour. Even at this time of the year, Mt Cook's peak was covered in snow, and together the lake and the mountain made for a spectacular sight. I found an epic spot at one of the lakefront freedom camping sites and decided to stay a couple of nights. I sat in my van, with the doors wide open, looking out onto the lake and snow-covered southern alps and had another "can't believe how beautiful this is" moment.

The next morning, I got the paddle board out and had the most amazing time gliding through the glassy water with undisturbed views of Mt Cook in the distance. A fellow traveller took some photos and shared them with me afterwards. As a solo traveller – one who isn't very good at taking selfies – I don't have a lot of photos of myself. I generally don't mind, given the scenery is usually way more beautiful than I am. However, I love having those photos of me paddle boarding on Lake Pukaki in front of Mt Cook. They are not only stunning photos but also the perfect reminder of how beautiful that summer was and how incredibly lucky and grateful I felt to have those experiences.

After almost two weeks inland, I made it back to the ocean and spent a couple of days in quirky Oamaru. This little town on the coast between Christchurch and Dunedin often gets overlooked when people plan their South Island travels, but it's absolutely worth a visit. The town is known as New Zealand's steampunk capital because of its somewhat random obsession with all things steampunk. There are elements of the genre throughout the town, as well as the fun and interactive Steampunk HQ museum. In addition, Oamaru has a gorgeous historic village and a beautiful waterfront. I planned to stay for only a night, but that turned into three because I enjoyed exploring this little town so much.

After I left Oamaru, I continued down the coast. I took my time, stopping at little bays and towns along the way. The coastline was beautiful, the weather was excellent, and I was in no rush. Eventually, I found myself at the NZMCA park in Dunedin, parked in precisely the spot where I was almost a year earlier when Covid had disrupted my South Island road trip. I hoped it wasn't a bad omen.

One day while in Dunedin, I made my way out to the Orokonui Ecosanctuary which is the flagship biodiversity project for the South Island. Within the sanctuary, multiple species of plants and animals are protected by a predator fence that surrounds 307 hectares of coastal Otago forest. Staff and volunteers have removed pests, enhanced habitats with weed control and planting, and re-introduced many rare and endangered species. The result is a magical place that's paradise for both the wildlife and human visitors. I spent the day strolling through the sanctuary, learning about the different species of plants and animals, and enjoyed being surrounded by such wholesome nature. As I was leaving, I ran into one of the staff members in the car park. He saw my van and asked about the setup with my boards on the side and the bike at the front. He introduced himself as Phil. We chatted for a bit and I told him about my lifestyle. At some point he said I should be writing a blog about my adventures, to which I replied "I do". I gave him the details of my blog and Instagram, and then we said goodbye and I left. I had no idea that this brief encounter would lead to an absolutely incredible experience.

The following day, I got a message from Phil, saying that

they were expecting a kiwi chick to arrive the next day, and asked if I wanted to come to meet the chick. For non-New Zealanders, it might be hard to understand what an incredible opportunity that is. Kiwi birds are the mascot of New Zealand. We love them and go to incredible lengths to keep them alive. They are endemic to New Zealand, which means you won't find them anywhere else in the world. Unfortunately, they have had a hard time ever since westerners brought various pests to New Zealand. Not being able to fly, the kiwi doesn't have much to protect itself from stoats, possums, cats and dogs. As a result, they are incredibly rare. They are also very shy. To see one requires patience and a lot of luck – as well as giving up sleep since they are nocturnal. To see a kiwi chick would be even more special. Needless to say, I jumped at the opportunity.

The next day, I drove back to Orokonui Ecosanctuary to meet Phil and the rest of the team. When I arrived, the young kiwi named Lochy was still on his/her way from the airport after flying in from Franz Joseph on the West Coast, but got there shortly after me. At one month old, no one knew yet if it's a male or female kiwi. They look the same, and only a DNA test would tell. Once they get older, males and females can easily be told apart based on weight and bill lengths – females are considerably larger! I had the feeling Lochy is male and since I don't want to refer to Lochy as "it", I will use "he" going forward – hopefully, she will forgive me if I got it wrong.

Lochy is a Haast Tokoeka Kiwi. This is the rarest of all kiwis, and only 5% of chicks reach adulthood in the wild. Lochy's parents are wild kiwis who live in the West Coast region of the South Island. Conservation workers took the egg before Lochy hatched. While that might seem cruel (poor mom and dad), it's ultimately a good thing as it massively increases the chances of the kiwi chick surviving. Unfortunately, kiwi chicks are pretty helpless. Once they are older, they have strong legs to kick off predators and defend themselves. But if born in the wild, there is a good chance that a young chick will fall victim to a predator like a stoat, possum or rat – or even an overly territorial fellow kiwi. They really don't make it easy on themselves. And apparently, kiwis are not overly maternal, so hopefully, they won't mind too much. According to the staff at Orokonui, it might actually increase the chances of them having another egg which would be a good thing.

Lochy hatched under the watchful eyes of conservation workers at the West Coast Wildlife Centre. When I met him, he was a month old, which meant it was time to start preparing him to be a wild kiwi. This usually happens in several steps. For the first little while, Lochy would have his own small fenced-off area at Orokonui. When the team is confident that he is getting stronger, Lochy will be allowed to roam around a bigger area within the sanctuary. Once he is big and strong enough (at least 1.2kg), the young kiwi will be taken to a predator-free island to grow even stronger before being released into the 'real' wild.

It was amazing to learn a bit more about this programme, and it's incredible how much effort the Department of Conservation (DOC) and people like the team at Orokonui put into making sure our national icon survives. The sad truth is, if it wasn't for this effort, there probably wouldn't be any kiwi birds anymore.

When Lochy arrived at Orokonui, he'd already had a long day. He was grabbed in Franz Joseph early in the morning, put in a little box and taken to Dunedin via plane. A big day for a little guy – especially given kiwis usually sleep during the day. I learned that kiwis easily get dehydrated when they are awake for this long and have stressful days. So, the first thing the team did after taking Lochy out of his little travel box was to inject fluids directly under the skin. This helps hydrate him and means he'll recover quicker. Lochy was surprisingly calm throughout the whole procedure – though he was probably too tired at this point to fight back. The team also attached a GPS tracker to Lochy's leg so they could find him again once he's free to roam around the sanctuary.

With extra fluids and a tracker, Lochy was ready to move into his new temporary home. The team had fenced off a little area in the bush, and they carried him over. I was feeling extremely fortunate and honoured to have the chance to experience all this. It was nothing like seeing a kiwi in the zoo or as part of some tourist tour. I had a chance to see how kiwi conservation really works. So when Phil asked if I wanted to hold Lochy and 'set him free', I couldn't believe it. What an incredible honour! The team explained how to grab Lochy's feet with one finger in between them and the others around with a tight hold (that little kiwi had surprisingly strong legs) and how to hold the body with my other hand. I carefully took him, and set Lochy down in his new home. I'm pretty sure he was glad when the lid on his little hut closed and he was left in peace.

I later learned that Lochy did really well and grew into a strong little Kiwi. Only a few months after I met him, he was big enough to move to Centre Island/Tihaka in Lake Te Anau, a pest free island where he will hopefully grow even stronger. I will never forget Lochy and this special day and still feel eternally grateful to Phil and the team at Okoronui for inviting me along for this once in a lifetime experience and answering all my questions.

It seemed very fitting that this all happened on the 17th of February – the anniversary of my arrival in New Zealand 14 years earlier.

———

After this amazing encounter in Dunedin, I continued south along the coast. In the idyllic seaside settlement called Taieri Mouth, south of Dunedin, I met Suzy. She was in her late 60s, retired and travelling around in her motorhome with her little pooch Walter. I think female solo travellers are somehow drawn to each other. I was always friendly and happy to chat with people I met at campgrounds. But whenever I saw a fellow solo female nomad, I made an extra effort to say hello. So that's how I met Suzy. After a quick chat, she asked if I wanted to join her and Walter for a walk on the beach. I was itching to get to what looked like a stunning beach anyway, so the three of us set off. We exchanged life stories, and I learned that Suzy had lost her husband just over a year ago. They had two sons. One was living in the UK and the other in Melbourne. Suzy shared that after her husband passed away, she had felt very lonely. Buying a motorhome and travelling the country together was something they had always talked about wanting to do one day, but they didn't get the chance. At some point, her sons suggested Suzy should live that dream for both of them. Initially, she was very reluctant about the idea, worrying about driving a big motorhome and being on the road on her own. But her son from Melbourne came over for a few weeks to help her find the right motorhome, and they embarked on the first trip together. Now, a year later, Suzy was feeling much more confident and was happy she had taken this step on her own.

"So, you don't have any kids, yet?" Suzy asked as we were

walking along the beach, and when I confirmed that I didn't, she followed up with, "still looking for a dad, huh?". "No", I replied. "I don't want to have children!"

I have had these conversations before and had given similar answers. However, I had never before been so confident about it. Usually, my response was something like, "I don't think I will have kids" or, "I probably won't have children". As I responded to Suzy with a clear and strong "No", I thought to myself, "WOW, where did that come from?" When exactly had I decided that I definitely won't have kids? The last time I had seriously thought about it two summers ago, I was leaning towards no, but I didn't feel like I was ready to make a final decision. I hadn't thought much about it since. I had been too busy losing Josie to rust, finding a new van, exploring the country, getting stuck in Covid lockdown, being overworked and stressed and then finding my balance again and just, you know, living life. It had also been a while since the topic had come up in conversations. When Suzy asked me that day, I responded without thinking. It just came out, and it felt right.

Apparently, somewhere along the way, I had decided that I won't have kids, and I had made peace with it. It felt good to say it out loud, without the maybe or probably. It felt genuine and right. It must have felt that way to Suzy, too, because for the first time I could remember, having this conversation with a stranger didn't result in them saying something like, "you might change your mind one day". Instead, Suzy told me how beautiful she thought it was that I knew what I wanted from life and that I was going after it.

Later that day, when I was alone in my van, my thoughts drifted back to that moment. Being the analytical person I am, I tried to pinpoint the moment I had decided that I definitely didn't want kids. Somehow, I always thought that a big decision like that should have been a deliberate one. I thought there would be a moment where I would sit down and weigh up all the pros and cons and then make a decision. But it hadn't happened like that at all. There was no deliberate moment. Two years ago, I didn't feel ready to make a final decision on the matter, so I decided to focus on living my best life until I was ready. And somehow, I had made the decision, it just didn't happen in one deliberate moment.

It felt right. Nevertheless, a part of me wanted to re-engineer the process. It wasn't enough for me to know that I definitely didn't want kids, I also wanted to know why. As I deliberated the pros and cons, I realised that what had happened wasn't so much a decision against children, but a decision for a way of life. Despite the ups and downs, the last three years had been absolutely amazing. I didn't know if I wanted to keep living in a van forever, but I knew I wanted this level of freedom and flexibility forever. And for me, that wouldn't be possible if I had children. So, in the end, I realised I hadn't decided not to have kids, I had decided that I wanted to live a certain way – and that required me to be childfree.

There was something else that dawned on me that day. Looking back, I realised that it wasn't so much a matter of having gained new insights or clarity that allowed me to now make a decision I wasn't ready for two years earlier. The main reason I was prepared to commit to a childfree life was that I was confident to be myself. Over the two years since I had last seriously thought about the question, I had found a new level of self-awareness and confidence, and I wasn't scared anymore that people would misunderstand or judge me. I realised that, in some ways, the 'maybe' and 'probably' had been for other people as much as they had been for me. Now, I didn't need them anymore. I felt strong and confident to own that choice – regardless of what people think.

I wondered if I would feel the same way if I hadn't been on this epic vanlife journey for the last three years. I had created this beautiful life that was so full of purpose and meaning, it showed me that I didn't need children in my life to be happy. And it wasn't just about living and travelling in a van. That was just how I translated the underlying beliefs and values into the real world for now. I didn't know how long I'd be living in a van. But I did know that the freedom, flexibility and independence that allowed me to live this way was there to stay – and that's what would enable me to create a happy life, no matter how or where I would end up living in the future. I knew there were hundreds of ways to have meaning and purpose in my life without having children – or the super successful career. That realisation made it easy to feel confident about my choices.

———

Suzy and I got along great, and since we were both heading south, we decided to travel together for a few days. We headed to Lake Waihola, where we waited out a couple of rainy and windy days at the holiday park. Suzy was my kind of travel companion. During the day, she seemed just as happy to mostly do her own things as I was. We went for walks together when the rain stopped and took turns cooking dinner for each other in the evenings, but other than that, we kept busy with our individual lives. Suzy was knitting a sweater for one of her grandkids who had a birthday coming up and had requested a sweater in the colours of his favourite rugby team. I used the time to catch up on work.

By this point, I had a pretty good work setup in my van. When Covid forced everyone to work remotely, video calls had become everyone's favourite activity. Many things that used to be an email now seemed to require an online meeting. I didn't mind. It was nice to see clients more – even if just on camera. However, it meant that I could no longer hotspot off my phone for internet like I had done the first two years on the road. I needed faster and more reliable internet, so I signed up for Netspeed, one of the mobile broadband providers in New Zealand. I now had a Wi-Fi modem in the van and plenty of data to do video calls and stream movies and TV shows at night. There were still many parts of New Zealand where I didn't have internet coverage – usually the beautiful, remote spots – but between Netspeed and my phone as a backup, I had coverage in a lot of places, and working had become easier.

Back in my old life, I always really liked having a dedicated work desk and setup, but over the last three years, I had gotten good at working from just about anywhere. All I needed was my laptop and a decent internet connection. For meetings, I would sit on my couch with the laptop on my swivel table. When I didn't need to look professional on camera, I would often just sit at the head of my couch, with my back leaning against the shelf, my feet up, and my laptop on my legs. Admittedly, not the most ergonomic setup, but it worked well for me. So that's how I spent most of those two rainy days at Lake Waihola.

Once the rain had passed, Suzy and I continued south along the coast. Our destination was an area south of Dunedin called the Catlins. I had been there almost exactly four years earlier when my sister visited. I fell in love with the area then and was excited to finally be back. The Catlins is one of those parts on New Zealand where there is something to see around every corner. There are so many beaches, walks, waterfalls, lighthouses and lookouts along the roads that you can spend days travelling a fairly short distance. Four years earlier, we had been on a schedule and were only able to stop at a couple of sights. This time, I wanted to take my time.

Our first stop in the Catlins was what is probably the most famous; Nugget Point. Nugget Point is a narrow landmass that reaches out into the ocean. At the end is the Nugget Point Lighthouse, perched at the top of the green and grey cliffs. Suzy and I decided to set up camp at nearby Kaka Point Campground and bike out to the lighthouse. Google maps promised a mostly flat ride, so we expected a cruisy trip. However, we realised quickly that Google's definition of "mostly flat" was somewhat different to ours. Suzy didn't mind. She turned up the levels on her fancy eBike and shot up the hill in front of me. Halfway up the second hill, I had to accept that I wouldn't be able to keep up, so I let her go ahead. She waited for me at the top, looking fresh and relaxed while I fought to get air into my lungs. According to Suzy, it was only fair she had an eBike, given she was almost twice my age. But at dinner, she gave me an extra-large serving to make up for it.

Luckily, the destination was more than worth the effort it took to get there. We chained up our bikes at the car park and continued on foot. There is a walkway along the top of the cliffs with amazing views of the coastline and the lighthouse. We were lucky to be there on a sunny day, and the scenery and colours around us were incredible. Ahead of us, at the end of the narrow walkway, was the white lighthouse at the top of the steep green cliffs. It glowed in the sun, making it look even brighter next to the dark green bushes and blue sky. Below the lighthouse, the cliffs dropped off steeply, sinking into the clear blue waters with several other big rocks and mini-islands poking out next to them. All around us, we could hear birdlife, and on the rocks below us, we could see a few seals soaking up the sun. As we stood there enjoying the views, I had another one of those "damn! New Zealand is beautiful" moments that were so frequent that summer.

After a night at Kaka Point, Suzy and I said goodbye. She was on a schedule, needing to be back home for a good friend's birthday in a few days. I had nowhere to be and wanted to take my time. I had enjoyed Suzy's company and her cheeky sense of humour, but I was also glad to be on my own again and to be able to go at my own speed without having to coordinate with someone else.

I decided to spend a few days at Pūrākaunui Bay, a remote beach south of Nugget Point. There was no internet or cell phone coverage, and I enjoyed a few days disconnected from the rest of the world. I went for walks on the beach, watched the tides come and go, and made friends (from a safe distance) with the local sea lion, who came each day at low tide to take a nap on the beach in the sun.

On my first morning at Pūrākaunui Bay, I had slept through sunrise and regretted it afterwards, so the second morning, I made sure to set an alarm. I had long ago learned that the best part of sunrise usually happens up to an hour before the sun starts to show on the horizon, so I set my alarm for 6 am, got up to make coffee, opened the rear doors of my van and then got back under the duvet to watch the day begin. It started with a dark orange line along the horizon that slowly spread out and coloured the few clouds in the sky all shades of yellow, orange and pink. Every time I looked away for a few seconds, the colours had changed. At some point, the sight before me was so beautiful that I got out of the van to get a wider view and take better photos. I realised I wasn't the only one who had gotten up early to watch the sun come up. My camp neighbours were also standing next to their van in PJs, admiring the views and taking photos. As we stood there, one of them said, "what a perfect start to autumn." I almost corrected him, thinking there was no way summer was already over, but it turned out he was right. It was the 1st of March, which meant summer had come to an end, and autumn was here.

The famous chapel at Lake Tekap

Parked up at Lake Pukaki with views of Mt Cook.

Standup paddle boarding on Lake Pukaki

To view these images in colour, and more photos
from my journey, visit my website.
lifedonedifferently.com/gallery

17

BITTERSWEET

AUTUMN 2021

Wanaka & Roy's Peak

Queenstown

Te Anau

Porpoise Bay & Fortrose

It might have officially been autumn in March, but it still felt very much like summer. If the fellow camper at Pūrākaunui Bay hadn't pointed it out, I probably wouldn't have even been aware that, officially, the seasons had changed. In the years to come, I would often talk about this time as "the epic summer on the South Island", even though half of it was technically in autumn. The weather was lovely most days, and it hadn't been a very hot summer (except for that brief heat wave that led me to discover Lake Tekapo), so I didn't notice much of a temperature difference either. It wasn't just the weather that didn't change much as the seasons changed. My epic South Island road trip also continued throughout autumn.

After spending a few days in beautiful Pūrākaunui Bay, I headed inland to Tawanui. I had heard about the Catlins River Walk, and since there weren't many long walks in the area, I decided to check it out. I stayed at the DOC campsite for two nights and spent the day in the middle walking the track. As the name suggests, it follows the river, and while the views weren't quite as stunning as those offered by some of the other tracks I did that summer, I enjoyed my day in the forest. The trail didn't cover a lot of elevation, but it was a constant up and down, and most of it was slippery with lots of roots to make you stumble. In other words, the track was a lot more demanding than it looked on paper, and by the end, I felt like I had earned my dinner.

From Tawanui, I headed back to the coast, stopping at the sleepy settlement of Papatowai, the impressive Cathedral Caves and Niagara. Eventually, I made my way to Porpoise Bay, a beach in the southern part of the Catlins that is famous for the Hector Dolphins that call the bay home. My sister and I had stopped here three years earlier and were lucky enough to be able to swim with the Dolphins. I was hoping to be that lucky again.

As I drove over the hill and Porpoise Bay came into view, I was excited to see a little wave peeling along, with otherwise glassy conditions. It would have been an excellent size wave to practice my longboard surfing. However, after short contemplation, I decided to take the paddle board out instead, as that would allow me to better see the dolphins, should they show up. As it turned out, I made the right choice. Within 10 minutes of being in the water, the pod came to check me out. They are curious by nature, and there are many stories from surfers, kayakers, paddle boarders and swimmers who were fortunate to encounter these fantastic creatures at Porpoise Bay. I paddled along for a bit, and the dolphins kept popping up all around me. After a while, I headed to the southern end of the beach, where the waves were small enough to surf on my paddle board. I had a lot of fun catching a few waves when the dolphins joined in. For the next half hour or so, I shared small, glassy, peeling waves with a pod of dolphins and no one else in sight — such an incredible experience. After a while, word must have gotten out, and a group of kids rocked up with their surfboards to join in. I decided I'd had my fun and paddled back towards where I had parked my van. Almost an hour later, as I was sitting on the beach eating my lunch, I could still see the dolphins playing in the waves, having a great time.

Over the following days, I continued south to Slope Point, the southernmost point of the South Island, and then on to Waipapa Point and Fortrose, the south-western end of the Catlins. I had heard about an awesome freedom camping spot in Fortrose, right by the estuary. However, people had also warned me that it could get very busy, so I made sure to arrive early. I didn't have to worry. There was lots of space and only ten or so campers, all spread out along the waterfront. It wasn't the first time that summer and autumn that freedom camping spots seemed empty compared to photos I'd seen and stories I'd heard. It was one of the signs that this wasn't an ordinary season in New Zealand. However, it would be a few more weeks before it really hit home just how unusual this year was.

In the afternoon of my second day in Fortrose, the wind picked up, giving me the chance to kiteboard on the beautiful estuary right in front of the van. One of the other campers took photos of me, and we started chatting afterwards. He was curious about kiteboarding and asked lots of questions about my gear and what it takes to learn. Eventually, he asked, "is it safe to do this on your own?". It was a valid question. I wouldn't say that kiteboarding is a high-risk sport. It probably looks much riskier than it actually is – assuming you know what you're doing and had proper safety training. But, if you get into trouble, for example, because of a gear malfunction, it can get ugly quickly. It's difficult for someone who doesn't know how the kite functions to help a kiteboarder who is in trouble, so it's definitely safer to go out with others who know what they are doing. However, having other kiters around often wasn't an option when travelling in these remote parts of New Zealand, and sometimes, the conditions and scenery were too good not to risk it. I am a confident kiter and only go out on my own in places where the conditions are safe and easy. For example, I would never go kiting on my own at one of the wild west coast beaches. In addition, whenever I go on my own, I take my Personal Locator Beacon with me so that if something happens and I find myself getting dragged out to sea, I can call for help. But at the end of the day, life comes with risks, no matter how you live it. Yes, doing certain things on your own adds an additional level of risk, but for me, it was a risk worth taking.

With a few days in Fortrose, I concluded my time in the Catlins. I had been looking forward to spending time there since I had visited for a few days three years earlier, and it more than lived up to my expectations. In Fortrose, I met a lovely couple from Wellington. In the three weeks I had travelled the hundred or so kilometres of the Catlins coastline, they had come all the way from Wellington to Fortrose, almost ten times the distance. Like so many others I met, they only had a limited number of weeks to travel and wanted to make the most of it by seeing as many places as possible. After chatting with the Wellington couple, I felt extra grateful that I had the opportunity to spend over three weeks exploring just one small part of the country, instead of rushing through like they had.

———

In the second half of March, I made my way to Invercargill and then said goodbye to the ocean and pointed the steering wheel inland. After a detour to remote Lake Hauroko, I arrived in Te Anau, a small town on the shores of a lake by the same name. This is another part of New Zealand I had rushed through on a previous trip, and I was looking forward to spending more time in the area. I loved Te Anau from the second I arrived. The town seemed lively without being busy, and the lake and surrounding mountains made for stunning scenery. However, there was something odd about Te Anau. There were lots of empty restaurants and cafes. The town seemed to have an unusually high number of eateries for its size. As I was ordering a Flat White at one of the cafes, I casually asked the woman taking my order if the town gets much busier in the middle of summer, which might explain the many cafes and restaurants. "Oh yes," she said, "it's definitely busier in summer. But in normal years, it's much, much busier than this almost year around."

In normal years! I felt a bit ashamed for having even asked the question. Of course, it's unusually quiet in Te Anau right now. In fact, many places I had visited seemed quiet. And more than once, I had briefly wondered why there were such huge car parks at some sights and attractions when they didn't seem to be needed. I couldn't believe how ignorant I had been. This wasn't a typical year – not for me and not for anyone. However, for me, it wasn't a normal year because I was on this epic road trip around the South Island, having the time of my life. For many others, it wasn't a normal year because the absence of international tourists was threatening their livelihoods.

At this time, the only Covid cases in New Zealand were in quarantine facilities. There was no Covid in the community, and our borders were closed to visitors. Citizens and permanent residents could come in, but they had to spend two weeks in managed isolation facilities and test negative for Covid multiple times before they could go out into the community. Without Covid, life seemed fairly normal in New Zealand at the time compared to many other parts of the world – unless you lived in a tourist town or worked in a tourism-related sector. In the year ending December 2019, over 3.8 million people from around the world visited New Zealand. That is a significant number, especially when you consider that only about 5.1 million people live here permanently. Many of these 3.8 million visitors ate in restaurants and cafes, visited tourist attractions and joined tours and other activities. Since March 2020, hardly any international tourists had visited the country. While Kiwis were travelling in their own backyard much more so than in other years, it wasn't anywhere near enough to make up for the gap. No other sector in New Zealand had been hit as hard by Covid as tourism, which was evident in Te Anau. The town is best known as the gateway to the world-famous Milford Sound, one of the must-dos on the South Island. Before Covid, almost a million people visited Milford Sound each year, and many of them would stop in Te Anau on their way in and out, buying food and paying for accommodation and tours. Needless to say, many people and businesses in Te Anau were struggling that year, and the empty restaurants and cafes were a sign of it.

It wasn't just Te Anau, either. Now that I had woken up to this reality, I saw all the sleepy towns I passed through and all the empty car parks and freedom camping sites in a different light. I loved that everything was quiet. I loved that it was easy to find car parks and that you didn't have to rock up before mid-day to secure a spot at popular freedom campsites. But during my time in Te Anau, I realised that every empty car park or restaurant represented struggling businesses, people and families. I was having the time of my life while they were fighting for their livelihoods. On top of that, the more selfish part of me realised that this was likely to be a once-in-a-lifetime experience and that I was incredibly lucky to be able to enjoy a quiet summer and autumn on the South Island. Most likely, it wouldn't be like this when I would come back in the future. Everything would be busy again, campsites would be packed, and personal space and privacy would be luxury again.

After realising all of this during my time in Te Anau, the rest of autumn had a bittersweet feeling to it. On the one hand, I was having the best time ever – partly because the borders were closed and it was quiet – but on the other hand, I was now acutely aware of all the people who had lost their jobs and struggled to keep their businesses going. I started to stay at paid campgrounds much more to do my part to support locals, and I also used it as an excellent reason to buy more coffees and eat out more often than I usually did. I knew the small amounts I was spending weren't really making a difference, but I wanted to do what I could. I also developed a whole new level of appreciation for how lucky I was that this was my life and that I had the opportunity to travel around New Zealand without tourists. I knew I had to make the most of it.

Te Anau is not only the gateway to Milford Sound but also to some of New Zealand's best hikes – including the Kepler Track, one of the Great Walks. Most people do the Kepler Track over four days, spending three nights in the huts along the way. Since it is a Great Walk, the huts are very well equipped, making the track a great option for people new to hiking who don't have all the gear yet – like me. Hiking was a new passion of mine that developed that summer after realising that some of the best views in the country are only accessible by foot. I enjoyed the quiet solitude of hiking, I loved being out in nature, and I liked that it was less weather dependent than many of my other activities. Yes, hiking is most fun in nice weather, but you can still go when it rains. With kitesurfing, surfing and paddle boarding, you need specific conditions, and you can't go without them, no matter how much you want to. Hiking was much easier in that regard. So far, I had only done day walks, but I felt ready for my first overnighter – and the Kepler Track looked like the perfect option.

In normal years, you have to book months in advance to get a spot in one of the huts along New Zealand's great walks. Usually, they book out within days (sometimes hours) of the

Department of Conservation (DOC) opening up bookings. However, 2021 wasn't a typical year, and I was able to secure a spot at Luxmore Hut at short notice. On the day, I started early and made it up to the hut just after lunchtime. I dropped my bag, claimed one of the bunks, and continued to Luxmore Summit. I covered over 20km and around 1400m elevation that day. Needless to say, I was shattered by the time I was back at the hut. But the views more than made up for it. I started walking in the cloud, but just as I emerged from the tree line, it cleared up, and the views over Lake Te Anau and the surrounding mountain ranges were nothing short of breathtaking. I didn't sleep well that night, struggling to get comfortable in the bunk and being disrupted by noise from the other 20 people in the room. But I didn't mind. The following day, I got up early and was treated to a spectacular sunrise, and when three of New Zealand's famous (but rare) alpine parrots, the Kea, showed up shortly after, I once again stood in total awe of New Zealand's beauty. On my way back down, I declared my first overnight tramp a full success.

A few days later, at the Mavora Lakes east of Te Anau, I experienced the first overnight frost. All summer, I had the idea in the back of my mind that I might also spend winter on the South Island. Photos showing snow on the mountains looked amazing, and I was keen to experience it. However, one night of frost, and I got over the idea very quickly. I don't usually feel chilly easily, but it was so cold that night I couldn't sleep. Sometime in the early hours, I got up and dug out my sleeping bag, which, of course, was tucked away in the hardest-to-reach corner under my bed. But even with a sleeping bag and my duvet, I was still freezing – and the minus one or two degrees we had that night were nothing compared to how cold it could get in winter. I turned on the gas heater a couple of times throughout the night, which warmed up the van, but thanks to a lack of decent insulation, the heat disappeared almost as fast as it came out of the heater vent. Besides, I had to be careful with how much gas I used as the next place to refill was a few days away. I didn't want to risk being stranded without the ability to make coffee (Yup, I'd rather be cold than without coffee!). So, as much as I liked the idea of spending a winter on the South Island, I had to accept that my van wasn't made for it. However, with some luck, I still had a month or so before overnight frost would become a regular occurrence, so I pointed my steering wheel north and headed to the South Island's tourism capital; Queenstown.

Believe it or not, this was my first proper visit to Queenstown. I had driven through before, but back then, I didn't have enough time to stop for more than a quick lunch. Given that Queenstown is usually one of the first places visitors to New Zealand want to see, it seemed a bit odd that even after 14 years in the country – more than three of which I had spent travelling full-time – I had never been in the area for more than a quick drive through. Fair to say, it was time to change that.

In mid-April, my friend Ava flew down to meet me, and we spent a week playing tourists. We rented an Airbnb in Queenstown and ticked off all the main sights and attractions in the area. One day we drove over the Crown Range to Wanaka, stopping at the famous Cardrona Hotel. On other days, we explored Arrowtown and Cromwell, did a tour at Goldfields Mining Centre, a cruise on Lake Wakatipu with a stop at Walter Peak Station where we had the most amazing lunch, and spent a day in Glenorchy. The week was a big change of pace for me. Usually, it would have taken me weeks to see all those places. However, it was a lot of fun. As much as I enjoy travelling on my own, it was nice to be able to share it with a good friend for a change – especially since one day that week marked my 37th birthday, and after a lockdown birthday the previous year, it was nice to be able to celebrate with someone.

After Ava left, I returned to Glenorchy for a few days and then made my way over the mountains to Wanaka, where I set up camp for a week. I was starting to feel a bit of travel fatigue. I had seen so many amazing new places that summer and autumn, and had so many incredible experiences. I think I was starting to feel a bit overwhelmed. It was time to slow down and give myself time to process it all. Besides, I took a week off work while Ava was visiting, and now I had a bit of catching up to do. So at the end of April, I found a beautiful spot at Glendhu Bay Motor Camp, just outside of Wanaka, and stayed put for a week. The campground was quiet, and I had a site right on the lake with stunning views.

I spent most of the week working, taking breaks to go paddle boarding on the lake or for walks around the lake-front. However, one day, I took a break from work to tick off one of my must-dos in the area. I set the alarm for 3:00 am, drove to the nearby starting point for the Roy's Peak track and started to climb. For the next three and half hours, I dragged myself up the mountain in the dark. It began as an exciting adventure, hiking in the dark, but after a while, the excitement was overshadowed by the relentless slog that is Roy's Peak track. It's one of the most popular day-hikes in New Zealand, but it's not the track itself that attracts people. For about eight kilometres, the path winds its way up the mountain, covering over 1,000 metres in elevation in a seemingly endless series of turns without much change in scenery. So why do thousands of people make their way up this pretty

LISA JANSEN

dull track each year? Because of the incredible views from the top.

The idea of that stunning view is what kept me going as I was slowing making my way up the mountain that day. I might be an active person, but I'm not particularly fit – and I've never been good with hills. The part of Germany where I grew up is famous for how flat it is. People often joke that you can see on Monday who will visit on Friday because it's so flat you can see them coming from miles away. Growing up, our idea of a big hill was the pedestrian bridge over the train tracks. Needless to say, 1,000 metres of elevation was a big challenge for me, and the last couple of kilometres were painful. However, I had predicted this and had allowed plenty of time to get to the top in time for sunrise.

To say I got rewarded for my efforts would be an understatement. Going up Roy's Peak for sunrise is a popular option. However, you never know if it will pay off. Sometimes, even when the forecast looks good, the sun can be hidden behind clouds early in the morning, and you won't get to see much. Luckily, on that day, I got to see lots. As the sun started to come up in the east, the sky was lit up in all shades of orange, red and pink. There were just enough clouds to make it spectacular. As the sun rose, it started to reflect on the snow-capped mountains in the distance and with Lake Wanaka below, it was simply stunning. What made it all even better was that just a small group of five of us were sitting at the lookout enjoying nature's show. In normal years, there would have been dozens. I've heard stories of people needing to line up to take photos at the famous viewpoint. That's how busy it can get. As I stood there, that now familiar bittersweet feeling crept in again. I was overwhelmed by how beautiful this moment was and how lucky I was to experience it. I almost felt grateful for Covid and closed borders for giving me moments like this. And then I felt guilty for feeling that way, remembering that Wanaka is yet another town where people had struggled since the borders closed. For me, the absence of crowds was a blessing. For them, it was a curse.

With Roy's Peak conquered, I had ticked off one of the last must-dos for this trip. It was also definitely getting colder now. During the week in Wanaka, I used up a full gas bottle (which usually lasts at least six weeks) because the heater ran so much – and I had still been cold. So with a heavy heart, I decided that it was time to make my way north to warmer climates. My original plan was to head north via the West Coast. However, I felt that it was too late in the year to enjoy it. I decided to head to the ferry in Picton via the most direct route, promising myself that I would be back next summer to continue where I left off. And so from Wanaka, I made my way north-east towards Christchurch and then up along the coast to Picton.

In the last week of autumn, my van and I were on the ferry heading to Wellington. Unlike my trip south in November, when the weather had been excellent, it was grey and gloomy all around this time. So instead of watching the sounds float by from the deck, I grabbed a seat near the window in the heated lounge and used the time to reflect on the last few months.

I've loved New Zealand from the moment I first arrived more than 14 years earlier, but I felt like this summer and autumn had taken that love to a whole new level. I felt so lucky and proud that I got to call this place home. The past six months had been nothing short of amazing. They had been the best vanlife months yet – maybe even the best time of my life. I didn't want it to end. I kept telling myself that I could come back next summer, but I knew there was a good chance it wouldn't be the same again. Tourists would most likely be back. Everything would be busy and crowded again. A part of me was worried that this summer and autumn had ruined vanlife for me. Before Covid, I often struggled with the lack of personal space and privacy that comes with the lifestyle. I had to learn to accept crowded and noisy campsites and people parking within a few centimetres of me. Before Covid, it was just part of this lifestyle. But now, I'd had a taste of how good it could be without the crowds. I was worried I would struggle to get used to it again once the masses returned. I wished things could stay exactly as they had been for the last six months. Of course, that was a selfish view, and I knew it. Many more people in the country were praying that this Covid nightmare would be over soon. Nevertheless, if I could take any six months from my life and turn it into an endless loop, it would be those six months on the South Island that summer and autumn. Unfortunately, my life isn't some weird version of Groundhog Day, so autumn turned into winter, and there was nothing I could do about it.

18

UNEXPECTED
WINTER 2021

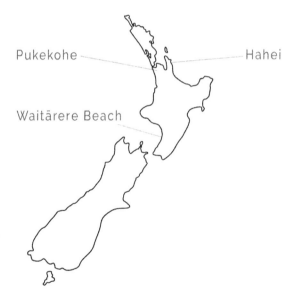

Pukekohe

Hahei

Waitārere Beach

As I was making my way north in the first week of June, I didn't have much of a plan for winter. I only had a simple goal; don't repeat the mistake from the previous years. This year, I promised myself, I would ensure I don't end up in that place again where I'm working too much and am not looking after myself. Work was going well at the time. I had two key clients who kept me busy for about 20-25 hours per week, plus a few other clients that needed the odd job done every now and then. I was set to have a winter working about 30 hours per week, which would be perfect. I would be able to save quite a bit, given my living costs were so low, but I would also still have plenty of time for the things that make me happy and keep me healthy.

Unlike in previous years, I hadn't committed to any housesitting jobs yet either. This was partly because there weren't many good options coming up. With the borders still closed, Kiwis weren't travelling internationally, and most had done their extensive domestic trips over summer or the previous winter. As a result, most housesitting jobs available were only for a week or two. For me, that wasn't as attractive, as I would have to move a lot and would never really settle anywhere. Therefore, I decided to spend more time in the van that year. In the Far North, the temperatures should be warm enough, and I was planning to mostly stay at campgrounds so I would have power and hot showers.

All in all, the plan for my fourth winter on the road was pretty simple; spend time in the Far North and work enough to save up money but not so much that it would be stressful and I wouldn't have time to look after myself. I felt pretty good about that plan. However, once again, life had other plans for me and presented me with an unexpected opportunity that was simply too good to ignore.

I was in Waitārere Beach on my way north when I got a message from fellow nomad Jackie. She and I had a lot in common. We both lived in vans, and we both wrote for the magazine Motorhomes, Caravans & Destinations and had also both published a book (two in Jackie's case). Unlike me, Jackie was travelling with her partner, and her van was even smaller than mine, but our values and mindset were very much aligned. We had been in touch over social media and I had interviewed Jackie and her partner for a podcast episode.

That day, Jackie reached out because she had been offered a writing job that she didn't have time for. Her publisher had asked if she would be interested in writing a guidebook about the nomad life in New Zealand. The book would be aimed at people interested in living and travelling in mobile homes in New Zealand – whether they do it part-time or full-time like Jackie and I. The publisher had released such a guidebook for Australia the previous year, and it had been such a big success that they now wanted a New Zealand version. Jackie felt like the timing and topic weren't right for her, so she asked if I would be interested – which, of course, I was.

Jackie gave my contact details to the publisher, who called the next day. The project sounded super interesting and like the perfect fit for me. Having lived on the road for almost four years at that stage, I had learned a lot, had many tips to share and knew where to get the information I didn't already have. I knew it would be a fun book to research and write. Besides, I had dreamed of writing another book, given how much I enjoyed the first one, so I was beyond excited to be offered this opportunity. There was just one problem; the book needed to be published by mid-November to leverage the Christmas gift-buying season. Given it takes time to edit, design, print and distribute a book, I would only have six weeks to write it. Easy and fun topic or not, six weeks is not a lot of time – especially when you're already committed to 25 hours of work for other clients.

"You promised you would have better balance this winter. You promised you wouldn't be overworked and stressed again," noted the cautious part of me that remembered the challenging previous winter well. "This is a once-in-a-lifetime opportunity. You want to be a writer. Here is your chance to be a writer. Besides, what's six weeks? You can have balance the other 46 weeks of the year," is what the ambitious and excited part of me was saying.

In the end, it was a no-brainer. As much as I hesitated and worried about ending up in that dark place again, there was no way I would pass up on an opportunity like this. I figured I would just have to find a way to do it all; write the book, do my client work and look after myself. Luckily, I was in a much better place emotionally. Earlier that year, I had discovered Intuitive Eating, which had helped me improve my relationship with food as well as my body image. In April, I had started seeing a psychologist specialising in disordered eating, intuitive eating and body positivity. While our sessions were mostly about food and body image, they often also covered other aspects of my life, and I felt confident that having her by my side would help me not neglect my health and happiness when I got busy.

I realised, however, that my new do-it-all plan would be much easier if I lived in a house while I was writing the book. As much as I loved my van, it wasn't a great place to be while juggling work, a book, winter and mental well-being. I would be spending a lot of time at the computer, and I didn't have a good setup for it in the van. In addition, it would be nice to be able to go out for a walk when I have the time, even if it's raining, knowing that I would have a hot shower and room to dry wet clothes afterwards. I had another look at housesitting jobs, but there still weren't any long-term ones, and I didn't want to add the stress of moving every couple of weeks to what would already be a busy winter. In the end, I decided to rent a place. I got word out to my network, hoping that someone might want to rent out their holiday home for a few weeks so that I could spend winter in a peaceful place, ideally close to the beach and some nice walks.

I got lucky! Friends offered me their holiday house in Hahei in the Coromandel. I had been there before, and it would be the perfect place. Hahei is a small town on the east coast of the Coromandel Peninsula. It can get crazy busy in summer, but it's peaceful and quiet in winter. There is a little shop in town, a good café (can't write a book without a steady supply of Flat Whites), a beautiful beach and some excellent walking tracks. The nearest bigger town, Whitianga, is only half an hour away and would provide everything I might need that I couldn't get in Hahei.

I moved to Hahei in the third week of June and stayed until the end of July. Even though I was very busy, I had a great time. I managed to get into a rhythm where I did client work Mondays through to Thursdays, Fridays and Saturdays I wrote, and on work days, I often spent a couple of hours in the evenings doing research or editing what I had already written. Sunday was my day off, and I made it a point not to touch my laptop if possible. Every day, I made sure I got out of the house, which was usually easy given there was a beautiful beach a few minutes away. On Sundays, I went on longer adventures, walking to the famous Cathedral Cove a couple of times, heading to Whitianga or exploring on my bike. I ate well, looked after myself, made time to read and journal most days, and reminded myself to take breaks regularly. It was a busy time, and there were definitely stressful days, especially as the book deadline got closer and closer. But overall, I felt strong and balanced. It was a relief to see I'd learned my lessons the previous years and found a way to look after my happiness and well-being even when I was busy and spending a lot of time at the computer.

I finished the book in the last week of July and handed it over to the publisher. My part was done, and it was up to them to get it ready for release in November. A few days later, I said goodbye to Hahei and headed inland. My friend Ava was celebrating her 40th birthday with a girls' weekend in Rotorua, and, of course, I couldn't miss that. Afterwards, I made my way to Auckland. I had decided to return to the South Island for summer but wanted to spend a couple of weeks in Auckland beforehand to catch up with friends and clients. Friends of friends had asked if I could housesit for them in Karaka on the outskirts of Auckland for two weeks, and it seemed perfect. Karaka is a peaceful, rural area that doesn't feel like Auckland, but I was close enough to town to see friends and clients when I wanted to.

It was during my second week in Karaka when things started to go south. As it turned out, the offer to write a book wasn't the only unexpected things to happen that winter. After being Covid-free for months, Auckland experienced a new outbreak. At first, word got out about an isolated case. However, within a day or two, it became clear that we were dealing with a significant outbreak, and the government decided to lock Auckland down. We were given 48 hours notice. After that, no one would be allowed in or out, unless they had good reasons. Obviously, this is a tricky situation when you're house and pet sitting for other people. It meant that I couldn't just leave. The homeowners were on the South Island and didn't immediately decide what they wanted to do. It wasn't the first time that a part of New Zealand would go into a snap lockdown, and in the past, these had only lasted for a couple of weeks. So the homeowners considered staying on the South Island – if I would be able to stay at the house until they are back. There was a bit of back and forth, but in the end, they decided it would be safer to come back home.

At that point, I could have left Auckland. In hindsight, I should have. But I had spent the last two weeks seeing lots of people all over Auckland – including in the part of the city where Covid seemed to be spreading. It was ironic really, considering how introverted I am most of the time. The one week all year when it would have been beneficial not to have had any contact with others was the one week I had been miss socialite. From the beginning, my main worry with Covid was the idea that I could pass it on to someone more vulnerable. I'm young and healthy, so I was confident that the risk to myself was pretty low. But not everyone is that lucky, and I did not want to be responsible for someone else's suffering if it could be avoided. I also really didn't want to be the one who brought this latest outbreak to communities outside of Auckland. Besides, I was having a hectic work week and was feeling a bit overwhelmed by it all.

So I decided to stay in Auckland, thinking it would probably just be for a week or two – like all the previous snap lockdowns since the first big one. I found a private property in Pukekohe, close to where I was housesitting, that welcomed NZMCA members to stay. I called them, and they confirmed I was welcome to stay for the duration of the lockdown and that I would also have access to power – which would be helpful given it was still winter. I was still nervous about it, though. I was going to a place I had never been before with people I didn't know, and I wouldn't be able to leave until the lockdown was lifted – and who knew when that would be. What if the place was really noisy? What if the owners or other campers made me feel uncomfortable? Of course, worst-case scenario, I could leave, but it would be challenging to find somewhere with power that was still welcoming new people. All the campgrounds around Auckland that I called had already closed their gates. I was lucky to have found this spot. There was no guarantee that I would find somewhere else if I didn't feel safe where I was going.

So with a bit of an uneasy feeling, I packed up my things, moved back into the van and headed to nearby Pukekohe. Luckily, I quickly realised that I had worried for nothing. I was welcomed by Viola and Mike, the lovely property owners, and I immediately felt comfortable with them. One other lady was already there with her bus, but she was tucked away in a corner, and Viola said they didn't see or hear much of her. The property was on the outskirts of Pukekohe town in a peaceful rural setting, and excessive noise would not be an issue. I started to relax a bit. I would be OK here for a few weeks.

Over the next couple of weeks, I settled into a routine. It wasn't where I had expected to be, but the unexpected wasn't all bad. Unlike during the first big lockdown the previous year, this time, work got busier instead of slowing down. By now, everyone was perfectly set up to work remotely, and it was almost like everyone decided they might as well use the downtime to get things done. It was fine by me. If I had to be stuck in Auckland for who knows how long, I might as well use the time to earn money. And so I spent most of my days working, going for walks around the neighbourhood in-between and having the odd chat with Mike and Viola whenever I ran into them. It wasn't what I had planned, but I felt I was making the most of the situation.

Nevertheless, I was anxious for this lockdown to be over. I was planning to make it back to the South Island by the middle of spring, and I couldn't wait to get going.

19

CONFINED
SPRING 2021

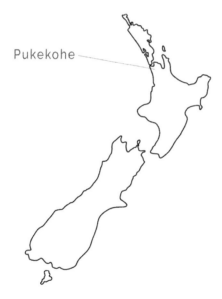

Pukekohe

S pring started with me being confined to my small van in Pukekohe in South Auckland. However, I was still feeling fairly positive about the whole situation. Of course, I would have much rather been travelling around the country, or at least be somewhere at the beach, but I decided to look at it as an opportunity to earn money, so I could work less over summer. Besides, I felt grateful to be in a safe, quiet spot with lovely hosts. I did, however, struggle a bit with the area around me. Pukekohe is technically part of Auckland, but it's almost an hour drive from the city centre (without traffic) and overall looks and feels much more like a small rural town instead of a part of New Zealand's biggest city. There is a small town centre, a circle of residential neighbourhoods around it and a much wider circle of farmland around that. When driving through this area, it's easy to see why Pukekohe and the surrounding area are sometimes referred to as the food basket of Auckland. A large chunk of the vegetables Aucklanders – and other New Zealanders – consume are grown here. On any day of the week, you will see farmers looking after their fields, growing potatoes, onions, cabbage, and much more.

The area around the property where I was parked up was the perfect representation of Pukekohe. Mike and Viola's place itself was a semi-rural lifestyle block with a good-sized family home, several sheds that were being used for their caravan repair and renovation business and several paddocks around it – one of which was my home that spring. If I turned left out of the driveway, I was surrounded by farmland. If I turned right, I soon found myself in a new residential neighbourhood, and if I kept walking for about 30 minutes, I was in the town centre. While all of this was a good combination of convenient and peaceful, it wasn't the most inspiring neighbourhood to explore. And when you're stuck in lockdown and aren't allowed to travel unless necessary, an uninspiring neigh-bourhood could quickly become an issue.

Knowing how important fresh air and movement are for my well-being, I made an effort to go for a walk every day. However, walking around residential neighbourhoods or on narrow roads through farmland on which people drive way too fast, started to get boring pretty quickly. In another example of bad timing, I had given away my old bike just before lockdown. It was in pretty bad shape and I was plan-ning to buy a new one to explore all the amazing cycle trails on the South Island that summer. Unfortunately, I hadn't gotten around to buying one yet, and with all shops closed during lockdown, it had to wait. I would have loved to have a bike during those weeks in Pukekohe as it would have allowed me to explore further afield. As it was, I walked more or less the same route every day, trying to distract myself with music or podcasts. But, truth be told, it wasn't working all that well.

Luckily, a couple of weeks into lockdown, I had a great idea. I invented a game that I called Lockdown A-Z. I started with A and worked my way through the alphabet, assigning a letter to each day. On the day, I went out on my walk looking for things that start with that letter. So on the first day, I went looking for things that start with A, the next day I was looking for things that start with B, then C the next day and so on. I took photos and shared them on my Facebook and Instagram pages and encouraged others to play along. I even got one of my clients involved and we shared photos via the team chat. Clearly I wasn't the only one whose lockdown walks felt a bit boring. Several people joined the game and we entertained and motivated each other with our photos of the day.

When I started my game of Lockdown A-Z, I hoped that we would never get all the way to Z. However, as we were nearing the end of the alphabet, the number of new daily Covid cases was still going up. As much as I hated to admit it, Covid was far from under control and the end of lockdown nowhere near in sight. By the time October rolled around, it became more challenging to stay positive. I had planned to be back on the South Island by now. Instead, I was stuck in Pukekohe, confined to my small van and an uninspiring neighbourhood around me. I tried to focus on the positive, telling myself that I was lucky work had ramped up, so I could at least use it to build up savings. But work had turned from being a welcomed distraction to being mostly stressful and frustrating, making it harder to see it as a blessing.

A light in the dark were my new lockdown buddies, Kate and Rob. They arrived a few weeks into lockdown, Kate with her modern motorhome and Rob in an iconic old Bedford bus. The two of them had spent the first few weeks of lockdown at a nearby freedom camping spot, but with restrictions dragging on, they wanted to be somewhere more private and secure. In their typical lovely manner, Viola and Mike welcomed them with open arms. Even introverted me had started to feel a bit lonely, and it was nice to have a few more people to chat with every now and then. In addition, after almost six weeks in Covid Alert Level 4 (the highest level), Auckland moved to Level 3. While that didn't mean I could leave, it at least allowed me to move around Auckland a bit more.

The first weekend after this change, I took the van to Karioitahi Beach, about half an hour west of Pukekohe. I clearly wasn't the only one excited to have a bit more freedom. The remote beach was as busy as I had ever seen it. Despite that, I got lucky and managed to grab one of the beach front car parks. I backed in, opened the rear doors and let the sun and fresh air in. After taking in a few big breath of salty air, I made a coffee, got comfortable and enjoyed the scenery. I had missed the ocean and it was so good to see and smell it again. Later that day, I went for a long walk on the beach and then put my wetsuit on and jumped in. It was too windy and messy for any surfable waves, so I just splashed around for a bit. It was wonderful to be back in the ocean. Afterwards, I made dinner in the van. I was tempted to try and get away with staying the night, but I didn't want to risk getting into trouble with the locals. So after enjoying a beautiful west coast sunset, I made my way back to Pukekohe.

The following weekend it was windy and I headed to Clarks Beach to go kitesurfing. After having been confined to the van and a small part of Pukekohe for weeks, flying over the water, powered by nothing but the wind and feeling the power of the kite above me was exactly what I needed. With shops now open again, I was also able to buy a new bike and started to explore further afield on two wheels. It was certainly nice to have a bit more freedom to move around. However, the excitement and relief of being allowed to move around Auckland again didn't last very long, and as October turned into November, I seriously considered making a run for it. I had heard stories of people who had managed to get out of Auckland, so I knew it was possible. But it wouldn't be easy.

It might be hard to imagine how a whole city can be locked down and its residents prevented from leaving. However, Auckland is a very narrow city. In fact, the narrowest point of New Zealand is in the Auckland suburb of Otahuhu where only one kilometre separates the Tāmaki River that's part of the east coast and the Manukau Harbour on the west. Because the city is on such a narrow landmass, there are only a few roads in and out in the north and the south. To the east and west, there is nothing but the open ocean. During lockdown, there were checkpoints on all the main roads and regular spot-checks on the side road. In other words, I couldn't just start driving south and expect to get away with it. However, people who were moving to another part of New Zealand permanently were allowed to leave Auckland – if they had the paperwork to prove that they were moving residency. Since I owned property in Christchurch, I probably could have gotten the necessary paperwork to get through the checkpoints. The temptation was huge. Only Auckland was still locked down. For the rest of New Zealand, it was mostly life as usual. With the weather getting warmer, people all over New Zealand were travelling again, sharing photos of their adventures on social media, making those of us stuck in Auckland jealous.

While measures like closed borders and strict lockdowns might seem extreme, they had served us well until then. Our death rates where significantly lower than most other countries, and we had enjoyed a Covid free year with hardly any restrictions at all. I could see the value in the rules and restrictions. Nevertheless, as the lockdown reached its tenth week, the temptation to try and make a run for it was strong.

In the end, I decided not to risk it. I was worried about unknowingly taking Covid to the rest of New Zealand. However, to be honest, that risk was minimal. I had hardly any interactions with people other than outside gatherings with my lockdown buddies. And I would have to show a negative test result anyway to get across the border. The main reason I decided to stay put was fear of getting caught. There had been a couple of high profile stories in the media about people who had broken the lockdown rules and left Auckland. Those people had been publicly named and shamed, their photos had been on the front page of newspapers, some had lost their jobs and probably some of their friends, not to mention the hate and threats they received from the public. I really didn't want to be them. Everyone knew I was in Auckland. If I would leave, I would've had to do so quietly and then hope that no one outside of Auckland recognises me or my van and starts asking questions. With my bike at the front and the two surfboards on the side, my van was highly recognisable, and I felt like it was only a matter of time until someone who knew I should be in Auckland would see me. Besides, with this risk hanging over me, I probably wouldn't have been able to enjoy my freedom anyway.

So I accepted the fact that I would be stuck in Pukekohe until the lockdown was officially lifted.

One day, I was talking to a friend on the phone, complaining about being confined to my van. "But you would be living in your van anyway, wouldn't you?", she asked. It was a fair point. I had been living in my van for almost four years at this point, and if I hadn't been stuck in Auckland, I would be living in my van elsewhere. But it felt smaller all of a sudden.

This whole experience made me realise that there is a big difference between vanlife and living in a van. For me, vanlife is all about travelling, exploring, seeing new places and having adventures. It's fun and exciting. While I was doing vanlife, it never bothered me that my home was tiny. It was like nature and the places I visited were my home and the van was only where I slept and ate. During this spring in 2021, I wasn't doing vanlife. I was just living in my van. There was no excitement and no new places to explore. Most days, I only got out of the van for an hour or two, and on rainy days not even that much. The rest of the time, I was working, eating, reading, watching TV or sleeping, and I was doing all of it in more or less the same spot. I was spending 90% of my time on a 70 x 200 cm bench that was my bed, couch, work and dining area. Maybe not surprisingly, I started to think about how much longer I might want to live in my van. I was highly aware that this was an unusual situation and I certainly wouldn't make any decision while in lockdown, but the thought was there, nonetheless.

I started to plan my summer as a way to keep positive and to have something to look forward to. Summer holidays are a big deal in New Zealand. Because we're in the southern hemisphere, Christmas is in summer and spending time at the beach is almost as much part of a traditional Christmas down here as trees and presents. Covid or no Covid, the government knew that keeping Auckland locked down over the holidays would essentially be political suicide. Therefore, everyone was confident that the lockdown would be lifted sometime before Christmas at the very latest.

I really wanted to be able to enjoy this summer. So much so, that I had decided to leave my biggest client. I had worked for them in different capacities for almost two years. The team was amazing and I loved being part of it. However, over the last twelve months or so, my role had grown significantly and I was now regularly doing 30 hours and more for them each week. Add to that work for my other clients and it didn't leave a lot of time. I realised that if I wanted to enjoy summer, I needed to let them go. When I told the General Manager, I found myself saying; "I really want time this summer to enjoy vanlife because it might be my last summer in the van." That statement kind of surprised me as I said it. Yes, things had been tough lately, but I hadn't realised that I was seriously thinking about my time as a full-time vanlifer coming to an end. I knew there was a good chance that I would fall in love with the lifestyle all over again as soon as I was free to roam. But once I had said it out loud, it was on my mind. The fact is, as much as I had loved the last four years and as much as I felt that living and travelling in my van was one of the best decisions I'd ever made, vanlife is not without challenges – even when you're not stuck in lockdown.

For starters, it's hard to be part of an 'in-person' community. Nomads are an amazing bunch of people. I was part of several online groups (mainly on Facebook), where campers inspire and support each other. It's a very welcoming and friendly community – but it's primarily online. By definition, nomads are free-spirited and move around a lot, so in-person meetings can be challenging. Even if you meet in person, it's usually only for a short time before everyone goes their own way again. It's very different to living in a fixed place where you know your neighbours and many of your friends live nearby. As a nomad, it's hard to get involved in the community. I often thought about joining groups to meet people with similar interests, but I was never around long enough. As someone who makes new friends slowly, I sometimes wished I had a more stable community around me, and I've heard other travellers talk about feeling the same. Maybe that's one of the reasons why many nomads get to a point where they stay put in one place for longer before moving on.

Along the same lines, I also found I was missing my friends more and more. As an introvert, I didn't need a lot of social interaction, but I do value quality time with close friends. It's hard to have that quality time when you only see each other a few times a year. I sometimes found myself missing those days when I would spontaneously see friends for breakfast or dinner on the weekends or to go to a show or movie together. In particular, I missed my kitesurfing friends. In Auckland, there was a great community of kitesurfers.

Whenever I went for a session in Auckland, I usually saw people I knew and we'd catch up and help each other with the launch and landing and share the excitement on the water. In the last four years, I'd often kited alone or with a small group of strangers. I'd still enjoyed it, but it wasn't quite the same. That was maybe why Auckland's Muriwai Beach was still my favourite kitesurfing spot even though I had kited in some epic locations around the country. Muriwai was my home spot, not just because of the amazing condition but also because of the people.

Another challenge of vanlife is that the lack of routine can be draining after a while. A nomad life, by definition, has a lot less routine than a 'normal' life, which means simple things often take more thought and energy. It's pretty amazing how much our brains can do on auto-pilot once something has become a habit. By doing things like driving the same route all the time, going to the same places and doing the same things, we form habits. Habits are great because they give our brains a break. Less brain power is needed to drive a route you know very well than driving a completely new one. Brushing your teeth takes a lot less effort and concentration than painting your nails, partly because we do the former multiple times a day (or at least we should).

As a nomad, you are constantly in a new environment. A nomad's brain constantly has to take in new information and make decisions: which route to take, where to go, where to stay, where to buy groceries, and many other decisions that most people who live in one place only make once or twice – and then keep repeating. Most of the time, I found this constant change exciting, but sometimes, it started to feel tiring. Every time I needed groceries, I had to figure out where the next supermarket was and how to get there. I then had to hope there would be parking suitable for my van and, once inside, I had to find my way around and hope they had the products I needed. Similarly, I had to constantly make decisions about where I would park for the night. There had been many days when at lunch time, I still had no idea where I would spend the night, and more than once I experienced decision paralysis because there were too many options to choose from. People living normal lives don't have these issues. They usually shop at the same supermarkets each week and know where they will be sleeping not just that night but most likely also next week, month and year.

I'm a creature of habit, and back when I was living in Auckland, I always had my go-to places for things like groceries, coffee, time at the beach, walks, takeaways and more. Exploring new places all the time has been one of the biggest joys of the nomad life, but sometimes I missed having my go-to places. There is just something comforting about familiar places, and knowing the coffee you're spending $5 on will be good. Not to mention the feeling of comfort that comes from being greeted by name and people knowing how you like your coffee without having to tell them.

All of these challenges had been there for a while, but until now, they had been insignificant compared to all the fun parts of the lifestyle. However, that spring, as I was confined to Pukekohe and my little van for months without knowing when it would end, they started to bother me more. In the absence of almost everything that makes vanlife amazing, I had way too much time to think about the downsides. But, I also knew that there was a very good chance that all of this would change very quickly as soon as this lockdown was over and I'd be free again – so I held out for that.

Nevertheless, there was one issue that I knew wouldn't go away that easily, and that is the lack of privacy and personal space. When you live and travel in a mobile home, you are always either in public spaces or on someone else's property. In other words, you are always at the mercy of others. You never control the environment around you. More than once, I've been parked up in a beautiful public park or by the beach, enjoying the scenery, just for someone else to come along and block my views, play music at full volume or feel the need to have a gathering outside until the early hours of the morning. I can't stop them. I can't even really complain. They have a right to be there just as much as I do. During the busy seasons, when campgrounds and especially freedom camping sites are packed, it's also perfectly normal for people to park so close to each other that you can touch your neighbour's van through the window. It's a safety risk (if there is ever a fire it would spread easily from one camper to the next) and for someone like me who values personal space, it's also uncomfortable. But it's all part of the lifestyle. You never know who your neighbours will be for that night or whether you will get along with the owners or manager of the property where you're parked. Of course, the big advantage is that if you don't like it somewhere, you can easily move on. But you're just moving on to another spot where you don't know what you'll get.

This lack of control over my environment hadn't bothered me at all for the first few years of travel. There was a night in Gisborne during my first year when a bunch of young tourists were having a party at a freedom campsite until way past midnight. There were other times when I felt like people were parking a bit too close for comfort. It was annoying, but they were just individual incidents, and at the time, I didn't see it as a big issue. However, over the past year or so, that had started to change. Somewhere along the way, I had become hyper aware of the fact that I never controlled my environment. If I wanted to have a quiet weekend, I could go to the most remote campsite, but all it took was one other person or group who wanted to have a party weekend and I would have to accept that I wouldn't be getting my quiet weekend. Yes, I could move on when that happened, but who knows what would wait for me at the next spot?

After almost four years living constantly in public and shared spaces, I had started to long for my own little place. A place where people can't just walk in and stare right into my home just because I have the doors open for fresh air. I knew deep inside that this longing wouldn't go away. It might be less intense once I would be back to travelling and would have the experiences again that make vanlife so special, but I knew it wouldn't go away completely. In fact, I was pretty sure it would grow stronger, especially once the Covid pandemic is behind us and mass tourism returns to New Zealand. I kind of knew that this was the one thing that would eventually make me want to stop vanlife. I just didn't know when.

Despite all the negative thoughts and the doubts that were creeping in about my lifestyle, I was beyond excited when, at the end of November, the government FINALLY announced the end of Auckland's lockdown. From the 15th of December, we would be allowed to leave. The autumn of 2021 had been by far the toughest months since I started vanlife. But at the end of November, things started to look up. I was more determined than ever to let nothing get in the way of another amazing summer on the South Island. Little did I know, there were more challenges standing in-between me and an epic summer.

20

FULL CIRCLE

SUMMER 2021 / 22

At the beginning of December, things were looking positive for summer. The end of lockdown was in sight, and I had managed to reduce work to a level that would allow me to enjoy travelling while still earning enough to cover my bills. I used the first two weeks of December to prepare for my departure to the South Island. At this point, we were allowed to socialise with people outside of our immediate bubbles again, so I spent time catching up with friends. I also got a few life admin things done, like renewing my driver's license, getting a haircut and seeing my doctor for repeat prescriptions. I also decided to get my van's Warrant of Fitness (WoF) done, even though it wasn't due until late January. I figured if I got it out of the way now, I wouldn't have to deal with it in January. This is the same regular safety check that had resulted in losing Josie, my first van, almost three years earlier. So needless to say that WoF time always made me nervous.

I dropped the van off and walked over to the hairdresser. As I sat in the chair waiting for the colour to soak in, the phone rang, showing a local number I didn't recognise. I had a bad feeling right away. Sure enough, Pete from the garage that was doing the WoF informed me that the van had failed. My old enemy, rust, was back again. Luckily, it wasn't as bad as it had been with Josie. If I had received the news at a different time, I probably would have just shrugged it off as part of the lifestyle. After all, if you buy a 20-year-old van, you can't be surprised when you have to invest in it every now and then. But the timing sucked! After almost four months stuck in Auckland, I was days away from finally being allowed to leave, and now this.

On top of that, the chances of finding someone who could do the repairs before Christmas were slim. Many panel beaters were still working through the backlog that had piled up during lockdown and weren't taking on any new work this side of the holidays. Those with some capacity could not guarantee that the work would be done before Christmas, and, of course, they wouldn't sacrifice their well-deserved summer holidays just because I wanted my van back. In short, if I tried to get it fixed before Christmas, there was a big risk that I'd end up without a van till well into the new year.

That evening, I sat in my van feeling defeated. The thought of a carefree, fun summer had kept me going through the tough lockdown months, but now it looked like summer would be just as challenging as spring, just in different ways. What made it better was that, unlike lockdown, this was a situation I had at least some control over. I couldn't change the fact that the van needed repairs, but I could control what I did about it and how I would let it impact my summer. Ultimately, I decided to head south anyway and get it sorted once there. I simply could not deal with being stuck in Auckland any longer. Besides, on the same day my van failed its WoF, a friend in Christchurch reached out to see if I would be interested in housesitting for friends of hers for two weeks at the beginning of January. It felt like a sign. The house was right by the beach, and I could stay there while the van would get fixed. Christchurch is New Zealand's second-largest city, so it shouldn't be hard to find someone who can do the work.

And so on the 15th of December, the day Auckland's Covid lockdown officially ended and we were allowed to leave, I said goodbye to Mike and Viola, thanked them again for being such fantastic hosts, and then headed south. Since Pukekohe is in south Auckland, it didn't take me long to get to Mercer, where, until the previous day, the border had been. For the last four months, there had been checkpoints here and pretty much everyone who wanted to get through needed to show some paperwork explaining why they were allowed to leave. There were no more signs of all of that as I was passing through. Some rules were still in place, including needing to be either double vaccinated or having a recent negative test result, so I was partly expecting some checks. But I drove past Mercer on the motorway the same way I had many times before and continued south on State Highway 1. About 20 minutes later, I got pulled over by police. I felt nervous for a minute, but they just asked to see my vaccine passport or negative test result and then wished me safe travels and a great summer.

I had booked a ferry crossing weeks earlier. Like many others, I was confident that we would be allowed to leave Auckland in time for the summer holidays at the very latest. I figured the ferry would book out very quickly once the dates were announced, so I took a chance and secured a spot weeks before the 15th of December was announced as the end date for Auckland's lockdown. I had booked the ferry for December 18th, the Saturday before Christmas, thinking that surely we would be allowed to travel again by then. That meant I had three days to get to Wellington. Once there, I spent the night at the NZMCA park in Plimmerton and then headed to the ferry on Saturday morning. This was my sixth crossing since I started vanlife, and it was by far the busiest. Clearly, I wasn't the only Kiwi excited about a summer on the South Island. It didn't help that construction work in the loading area around the ferries took up some of the space used for lining up and organising vehicles before boarding. What usually looks like 4 or 5 pretty straight lines of cars and campers waiting to drive onto the ferry was utter chaos that day. There were vehicles everywhere, and we were squeezed in so much that some couldn't open their doors. However, when the time came to board, a young man took control of the chaos and somehow managed to get all of us on the ferry in an orderly fashion. He did so with a big smile and while joking with everyone, making the whole experience fun for all of us.

Once on the South Island, I spent a few days around Picton, soaking up the beautiful early summer weather. After that, I made my way to Blenheim. I had committed to house- and cat- sit on a lovely rural property surrounded by vineyards for ten days over Christmas and New Year. At first, I was reluctant when the opportunity presented itself. After being stuck in Auckland for so long, I was eager to travel again. However, for a week or so around Christmas and New Year New Zealand tends to go crazy. Just about all campgrounds, beaches and parks are packed to the rafters. Absolutely everyone who can take time off over the holidays does. Most offices and trades are closed, and just about the entire population of New Zealand heads to the beach. Kiwis love the outdoors and camping, so even those campgrounds that are very quiet most of the time turn into hives of activity. It's actually quite a fun thing to watch. If you ever have the opportunity, I recommend setting up camp at a popular holiday spot a few days before Christmas, and then sit back and watch the place turn into a tent and caravan city as more and more people arrive and set up their temporary summer homes.

As much as it was fun to watch this happen, I never enjoyed being there once the tent cities come alive. It's just too crowded for me. I figured there was a good chance this year would be particularly busy with international travel still not an option and Aucklanders feeling the need to make up for the time lost to the long lockdown. In addition, everything felt a bit more tense than usual during those first weeks of summer. While Covid had been a global issue for almost two years by now, New Zealand had been very lucky for the most part. The previous summer, we had been Covid-free, and life had been more or less normal (minus the international visitors). This summer was different. At some point during the Auckland lockdown, everyone gave up on returning to zero Covid cases. Clearly, that wasn't going to happen with the much more transmissible Omicron variant. The primary purpose of the Auckland lockdown became containing the virus long enough for the vaccine programme to roll out. That summer, Covid was in the community and with it a number of restrictions and challenges. Masks were mandatory in many situations and venues, certain limitations were in place for those who chose not to get vaccinated, and we even had vaccine mandates for some professions. As everywhere in the world, not everyone agreed with these measures. That, plus the general uncertainty, frustration and fear, had created a somewhat tense and challenging environment.

I'm not a people person at the best of times, but that summer, I kept my distance even more. I found it challenging to deal with the tenseness and conflict that seemed to linger in the air. More than once, a friendly chat with camp neighbours turned into a charged political discussion about whether the measures our government was taking to keep Covid under control were justified. And there didn't seem to be any middle ground or compromise. People who were usually well capable of disagreeing on something without it turning nasty, seemed unable to do so when it came to Covid.

So, long story short, I decided that no matter how much I was looking forward to travelling again, I probably wouldn't enjoy it very much over the peak Christmas period, and housesitting would be the better option. Besides, I liked Blenheim, but I hadn't spent much time there yet. Housesitting near the town for ten days felt like the perfect opportunity to get to know the area better.

I had a great time in Blenheim, going for walks in the Wither Hills, riding my bike through the almost endless vineyards and along the river, occasionally visiting town for supplies and Flat Whites and otherwise just relaxing at the beautiful property. It had been a crazy year. I'd travelled all over the South Island, written another book and gotten stuck in Auckland for four months. I felt like my body and mind needed rest. So I let myself sleep in, cooked and ate good food and did nothing but daydream for hours. I had put the van issues in the back of my mind. I couldn't do anything about it until New Zealand returned to work at the beginning of January, so there was no point worrying. It was future Lisa's problem, as my dear friend Celine could say.

In the first week of January, future Lisa's problem became present Lisa's problem. I made my way to Christchurch with a short stop in Kaikoura. Once I had settled in at the house in Christchurch's Southshore, it was time to deal with the van. Before Christmas, I had lined up a panel beater to do the work, so once I arrived in town, I dropped the van off and hoped for the best. I was housesitting for two weeks and hoped the van would be fixed by the end of that. Unfortunately, I wouldn't be so lucky.

I really thought four months confined to my van in Pukekohe was enough of a test of my patience and ability to deal with challenges, but clearly some higher being thought, I had more to learn in that department. The panel beater quickly identified the issue with the van and informed me that the work, while time-consuming, wouldn't be that tricky. The problem would be getting the parts. Essentially, the panels at the front by the engine behind the mudguards on both sides had several rust spots. They recommended replacing the full panels, saying that simply removing the rust would mean there was a good chance it would be back next to the repaired bits within months. It sounded like a sensible plan. It wouldn't be cheap, but given I had spent four months in Auckland doing basically nothing but work, I wasn't too concerned about the money. I was worried about how long it would take.

By the time my housesit in Southshore ended, the panel beater still hadn't been able to find the parts needed. I was frustrated, but working hard to focus on the positive things happening in my life. Another week-long housesit had come up in nearby Sumner. The house was up on the hill and had epic views over Sumner and New Brighton beach, and I got to hang out with two super cute cats that were half Maine Coon, and accordingly big and fluffy. I had a great time in Sumner, but when there was still no real progress during that week, it became harder to stay positive. Clearly, the parts weren't easy to come by, and there was no way of knowing how much longer it would take. The van was taken apart at the panel beater's, so I couldn't get it back while we waited for parts either. On top of that, I felt like the panel beater didn't care. Their communication was poor, they looked for parts in one place after another instead of trying all options at once, and whenever I talked to them, I didn't feel like they had any sympathy for the fact that the van wasn't just a holiday camper but my home.

Still, I refused to let it get me down. I decided to book a rental car and an Airbnb and spent a few days exploring the nearby Banks Peninsula. I found a cute little cottage with river and mountain views to use as a base. Over the next few days, I hiked up to Packhorse Hut, explored famous Akaroa, went for a scenic drive along Summit Road and visited some of the more remote bays.

After my time on the peninsula, I found a cheap Airbnb in Christchurch. It was here that I gave up on staying positive – at least for a while. I felt like everything was out of my control. The parts for my van still hadn't been found, and I felt like the panel beater didn't care. For him, it didn't matter when the parts would show up. He had plenty of other work to keep the team busy. And no matter how often I told him that the van was my home and that I needed it back, it didn't seem to make any difference.

One night, I was sitting on the bed in the Airbnb, trying hard to keep positive and convince myself that it would all work out, but I simply couldn't. I felt lost without my little home on wheels. The part I hated most was the uncertainty. No one could tell me when the van would be fixed. "I hate being homeless", I thought to myself. Even as I thought it, I cringed. I realised how incredibly lucky I was that my idea of being homeless involved sleeping in a comfortable bed in a safe place with a rental car parked outside. There are people in this very country who are struggling with real homelessness. I felt ashamed for feeling so sorry for myself when I really didn't have a reason to, in the grand scheme of things. But then, I just laughed. For a good five minutes, I laughed in a hysterical 'I'm losing my mind' kind of way. I couldn't stop. The whole situation just seemed so ridiculous all of a sudden. First, I was stuck in Auckland for four months, and now this. Somewhere along the way, I must have really pissed off the goddess of freedom and adventure to deserve so much bad luck in such a short time.

I think I kind of accepted my fate that night. There wasn't anything I could do about it, so I might as well stop fighting it. I wouldn't say that this acceptance made it any less challenging, but I stopped trying to control something I couldn't. I ended up floating around Christchurch for another two weeks. I stayed at a friend's place for a bit and then did two more short housesits until I finally got my van back at the end of the first week of February. In the end, they did find the parts. It cost me a small fortune, but it felt worth it. I finally had my home on wheels back and was ready to enjoy the South Island and what was left of summer. Surely, with all the challenging times I had been through, I deserved a bit of good luck.

I left Christchurch at the end of the first week of February and headed inland towards Lake Tekapo and Mackenzie. I had discovered this part of New Zealand more or less by coincidence the previous summer and was eager to return. One of the things the area is famous for is the Alps2Ocean cycling trail that starts at the base of Mt Cook, New Zealand's highest mountain, and takes you all the way to Oamaru on the east coast. In spring, I had treated myself to a new bike and opted for an eBike, specifically with the fantastic cycle trails on the South Island in mind. They are designed to be done over multiple days, with accommodation options along the way. However, given I had my own portable home, I didn't want to pay to stay elsewhere. I also liked the idea of being able to sleep in my own bed each night. Therefore, I decided to do return trips over multiple days. It meant long distances, but the new eBike made that possible.

One day, I biked from Twizel all the way to Lake Ōhau Lodge and back. It was a long day, but the stunning scenery around me made it more than worth it. However, my favourite section of the Alps2Ocean trail was from Omarama to

Benmore. I started early in the morning, knowing I had some distance to cover that day. The first part of the trail wasn't all that exciting, essentially following State Highway 83 through the countryside. However, after about six or seven kilometres, the track meets Lake Benmore and follows the lake's edge south from there. The most stunning section took me up onto the hills with incredible views over the lake and the surrounding mountains. I could even see the snow-covered peak of Mount Cook in the distance. It was a beautiful sunny day, and I was soaking it up. This was the summer I'd had dreamed about during the long lockdown months. Out in nature, exploring, and standing in awe of how beautiful New Zealand is. All the challenges from the last few months were forgotten, and I was living life to the fullest again.

After a few weeks on and around the Alps2Ocean trail, I headed towards Central Otago – another area famous for cycling trails. One track, in particular, was high on my list. The new Lake Dunstan cycling trail had opened the previous year, and the reviews so far were excellent. Of course, that was something I had to see for myself. And this time, I would have company for a change. Simon, a fellow nomad who was based in nearby Arrowtown at the time, and I had been in touch over social media for a while. When I mentioned to Simon that I was planning to ride the Lake Dunstan trail, he was keen to come along. As it so happened, his nephew was visiting on the day, and he joined as well. So, on a beautiful Saturday morning, the two hired eBikes from Cromwell and we set off.

The track is about 37km long and connects the townships of Cromwell and Clyde. The first half is a leisurely ride along the scenic lakefront. After about 19km, we reached the famous floating café and burger bar, which was the perfect excuse for a break. Who doesn't like a barista-made coffee halfway through a 40km bike ride? After this refuelling stop, the ride got more challenging – but also more exciting. The trail took us up into the cliffs (thank god for eBikes) with steep drop-offs in some parts. We crossed several bridges and pathways attached to the side of the cliffs. The whole way, we had the lake to our left, cliffs and mountains all around us and blue skies above. We all marvelled at the scenery as well as the engineering feat that building this trail must have been.

Once in Clyde, we had a late lunch at one of the cafes to reward us for our efforts and then waited for the shuttle services to take us back to Cromwell. If I had been on my own, I probably would have cycled the trail in two return trips, going halfway from Cromwell on one day and then halfway from Clyde on another. But the transport had come as part of the package for Simon and this nephew's rented eBikes and offered an opportunity to do the whole trail in one day.

After our Lake Dunstan cycle adventures, I spent a week exploring the Central Otago area. In Alexandra, I was lucky to cross paths with Suzy, who I had met at Taieri Mouth the previous summer. She lived near Oamaru and was on her way back from visiting friends in Wanaka. When she heard that I was in Central Otago, she made a little detour to meet up with me. We had such a great time travelling together for a few days last year, and I was excited to see her again. We greeted each other with big hugs like old friends, and even her little pooch Walter seemed to remember me. Like last time, we decided to take turns cooking dinner for each other, so later that first day, I was sitting in Suzy's camper enjoying a delicious stew she had made in her slow cooker. We caught each other up on our lives and travels since we'd parted ways in the

Catlins last year. I told Suzy about my lockdown experience and the van troubles, and she told me about her trip to Golden Bay and gave me tips for when I would get there in a few weeks.

At some point, Suzy turned to me and asked, "are you happy?". I was a bit taken aback. Asking direct and confronting questions was usually my speciality. It was weird to be on the receiving end for a change. But, I didn't have to think long about this specific question; "Yes, I'm very happy," I replied and wanted to know why Suzy had asked. "No real reason," she said. "Your light just doesn't seem to shine quite as bright compared to when I last saw you". Slightly confused, I asked what she meant by that. "When I first met you, I thought you seemed like one of the happiest, most alive people I've ever met. You still have that spark, but it's not shining quite as bright anymore," Suzy explained.

It was weird to hear her say that. Somehow, Suzy had found a way to articulate what I had struggled to put into words for the last few weeks. The spark was still there, it just wasn't quite as bright anymore. I was happy and was having a great time travelling and exploring again, but life wasn't quite as bright anymore as it had been the previous year when I'd first met her. I told Suzy that I had been feeling this way for a while, but that I thought it was mostly because of all the bad luck lately with lockdowns and lengthy van repairs. For all those months, I thought my love and passion for the lifestyle would return once I was free to roam again. But here I was, doing exactly what I'd wanted to do and having a great time doing so, yet the spark still hadn't fully returned. I confided in Suzy that I had started to think that my vanlife days might be coming to an end – at least for now. It wasn't that I didn't like living in my van anymore. But somehow, I felt that it might be time for change.

"What would you want to do if you're no longer living and travelling in your van"? Suzy wanted to know, and that was the million-dollar question. As much as I felt it might be time for change, I didn't know what I wanted to do next. But I was OK with that. I didn't have to know, I could just keep doing what I'm doing, and if it really is time for change, I'm sure something else will come along that feels right. Suzy, a 'live in the moment' person herself, could fully relate to that.

"Would you still keep Life Done Differently going?" was Suzy's next question. Like many others I met on my travels, she knew me as Life Done Differently before she knew me as Lisa. For the last five years, I had shared my journey on my blog called Life Done Differently, and I also had Facebook and Instagram accounts with the same name. Somewhere along the way, the name had become my alter ego. The nomad community in New Zealand is small, and while vanlife bloggers and social media accounts are a dime a dozen in many other parts of the world, you could still count the Kiwis sharing their vanlife and nomad life publicly on a couple of hands. As a result, word usually got around, and those who had blogs, YouTube channels or social accounts were often known by others in the community. More than once, I have been greeted by strangers with, "you're Life Done Differently, right?". It always made me feel a bit awkward. I had no ambition to be famous or an influencer. The blog and social media accounts were for fun, and I sometimes felt uncomfortable with being recognised by strangers. However, I did like how it had connected me with like-minded people like Suzy.

While I couldn't answer the "what's next?" question, answering this question was easy. Life Done Differently was never just about vanlife. "I actually picked the name and started the blog before I knew I would live in a campervan," I told Suzy. When I started the blog, I was feeling lost and had no idea what I wanted to do with my life. All my friends were getting married and starting families, and society was telling me that's what I should want, too. But it didn't feel right to me, so I began to wonder what else there is. That's how Life Done Differently started. I was about to embark on this journey to figure out what there is to life when you don't want to follow the traditional path around marriage, kids and career, and I wanted to write about it. The idea to live in a van came a few months after I started the blog, and, naturally, it became a big part of it over the four and a half years since. But at its core, Life Done Differently was always about something else. It was – and is – about living with intent and being fully awake instead of living in some kind of autopilot mode. It's about questioning things and making choices based on who I am and what I truly want, not what everyone else around me is doing or what society tells me I should want. "I might not know what I want to do next," I said to Suzy, "but it will still be Life Done Differently. You don't have to worry about me just doing what everyone else is doing without questioning it." Suzy seemed relieved to hear this.

Later that night, when I was back in the little van that had been my home for almost three years, my mind drifted back to that conversation with Suzy. "What would I do next?" was the big question on my mind. I couldn't help but chuckle when I realised how familiar this situation was. Isn't this the same question that had started all of this almost five years earlier? And wasn't the whole point of this to find an answer? For over four years, I felt like I had found the answer, but here I was, asking the same question again. "It's like I've come full-circle," I thought to myself. However, while the question on my mind was similar, almost everything else about the situation was different.

Five years ago, not knowing the answer had scared me – so

much so that I quit my job and set off in my camper, desperate to find answers. This time, not knowing the answer felt OK – exciting even. Five years ago, I believed that one day I would figure out what I wanted to do with my life and then that would be it. From that day on, I would always know what's next. But at some point over the years since, I have come to understand that one never really figures life out. There might be times when I know exactly where I want to go and who I want to be, but those times will only ever last for so long. Sooner or later, there will be doubts, and I will ask myself, "what's next?" again. In the past, I had been uncomfortable with that kind of uncertainty. I wanted to have all the answers and know the plan. But that summer, I could feel change coming again, and while it was daunting in a way, it was also exciting. There were so many things I could be doing next. But for now, I wanted to continue to enjoy the South Island.

Suzy and I spent a couple more days together in Alexandra before going our separate ways. Suzy was heading east to Oamaru, and I was going west. I planned to travel north along the West Coast and then spend some time around Golden Bay and Abel Tasman, three big parts of the South Island I didn't have time for the previous year.

21

GRATITUDE
AUTUMN 2022

Farewell Spit

Gentle Annie

Franz Josef
Glacier

Fox Glacier

Haast

Pakawau
Beach

Abel Tasman

Nelson

The West Coast was incredible. It's an area known for lots of rain and unpredictable weather, but I got lucky. It rained on only three or four days in the entire three weeks it took me to travel from Haast in the south of the West Coast to Gentle Annie in the north. The rest of the time, I enjoyed beautiful days that could easily make you forget that summer was technically over. I slowed down, and made the most of it.

After a few days near Haast, I spent a week in Glacier Country, where I admired some of the world's most accessible glaciers. Franz Josef Glacier and Fox Glacier are only a thirty-minute drive apart, and both are visible from the townships of the same name. Seeing them was a beautiful but also sobering experience. I had been in the area a little over five years earlier, and it was shocking to see how much the glaciers had declined in such a short time. At some point, I went back through old photos, just to make sure my memory wasn't playing tricks on me. But there they were; pictures of the same views from five years earlier with significantly larger glaciers. There was no denying global warming. Future generations of Kiwis and visitors will likely only be able to see the glaciers in photos and videos. I felt sad but also grateful that I had a chance to experience them before it was too late.

There was also no denying that we were still in the middle of a global pandemic. Franz Josef and Fox Glacier are extremely popular tourist destinations. There aren't many other places in the world where glaciers are as accessible as they are here, and that usually brings thousands of visitors each year. However, with the international borders still closed, the towns were almost eerily quiet. I chatted with a few locals, and it was obvious that the last couple of years had been tough for the communities. Everyone was praying that tourists would return the following summer.

After my time at the glaciers, I continued north. I stopped in Hokitika for a few days to wait out some wet weather and to get my van's Electrical Warrant of Fitness and Self-Contained Certification renewed. After all the bad luck lately, I was nervous about these inspections, but the van passed both with flying colours. With that out of the way, I continued to Cape Foulwind and eventually made it to Gentle Annie, where I met up with Kate and Rob, my Pukekohe lockdown buddies (the fact that I now had Christchurch lockdown buddies and Pukekohe lockdown buddies tells you a lot about the couple of years we've all had). It was great to see Kate and Rob again and to spend a couple of nights together in the remote but beautiful spot known as Gentle Annie. I cruised up the river on my paddle board and then drifted back with the tide, went for swims with Kate, explored on my bike and enjoyed catching up with my friends.

Over the past few weeks since I had said goodbye to Suzy in Alexandra, I had been busy exploring and enjoying the West Coast, but as life slowed down a bit in Gentle Annie, the "what's next?" question popped up again. It was the perfect place for reflection and soul-searching, so I got my notebook out and started writing about what I could do next.

Writing is my way of thinking and processing. Whenever I'm stuck on something, I get my journal out and just start writing. Usually, by the end of it, I have much more clarity – sometimes even all the answers. I didn't get to any firm decisions while at Gentle Annie, but some ideas did start to shape. I realised that what I was craving more than anything was a bit more stability. I certainly didn't want to return to a 'normal' life in the city with a 9-5 job in an office. I still wanted to be independent and flexible, and I also wanted to keep exploring, but I felt like I had to slow it down a bit. "Maybe I would just spend a few weeks or even months in one place instead of moving around all the time," I thought to myself. While that idea sounded good in theory, something about it didn't feel right. I realised I also wanted a little bit more space. I didn't want to live in a big house. In fact, whenever I had been staying in regular homes lately, I felt a bit lost. After living in a tiny home on wheels for so long, having a lot of space had become uncomfortable somehow. I also didn't like how much more effort it took to keep a big house clean. I preferred small and cosy spaces that are low maintenance. But I had to admit that the idea of a permanent bed was appealing, as was the thought of having an oven and a shower I could stand upright in, plus a water tank that allowed for more than the world's quickest showers.

Even though I wanted a bit more space, I also knew I wanted to keep life simple and minimalistic. One of the most valuable lessons vanlife had taught me was how little I needed to be happy. I wanted to hold on to that feeling. If anything, I wanted an even simpler life. You see, vanlife is minimalistic (depending on how you do it, of course), but it's often not simple. There are a lot of decisions you have to make every day, starting with where to go and where to spend the night, where to get food and water, and so much more. There is a lot of additional uncertainty that you don't have in an ordinary life. And when you run into issues, like your van needing repairs, it can be anything but simple. I realised that one of the reasons I was thinking of my vanlife years coming to an end was that I wanted a simpler life. I wanted less uncertainty and fewer daily decisions.

I had been telling a few people lately that I thought my days as a full-time vanlifer might be over soon. I think many automatically jumped to the conclusion that it meant I wanted to return to the life I had before. It felt like many of them had always thought of vanlife as a phase and that, sooner or later, I would return to the career-focused life. So when I talked about wanting to change my lifestyle, it made sense to them. They saw it as the moment they had been waiting for when the vanlife phase in my life ends, and I go back to living a more normal life. However, it all felt very different to me. I didn't want to return to my old life – or any kind of ordinary life. To me, it all felt much more like a natural evolution. I had lived in my van for over four years. I loved it, but now it was time for the next phase. I didn't think of it as going back. I thought of it as moving forward. I wanted a life that would give me more of what I loved most about vanlife – minimalism, freedom and time – while also giving me more of the things I had begun to miss – stability and space.

By the time I was getting ready to leave Gentle Annie, I had a rough idea of what I wanted next. More stability, a bit more space (but not too much), the freedom to keep adventuring when I felt like it, and simplicity. It wasn't exactly a plan, but it was a start, and I didn't feel any particular rush to work it all out right away. I was having a great time travelling and wanted to enjoy it while it lasted. With that attitude, I said goodbye to the little paradise called Gentle Annie and made my way to Murchison and then on to Nelson.

———

From Nelson, I flew to Auckland for a few days at the end of March. Friends of mine were getting married, and I didn't want to miss the celebrations. In addition, the annual event that my friend Ava runs happened to be on the same weekend, and it was great that I could be there to support her. I flew up on Wednesday, spent the day catching up with one of my clients, then helped out at the event on Thursday and Friday, attended the Wedding on Saturday and flew back south on Sunday. It was a whirlwind trip. I thought about staying in Auckland longer, but I wanted to make the most of the good weather on the South Island while it lasted.

After I landed back in Nelson, I picked up my van, which I had stored at a campground in town, and then headed north. I was looking forward to spending a few weeks exploring Golden Bay and Abel Tasman. I had been there once before, fifteen years earlier during my first year in New Zealand. Back then, me and two friends had travelled like true tourists, which meant we spent all of two days in the area before rushing to the next destination. This time, I planned to take my time. After a short stop in Motueka, I made my way to Pakawau Beach, where I set up camp for five nights. It was the perfect spot to use as a base. The campground was small and quiet, and I had the most beautiful views from my site, with the beach only a handful of steps away. As a bonus, I was able to connect to power. Over the last couple of months, I had noticed my batteries losing power much faster than they used to, suggesting they might need replacing soon. With the days getting shorter at this time of the year, my solar panels no longer generated enough power to keep the batteries charged for more than a day or two. I could easily top up the batteries by driving, but if I wanted to stay put for a few days, a power connection was key to keeping the fridge running and the lights on.

I loved Pakawau Beach and the whole area. One day, I went on a big cycling and walking adventure, riding my bike to the Farewell Spit car park, where a 90-minute loop track starts. I left the bike behind and followed the path up the hills. From the top, I had amazing views over Farewell Spit, a 25km long sandspit at the very top of the South Island. It is one of the longest natural sandbanks in the world. Thousands of migratory birds come here each summer to feed on the fertile sand flats. From mid-spring to mid-autumn, gannets, godwits, white herons, oystercatchers, spoonbills, and more can be found on and around Farewell Spit. The view from above was breathtaking; once again, I stood in awe of the beauty around me.

Once I was back at the car park, I continued west on my bike. I felt energised by the sunshine and the stunning scenery around me and wanted more. I made my way to Wharariki Beach, which is often included on lists of New Zealand's most spectacular beaches. I left the bike at the car park and set off on the 20-minute walk over the dunes to the beach. On the other side, majestic white dunes stretched out before me, meeting impressive cliffs, rock pools, a river mouth and, of course, the endless ocean. I sat down in the warm sand and enjoyed being in this magical place for a while before making my way back to my bike and then back to the camper. As I was riding the last few kilometres, I was equally tired and excited. It had been such a fantastic day, and I couldn't help but wonder, "do I really want to give this up? Am I really ready to say goodbye to vanlife?"

After seeing the impressive Farewell Spit from above that day, I wanted to get a closer look. While you can get onto the spit on your own, you are only allowed to walk up the beach for about four kilometres. Public access is not permitted beyond that point to protect the wildlife. But even if you were allowed further on your own, walking all the way to the lighthouse near the end of the spit would be quite a mission. A much better way to explore Farewell Spit is with a tour. In all my years of travel, I rarely joined tours. I usually preferred to discover places at my own speed. However, I felt it was worth making an exception for Farewell Spit. And so, two days after my cycling and walking adventure, the small tour bus picked me up from outside the campground in the morning, and we spent the day visiting Cape Farewell and then driving up the spit to the lighthouse. Along the way, we saw many rare birds, as well as some seals and other wildlife, and learned about the area and the conservation efforts from our knowledgeable guide. Once we got to the lighthouse, everyone headed for the snacks and drinks waiting for us, but I had other priorities. I walked back to the beach, got into my swimsuit and dived into the ocean. It was just too beautiful a scene not to. How often do you get a 25-kilometre stretch of white sandy beach and clear blue sea all to yourself? Refreshed from my swim, I headed for the muffins and coffee, only to find none were left. I didn't mind. I would take a swim in crystal clear waters on a remote, stunning beach over muffins any day.

The next day, I left Pakawau Beach and made my way over to the remote west coast. For the most part, the road follows Whanganui Inlet, the first estuary in New Zealand to be protected by a combination of marine and wildlife reserves. The Westhaven (Te Tai Tapu) Marine Reserve covers 536 hectares of tidal sandflats and channels within Whanganui Inlet and protects all plant and animal life within its boundaries. Fishing and shooting are not permitted in the marine reserve, but you are allowed to explore by watercraft, so I found a spot to pull over and got the paddle board out. I spent almost two hours exploring the inlet before I continued west until I reached Paturau Beach, where I set up camp for the night. This part of New Zealand is about as remote as it gets. There is no cell phone coverage and no shops or restaurants. The nearest (small) shop is in Collingwood, over an hour's drive away. For a big supermarket and a small hardware store, you would have to travel all the way to Tākaka, an hour and a half away, and even then, your options would be limited. The next big town is Nelson, about three hours away. I love remote places like this. I went for a walk on the beach and then got comfortable in my van to enjoy the spectacular west coast sunset.

During those magical days in Golden Bay that April, any thoughts of vanlife coming to an end had drifted far to the back of my mind. I was having the best time and didn't want it to end. However, as I drove south towards Tākaka and Abel Tasman, I reflected on those past two golden weeks in Golden Bay. "It feels a bit like I'm on a farewell trip," I thought to myself. I was having a great time and was loving vanlife, but it hadn't changed the fact that I could feel change coming. It was a weird situation. It wasn't so much that I didn't want to live in my van anymore, but I felt like there was something else I wanted to do. In many ways, it wasn't that different from where I had been five years earlier. Back then, just like now, life was good, and I was happy, but there was an inner voice telling me that there was more out there, and that I should look for it. Doing so has been one of the best decisions of my life, which made me think that I should listen to that voice this time, too.

I spent the next two weeks in and around Abel Tasman, New Zealand's smallest national park. With the weather still beautiful, I spent my days hiking around the park, going paddle boarding and swimming in the ocean. Work had started to pick up a bit, too, but in a good way. I had enough work to keep me busy but still plenty of time to have fun. In my downtime, I spent more and more time reflecting on the last five years and thinking about what might be next. I hadn't said it out loud yet, but at this point, I knew in my heart that my full-time vanlife days were ending – at least for now. I still didn't know what that would mean, though. Would I sell the van?

Or keep it for shorter trips, but not to live in? And where would I live?

I started to accept housesitting jobs in Auckland for late autumn and winter. I planned to return to the city, and then figure out my next steps. I picked Auckland because that's where housesitting and finding work would be the easiest, but I also longed for a sense of home. It had been almost five years since I lived in Auckland, but it was still the place that felt the most like home. I didn't like being in the busy city, and I had no plans to settle there permanently, but during this time, as I was trying to decide what I might want to do next, I liked the idea of being somewhere familiar. Also, as New Zealand's biggest city, Auckland is the place that offers the most options, so it seemed like a good place to figure out my next steps.

With that decision made, I couldn't help but feel a bit nostalgic. What an incredible period of my life the last five years had been. I saw New Zealand in a way few people have. I had so many experiences and moments that I was sure I would remember for the rest of my life. I could see myself being 80 and still telling stories from the years I lived in a van. But what was worth even more than all the fantastic moments and memories was what I had learned about life and about myself in these years.

When I looked back, I realised how much of my life up until five years earlier had been on autopilot. I went to school and university and then started working 40+ hours a week without ever really asking myself "why?", or considering what else I could be doing with my life. I had blindly followed that traditional path, and I had no idea how much awesomeness there was to be found on either side of that path.

One night during my time in Abel Tasman, I started to think about what had woken me up. What was it that had made me question that traditional path? What had made me leave it? I thought about it for a bit, but the answer was obvious; the kids question. I was pretty sure that, if I'd had a strong desire to be a mum, I would still be living the auto-pilot life. That's not to say that every parent lives their life on auto-pilot. I just felt like I probably would have, given it's what I had done until then. It was only when my lack of desire for children clearly set me apart from my friends that I started to question things. Without that, I probably would have gotten married and started a family without ever really thinking about all the other ways in which I could live my life.

I have often felt grateful that I don't have the desire to be a mum just because of how much work and responsibility kids are. But in that moment, I felt grateful for a whole new reason. I felt grateful that it had woken me up and that it had made me question things. I also felt grateful that I had the opportunity to make this choice. I was acutely aware, there still are countries and cultures where women don't really have much control over their lives. And even in western countries, choosing not to get married and have children wasn't really an option for most women not long ago. Even just going back one generation, it was a very different story. While women of my mother's age may have theoretically had the choice, it certainly would have been much harder for them than it was for me today. More so, I had also become aware that this choice had been much easier for me than it was for many other women of my generation.

Over the last year or two, I'd started to connect with more childfree by choice people from around the world. I'd joined the online community We Are Childfree, read books and listened to podcasts. It had been quite an eye-opening experience. I quickly learned that many people experience a lot more resistance to their choice to be childfree than I had. I heard stories from people, especially women, whose families and friends openly challenged them and tried to change their minds. I heard stories from women who had to repeatedly defend their choice to healthcare professionals. I listened to people share how much they grappled with the choice, how lonely they felt and how they questioned whether there was something wrong with them for not wanting what everyone else wanted. I heard stories from people verbally abused and attacked by strangers on the internet who thought that having children was the only valid way of life, and that anyone who chooses differently is selfish or that there is something wrong with them.

It's not just about choosing to be childfree either. I had also heard people who chose other untraditional paths in life talk about how much criticism they received, and how they constantly had to justify their choices. From people who quit safe jobs to travel, to ones who gave up their corporate careers to start their own business, families who chose to home-school their kids, couples who got married but didn't want to live together and many more. Doing life differently is often tough, no matter what that 'different' looks like. It made me sad to think about how much society often struggles to accept and support anyone who is different. At the same time, I felt grateful for how relatively easy it had been for me.

My mom and dad were never the overly involved type of parents. They didn't get involved when I had to choose a career and a university, when I had to decide where to study abroad, when I had to choose jobs or when I decided to quit my job to live in a campervan. In the same way, they never questioned or criticised me when I started talking about not wanting children. It sometimes surprised me when people asked how my parents feel about that fact that I won't be giving them grandchildren. I was so used to my parents staying out of my life decisions that is surprised me when others thought they should have an opinion on the topic. To be honest, I don't know how they truly feel about it, but they never said anything to me that made me feel pressured to give them grandchildren or to live a certain way. My friends were the same for the most part. I'm sure they did wonder about it sometimes, and many probably thought I would change my mind eventually, but I never felt like they weren't supportive of my choices. Funnily enough, it was usually strangers who were the most critical, maybe simply because they didn't know me.

It probably helped that I was never in a long-term relationship that looked like it would lead to marriage and kids. I could imagine that people in committed relationships experience more pressure to take what society considers the logical next steps. I guess choosing to have a child on your own is about as unusual as being childfree in our society (maybe even less common). No one seemed to expect me to have a child before I had a partner. Maybe that's why I felt much more pressure to change my single status than the no-kids part. For quite a while, friends would try to play match-maker or encourage me to date more. I also remember friends asking me about this occasionally. "But don't you want to find someone to share your life with?" was a common question. However, as time went on and I stayed my course, and especially after I set off on my vanlife adventure, those voices quieted down more and more, and at that point in autumn 2022, I hardly ever heard those questions anymore. It felt like everyone in my life simply accepted my choices and moved on.

Hearing other people talk about how much harder they had to fight for that acceptance always made me feel incredibly grateful for how easy it had been for me to do life differently. I felt grateful that I had people in my life who supported me, even when I made unusual choices. But maybe even more so, I felt grateful that I was the kind of person who wasn't scared of swimming against the current. I wasn't afraid to be different, to not fit in. Yes, it felt lonely sometimes, but I didn't let that stop me. That stubbornness and independence was what had allowed me to create this incredible life that I now called my own.

That life and that confidence to follow my own path had come at a price. I had drifted apart from good friends simply because our lives differed so much. Despite them supporting my choices, and despite my best intentions, it was hard sometimes to feel connected to people who had chosen such different paths. Their priorities and values were so different from mine. What made it harder was that almost all the people I had been friends with since before vanlife had chosen very similar ways of life. They had all moved in the same direction, only I hadn't. At times, I felt left out simply because I didn't have a family.

That was the one big thing I didn't like about my Life Done Differently – the fact that it had separated me from people I cared about. But the most important people were still there. And I had made new friends and met many amazing people along the way. I sometimes wished I was more extroverted and had more people energy so I could have invested more time into getting to know all the travellers and locals I met along the way. But even though I didn't really get to know many of them, I felt grateful to have met them and to know that there are like-minded souls out there.

I thought about all this as I was hiking along the Abel Tasman coastal track on Easter weekend in April – which also happened to be my 38th birthday. The following week, I would make my way to Picton and take the ferry back to the North Island. Then, in two weeks, I would start house and cat sitting for friends in Auckland. I knew in my heart that these were the last moments of full-time vanlife – at least for now. I was trying my hardest to be present and enjoy the moments, but I couldn't stop my mind from dwelling on the past and reflecting on the journey I had been on since the last time my birthday had fallen on Easter weekend.

If I were asked to summarise the last five years in one word, it would be gratitude. Yes, there had been challenges along the way, and I paid a price for the choices I'd made, but at the end of the day, I always returned to a feeling of intense gratitude. I felt so grateful that I had the opportunity to have these four and half years on the road and that I had the courage to make the most of the opportunity. I felt grateful for the people I met and the places I saw. I felt grateful for what all of it taught me – about life and myself. I felt grateful to be living in a country that is not only incredibly beautiful but also safe and easy to explore as a solo traveller. I felt grateful for all the challenges and setbacks because all of them had led me here. All of it had led to me sitting on a bench in Abel Tasman National Park, on a sunny Saturday in the middle of April, taking in the spectacular views and celebrating my 38th birthday. It had been an amazing ride to get here, and I couldn't wait to see what the future would hold for me.

I didn't know what I wanted to do next. I was tempted to say that I definitely won't ever return to living in the city working a 9-5 office job. However, as much as I believed that to be true at the time, one of the things I had learned over the last five years was that things change. The same things that make me happy today might not do so in the future. So maybe I will settle down one day and return to what most people would call a normal life. If there ever comes a day when that will make me the happiest, then I want to be open to that. I don't want to deny myself happiness just because I promised I would never return to that life.

After all, Life Done Differently was never about living in a van. It was never even about living a different kind of life. At its core, it was always about living with intent. It was, and is, about being awake, about knowing myself and allowing myself to live life the way that makes me happy – whether that's living in a van or living the way everyone else is. I don't want to swim against the stream just for the sake of it. I only want to swim against the stream as long as that makes me happy.

EPILOGUE

Two weeks after celebrating my birthday in Abel Tasman National Park, I made it back to Auckland, where I stayed for several months, housesitting in various places around town. I was set in my decision that full-time vanlife was over (for now) but I still had a hard time letting go.

In June, I reluctantly listed my van for sale. A few people came to look at it, but no one made an offer. Since I was still a bit unsure about whether I really wanted to sell it, I had priced it relatively high, which was probably why there were no offers. Eventually, I decided to let it go. As much as I would have loved to keep it for shorter trips and to have a place to stay in between housesits, it was too expensive in upkeep – especially since it was reaching that age where the next big repair was a matter of when, not if. So I lowered the price, and then everything happened very fast.

One Saturday morning in August, a few days after I had reduced the price, a lovely couple came around to view the van. They liked the look of it, took it for a drive and then made an offer. I accepted, they handed over the money, I handed over the keys and then they drove off in my van – all in less than an hour. I felt completely unprepared. A part of me wanted to ask if I could keep the van for another day or two just so I could say goodbye and prepare myself for letting it go. But I didn't, and so I stood on the side of the road with a weird feeling, watching my little home on wheels disappear around the corner. I had to rush off to meet a friend, but later that day, I sat on the deck where I was housesitting at the time, and it all sunk in. After almost exactly five years as a van owner, I was on my own. I felt like I had just said a permanent goodbye to a good friend. It was what I wanted, but I still felt sad and a bit lost. It well and truly was the end of an era.

Five years ago, I'd embarked on a journey to figure out what life has to offer when you don't want to follow the traditional path around marriage, mortgages, kids and career. At the time, I wasn't sure if I would ever want that kind of life. All I knew was that I wasn't ready to commit to it at that point in my life. However, I struggled to see any alternatives. With a lack of role models showing me what life would be like without all those traditional goals and priorities, I decided to find out for myself.

So, what does life have to offer when you don't want to follow that traditional path? It offers freedom, flexibility, independence and adventure. It also offers challenges, setbacks, doubts, and loneliness. It's not perfect, it's not always fun, and it's no guarantee for happiness – just like the traditional life isn't. Can you be happy without a partner and kids? YES! Can you be happy with a partner and kids? Also YES! Can you be unhappy with either? Another YES!

However, we live in a society that often has a hard time with anyone doing things differently – whether that's choosing not to have children, living in a van, or anything else that isn't a more or less direct replica of what the majority is doing. We're not very good at embracing and celebrating our differences. Instead, we're often scared and intimidated by anything that's different and that we don't understand. That is why it's so hard to swim against the current. It makes you an outsider in a society that values conformity and fitting in.

Over the last five years, I've learned a lot about being different and not fitting in. I've shared many of those lessons throughout this book in the hope that they will help others who want to embark on a different path in life – whether that path is similar to mine or completely different. So here is the last piece of advice I want to leave you with.

There is no guarantee for happiness no matter how you live your life. However, I do believe that there is a fast track to unhappiness, and that's not being true to yourself. You are who you are! Living in a way that doesn't honour who you truly are will not lead to happiness, no matter how much society wants you to believe it will.

So if you want to do life differently, then go for it. And if you want to live the most traditional life anyone has ever lived, then go for that.

Whatever you want from life, just do you!

FIND OUT WHAT HAPPENED NEXT

Curious to know what happened next?

Did I settle down? Did I decide to continue the nomadic life?
Or did life have something else entirely in store for me?

Access the next chapter in my story for free via my website.

lifedonedifferently.com/next

PLEASE LEAVE A REVIEW

If you enjoyed this book, please take a moment to leave a review, either on the platform where you bought the book or on Amazon or Goodreads.

It's one of the easiest ways for readers to support authors as it will help others discover the book.

Thank you very much!

FOLLOW ME AS MY LIFE DONE DIFFERENTLY CONTINUES

facebook.com/LifeDoneDifferentlyNZ

instagram.com/lifedonedifferentlynz

ACKNOWLEDGMENTS

Writing this book has been a journey almost as tumultuous as the one shared on its pages, and I almost gave up multiple times. More than anything, I wanted this book to be authentic. But that required being vulnerable – which proved scary and difficult at times. I don't think I would have ever been able to finish this book, let alone gather the courage to publish it, if it hadn't been for the support of some incredible people. I want to take this opportunity to say thank you.

First and foremost, I want to thank a very special group of people without whom this book wouldn't be what it is; My amazing beta readers, who shared invaluable feedback that helped me improve the book. But even more importantly, your kind words and encouragement gave me the confidence to put it out into the world.

Shirely-Joy, Jules, Kae, Julie, Maureen, Staci, Carolyn W., and Carolyn L., who read early drafts (or parts thereof). Your feedback gave me the motivation to keep going.

Angela, Kathleen, Nicole, Daphne, and my brother Ole, who read through the first full draft and provided suggestions and inspiration to fine-tune the story and storytelling approach.

Christa, Clare, Rachael, Medha, Olivia, and Ana, who helped me polish it off and whose positive feedback gave me that last little push I needed to put my story out into the world.

All of you played a huge part in making this book happen,

and I am incredibly grateful for your feedback, ideas and encouragement. Thank you for making the time to support me.

I also want to thank Aleksandar Milosavljevic (Alek) for creating the beautiful cover design that captures the essence of this book so perfectly.

My best friend, Rachel ;) – the perfect yang to my unconventional ying. We're so different, and I'm sure you sometimes question my sanity, but that never stops you from supporting me. I wouldn't be who I am today without you!

My Life Done Differently community, many of whom have been following my journey for many years and have encouraged and supported me every step of the way. When I started this journey, I decided to write about it on a blog, mainly because I was hoping that it would connect me to like-minded people. It definitely has done that, and your messages of encouragement and signs of understanding mean the world to me. I don't think I would have written this book if I hadn't known that I'm not the only one who questions many parts of conventional life.

My sister, who is probably my biggest supporter, and the rest of my family, who made it so easy for me to make these unconventional choices.

My amazing group of friends, who I call my saltwater family. Our lives have drifted apart these last few years as I have chosen a way of life so different from yours. But I still feel a very special bond with all of you and am so grateful for your support and encouragement.

Last but by no means least, thank you to all the amazing people I have met on this journey, some of which have become close friends. Ava, Suzy, Marie and Thomas, Julie-Ann, Deb and Frank, Logan, my Christchurch lockdown buddies, Sarah and Bruno, and my Pukekohe lockdown buddies, Mike, Viola,

Kate and Rob, Bianca and Chris (you all know your real names) and many more. Your stories and our conversations helped me figure things out, made me see things from a new perspective, challenged me, made me laugh, sometimes made me cry, and almost always inspired and entertained me.

ABOUT THE AUTHOR

Lisa Jansen is a writer and digital nomad based in New Zealand. In 2017, at the age of 33, she quit her well-paying job to figure out what life has to offer when you're not sure if you want to follow the traditional path around marriage, kids, mortgages and careers. She spent five years living in her campervan, travelling around beautiful New Zealand. Along the way, she found herself and the answers she was looking for.

Lisa's first book, One Size Does Not Fit All: Discover Your Personal Path to a Happier Life, was published by Mortens Media Group in 2019. Her second book, The Nomad's Ultimate Guide to New Zealand, was published by New Holland Publishers in 2021. In addition, Lisa writes for a travel magazine called Motorhomes, Caravans & Destinations, and also writes a blog www.lifedonedifferently.com.

When she is not writing, Lisa works as a virtual marketing consultant.

facebook.com/LifeDoneDifferentlyNZ

instagram.com/lifedonedifferentlynz

ALSO BY LISA JANSEN

One Size Does Not Fit All: Discover Your Personal Path to a Happier Life

One Size Does Not Fit All offers a fresh perspective on a very popular topic: finding happiness. Instead of providing generic, one-size-fits-all advice and tactics, Lisa Jansen guides readers through an empowering journey and process to design their own strategy for a happier life-based on their unique personality, values, and strengths and weaknesses.

Drawing on extensive research and the author's personal experience of turning her life around, this book offers a real-life, jargon-free perspective on finding happiness. Written in an easy to understand, engaging way and incorporating numerous practical and fun exercises, it will be extremely attractive to anyone who is looking for new insights in finding happiness and who wants practical advice on how to live their best possible life.

The Nomad's Ultimate Guide to New Zealand

The Nomad's Ultimate Guide to New Zealand is the one-stop-guide for anyone who wants to learn more about travelling New Zealand in a mobile home – part-time or full-time, and whether that's a van, motorhome caravan, bus or anything in between.

The book covers:

- The pros and cons of the lifestyle
- Preparing yourself and your life for the new adventure
- Finding the right mobile home
- Getting ready for your first trip
- Navigating life on the road
- Finding campgrounds and more
- Where (and how) to meet people
- The highlights and hidden gems of each region of New Zealand
- And much more

Printed in Great Britain
by Amazon